Fair Representation

Fair Representation.
Meeting the Ideal of One Man, One Vote

MICHEL L. BALINSKI AND
H. PEYTON YOUNG

NEW HAVEN AND LONDON
YALE UNIVERSITY PRESS

Published with assistance from the
Louis Stern Memorial Fund.

Designed by James J. Johnson
and set in Times Roman type.
Printed in the United States of America by
Halliday Lithograph, West Hanover, Mass.

Library of Congress Cataloging in Publication Data

Balinski, M. L.
   Fair representation.

   Includes bibliographical references and index.
   1. Proportional representation—United States—History.
2. Representative government and representation—United
States—History.   3. Apportionment (Election law)—
United States—History. I. Young, H. Peyton, 1945–
II. Title.
JF1075.U6B3   328.73′0734′09   81–11518
ISBN 0–300–02724–9   AACR2

10 9 8 7 6 5 4 3 2 1

Contents

List of Tables and Figures

FIGURES

Preface

This book concerns a problem of national policy that is both political and mathematical: how to divide the seats in a legislature fairly according to the populations of federal states or party votes. It is a problem universal to representative systems of government and deals with the very substance of political power. Innocent as it may seem at first glance, it involves technical difficulties that have baffled politicians and mathematicians for almost two centuries. It is a matter of concern today: as this book goes to press, the accuracy of the 1980 census is being challenged in the courts, and the United States Congress has renewed discussion of the problem and introduced legislation to change the apportionment law. The root of the difficulty is that a perfectly fair division is impossible to achieve owing to the indivisibility of seats. Some compromise must be made. Finding the best compromise forms a fascinating historical and scientific tale.

We first became interested in the problem through the elegant work of E. V. Huntington, who spent much of his life crusading for the method of apportionment now used in the United States. His approach is a highly original and early example of what would now be called operations research. It shows more sensitivity to the practical demands of the problem than much of the modern work in this field, which too often pretends to model a problem by simply imposing constraints and an objective to optimize. Nevertheless, Huntington was ultimately led astray by not paying adequate attention to empirical data.

The aim of our book is to establish a solid logical foundation for choosing among the available methods of apportioning power in representative systems. It is an example of mathematical reasoning applied to a problem of public policy. The style of analysis is similar to the axiomatic approach used in mathematics, where the object is to discover the logical consequences of certain general principles. The validity of the approach depends on identifying the right principles as revealed through history, political debate, and common sense.

No one method suits in all respects. For the skeptic, there is even an impossibility theorem to show that the problem cannot be "solved." Nevertheless, seats must be apportioned and are. As Daniel Webster pointed out 150 years ago, the challenge is not to find a perfectly fair solution—which is impossible—but to come as near perfection as may be. The choice of principles to follow and compromises to accept is, of course, ultimately a question of political legitimacy and should be made by a nation's legislators. Our intent is to clarify the consequences of these choices.

The appeal of the problem lies in its unique combination of history, politics, and mathematics. Although its mathematics are surprisingly challenging, the problem requires no more than simple arithmetic to understand. It is easily accessible to the social scientist, the politician, the student, and the merely curious citizen. To back up the arguments advanced in the text, rather sophisticated mathematical arguments are ultimately required. These are treated separately in an appendix, but even there little more is presumed than some elementary algebra and probability theory—plus a taste for combinatorial reasoning. Appendix A expands and makes explicit the technical points and definitions of the text and contains numerous exercises presented as propositions to be verified. Scientifically inclined readers may wish to read the appendixes in conjunction with the text. The text itself stands on its own.

Although apportionment is a problem common to all systems of representative government, we have chosen to study it primarily through the experience in the United States, where it has the longest and richest history. The difficulty of the problem was already clear to the members of the Constitutional Convention in 1787:

> The greater the difficulty we find in fixing a proper rule of Representation, the more unwilling ought we to be to throw the task from ourselves on the Gen.[1] Legisl[re]. . . . A Revision from time to time according to some permanent and precise standard [is] essential to ye fair representation.*

---

*George Mason, delegate from Virginia, as quoted by James Madison (Max Farrand, ed., *The Records of the Federal Convention of 1787* [New Haven: Yale University Press, 1911], 1:179).

Acknowledgments

This book was written over a period of a few years during which we were affiliated with institutions on opposite sides of the Atlantic. We are deeply indebted to our families and to our friends, most notably Mrs. Joseph L. Delafield, for the generous hospitality that permitted us to work together.

The criticisms and suggestions of several of our colleagues W. Brian Arthur, Peter de Janosi, William Lucas, and Albert W. Tucker —and of the anonymous reviewers were particularly helpful, and we are happy to acknowledge our debt to them.

Special thanks go to Edith Gruber and Denise Fennelly for their patient and careful preparation of the succeeding drafts of the manuscript, to Thomas Czarnowski and Philetus Holt for the design and realization of the figures, and to Lane Hemachandra for an excellent job in carrying out the extensive computations.

Finally, we wish to acknowledge the generous research support of the Army Research Office and the National Science Foundation, as well as the institutions where we worked—the Graduate School of the City University of New York, Yale University, the Institut Auguste Comte, and especially the International Institute for Applied Systems Analysis.

M.L.B.
H.P.Y.

CHAPTER 1

Apportionment

The matter of competition is often Indivisible. An office, or a Mistress, can't be Apportion'd out like a Common.
            JEREMY COLLIER, *Essays Upon Several Moral Subjects*

The ideal of representative democracy—one-man, one-vote—is simple, but to meet it is not. The nations that practice it have tried many models, but in essence they all rely either on one of two systems—a federal system or a proportional representation system—or on a combination of both. In the federal system, the unit of representation is regional: a state or province receives seats according to its population. In the proportional representation system, the unit is political: a party wins seats according to its vote. The United States has a federal system, Israel a proportional representation system, and Germany and Switzerland have combinations that are directly bound both to territory and to party.

Everywhere the stated or unstated understanding is one-man, one-vote. No man should have a greater voice than another: a state should receive a number of representatives in proportion to its population or a party in proportion to its total vote. It seems that to say ''proportional'' is enough to solve the *problem of apportionment*—to make a precise allocation of seats to states or to parties—but it is not. The difficulty is what to do about the fractions. This has vexed both mathematicians and politicians for hundreds of years.

Some nations resolve the problem in smoke-filled rooms. Some have established nonpartisan commissions to do the job. Others have used mathematical formulas. But rotten boroughs, legal challenges, and good old-fashioned political fights have continuously hounded the problem, for it touches the lifeblood of the politician: his job.

The country that has had the most intense debates over the choice of method to solve the apportionment problem is the United States. The

1

argument began at the Constitutional Convention in 1787, flared again when the results of the first census were reported in 1791, and was regularly discussed thereafter every ten years.

Apportionment determines the power of the states in Congress and, through the electoral college, directly affects the selection of the president. It determines the number of congressional districts in each state, but it leaves to the states themselves the problem of how to draw the district lines (sometimes called ''reapportionment,'' sometimes ''gerrymandering''). The Constitution makes Congress responsible for fair representation, saying only that it is to be made ''according to'' the populations of the states. It does not specify any exact rule. The problem of interpreting the Constitution on this point has gone on for nearly two centuries and makes the United States history of apportionment one of the most interesting to study as a case.

Each state is guaranteed at least one representative, but whether a state gets 1 versus 2 or 39 versus 42 is a matter of considerable importance to its influence in national affairs. In 1970, for example, Oregon's exact share of 435 House seats was 4.500. Should it have gotten 4 or 5 seats? If the number were rounded up to 5 seats, giving its citizens a larger voice than they deserved, another state—say, one with a 4.450 share—might get only 4 seats and therefore less representation than it deserved. One-man, one-vote is in fact a mathematical impossibility.

What is to be done to find a fair solution? This is no small question. The effects of different formulas on Congress's composition can be dramatic. This may be seen by comparing the first rule used, one advanced by Thomas Jefferson, with another proposed later by John Quincy Adams, and applying them to the 1970 census figures. Jefferson's method would give New York 41 seats, while Adams's would give it only 37. Overall the results would differ in 27 states and involve 18 seats.

In virtually every Congress at least one-half of the states have received 7 seats or less, and for those the difference of even one seat is great. These differences depend on which apportionment rule is used. The issue resurfaces with the completion of every census. Important population changes in some states, and so in the balance of power in the House and in the electoral college, have invariably occurred, and will again.

The history of apportionment in the United States teaches two major lessons. The first is the importance of the problem. Political ''realists'' may belittle the difference of a few seats here or there, yet the effects can be of consequence. One possibility is that the outcome of a presidential election can be changed because of the electoral college, since apportionment determines the number of a state's electors. Indeed, one has been changed: the malapportionment of the 1870s was directly responsible for the 1876 election of Rutherford B. Hayes, although his opponent enjoyed 51.6 percent of the vote. Another danger is a significant shift of seats from small rural states to large industrial states—or the reverse—depending upon the method used. The fact is that political realists from Alexander Hamilton in 1792 to Arthur Vandenberg in 1941 have engaged in bitter conflicts over methods of apportionment whose effects were to transfer as few as *one* seat. More fundamentally, of course, the problem is one of political legitimacy: solutions must be acceptable to the nation.

The second major lesson of history is how political acumen—or plain, good common sense—determines whether a method is fair or not. Al most two hundred years of accumulated experience of apportionment are available, spanning nineteen apportionments. This experience provides numbers—the populations and the size of House—on which to test methods. It also provides a collective accumulation of insight into how methods work in practice. Can a method cause a state to lose a seat when the size of the House increases? Can one deprive a state that has grown to benefit a state that has shrunk? Does a method systematically favor the smaller states at the expense of the larger states? Is it fair that New York, with a proportional share by the 1830 census of 38.593, actually received 40 seats? These are questions that have been raised in the face of what some methods actually did and of what one would naturally want them to do.

In short, history and common sense together suggest a set of princi ples for what methods of apportionment should do and what they should avoid doing. Armed with these principles one can, by logical elimination, deduce which methods are acceptable and which are not. A general theory of apportionment—of what *fair representation means*—emerges from these commonsense principles.

The theory leads to three major conclusions. There are methods in use that may take a seat away from a party whose votes have increased to give it to one whose votes have decreased. There are methods that can take seats away from a state when populations stay the same and more seats are added to the house. To avoid these and other paradoxes, the choice must be restricted to a family of methods called "divisor methods." These include most of the methods that have ever been used, but not all. This conclusion applies to both federal and proportional representation systems, because the principles upon which it is based are the very heart of the concept of fairness.

How large a deviation from one-man, one-vote can be tolerated? Some countries, such as France and England, use no method of appor- tionment: solutions are negotiated. If, however, the intent is to eliminate any systematic advantage to either the small or the large, then only one method, first proposed by Daniel Webster in 1832, will do. In the United States, the case for choosing Webster's method is particularly clear because of the strict standards established by the Supreme Court on one-man, one vote. In 1973 the Court overturned a state's congressional district plan because the deviations "were not 'unavoidable' and the districts were not as mathematically equal as reasonably possible."[1] This ruling, and other like ones, concerned deviations in representation between electoral districts *within* states. But until now no one seems to have realized that the deviations in representation *between* states caused by the use of the present method of apportionment are worse. This method systematically discriminates against the larger states in a way that is avoidable.

For proportional representation systems, on the other hand, it may sometimes be desirable to sacrifice evenhandedness and deliberately give an advantage to the larger parties so as to encourage the formation of coalitions. To maintain political stability, no advantage in representation should accrue to a party that splinters, and very small parties should be discouraged. If this is the primary desire, then only one method, first proposed by Thomas Jefferson in 1791, will do.

CHAPTER 2

Representation in the United States

In the United States the problem of fair representation is stated in article I, section 2 of the Constitution:

> Representatives and direct Taxes shall be apportioned among the several States which may be included within this Union, according to their respective Numbers, which shall be determined by adding to the whole Number of free Persons, including those bound to Service for a Term of Years, and excluding Indians not taxed, three fifths of all other Persons. The actual Enumeration shall be made within three years after the first meeting of the Congress of the United States, and within every subsequent Term of ten Years, in such manner as they shall by Law direct. The Number of Representatives shall not exceed one for every thirty thousand, but each State shall have at least one Representative.

The essential intent of the article seems clear—at first blush. It is to share representation—and taxation—fairly among the states. Yet it does not expressly say how this is to be done. No permanent and precise standard fixing a proper rule of representation is given. It is partly our purpose to fill this omission which foresight failed to anticipate.

What is to be found in the language of the Constitution itself? Representatives and direct taxes shall be *apportioned* according to the respective populations of the states. *Proportionality* is the ideal. Taxes may be so apportioned since money is divisible exactly to the penny. But representation cannot be so apportioned because representatives are indivisible. The proportional share of representative power due the Commonwealth of Virginia following the first census, was 18.310 in a House of 105 seats, whereas Delaware's was 1.613. The first apportionment gave Virginia 19 seats and only 1 to Delaware. Does this meet the ideal of proportionality?

The antecedents of proportionality in representation are as old as the concept of democratic government itself. The Greeks believed in it and applied it as early as the fifth century B.C.[1] John Locke advanced the same idea:

> If therefore the Executive . . . observing rather the true proportion than fashion of *Representation,* regulates, not by old custom, but true reason, the *number* of *Members,* in all places, that have a right to be distinctly represented . . . it cannot be judg'd, to have set up a new Legislative, but to have restored the old and true one, and to have rectified the disorders. . . . For it being the interest, as well as the intention of the People, to have a fair and *equal Representative;* whoever brings it nearest to that, is an undoubted friend to, and Establisher of, the Government, and cannot miss the Consent and Approbation of the Community.[2]

The Delegates to the Constitutional Convention, which met in the summer of 1787, were imbued with the political philosophy of Locke and the Age of Enlightenment. Madison reminded the delegates "of the Lycian Confederacy in which the component members had votes proportioned to their importance, and which Montesquieu recommends as the fittest model for that form of Government."[3] Indeed, the problem of apportionment was viewed as one of the most fundamental issues to be decided at the Convention. "If a fair representation of the people be not secured, the injustice of the Gov.ᵗ will shake to its foundation."[4]

But what is representation supposed to be proportional to? For the United States, the Constitution answers, according to specially defined populations. The *basis of apportionment,* which greatly agitated the Convention, was the result of compromise, and it continues to be an issue to this day. A substantial body of opinion held that property as well as persons had to be represented. Representing persons independently of property was a radical departure, and well into the nineteenth century some states continued to impose property qualifications on suffrage. Leaving aside property, should representation be apportioned to voters only, or to the total number of persons in each state?

The 1787 Convention adopted a compromise from the thicket of proposals by taking *representative populations* as the basis of apportionment, numbers found by counting the total number of persons in each state, discounting slaves by 40 percent, and excluding all Indians not subject to taxation. Instead of the number of voters, a less ambiguous basis was chosen that reflected more closely the distribution of property holdings. The special treatment of slaves represented a peculiar balance between Southern and Northern interests. The twin blade of taxation and representation cut two ways: more representation, more taxation. On balance the three-fifths rule was a concession to the South, taxation having—at that distant time—less bite than representation. Joseph Story, the Supreme Court justice, later commented: "It might have been contended, with full as much propriety, that rice, or cotton, or tobacco, or potatoes, should have been exclusively taken into account in apportioning the representation. The truth is that the arrangement adopted by the Constitution was a matter of compromise and concession, confessedly unequal in its operation, but a necessary sacrifice to that spirit of concilia tion, which was indispensable to the union of States having a great diversity of interest, and physical condition, and political institutions."[5]

The basis of representation has, of course, changed in the course of United States history, and may change again. In 1868 the passage of the Fourteenth Amendment abolished the three-fifths rule and changed the basis to, "Representatives shall be apportioned among the several States according to their respective numbers, counting the whole number of persons in each State excluding Indians not taxed. . . ." It was not until the census of 1940 that all Indians came to be included in the representative population. In 1970, for the first time, parts of the overseas population of United States citizens—having been granted the right to vote in presidential elections—were allocated to their "home" states and added to the populations of those states for purposes of apportionment. The new definition of representative population resulted in an increase of less than 1 percent in the total population but actually changed the outcome: Connecticut lost one seat and Oklahoma gained one. The issue is very much alive today, the bone of contention being whether to count "illegal aliens."

How should shifts in population be accounted for as a nation grows? The Constitution answers that after the first enumeration, to be made within three years of the first sitting of Congress, a new census should be taken every ten years. Similar provisions for regularly updating the basis of representation are found in many nations.

In concluding the guiding clause on representation, the Constitution imposes limitations on the number of members. The number of representatives is not to exceed one for every thirty thousand people and each state is assured of at least one representative, thus imposing both a top limit and a bottom limit to representation. Each state, no matter how small its proportional share, is guaranteed one seat. Yet the number of representatives cannot exceed the representative population divided by thirty thousand. From the context it seems that this clause is to apply to each state individually, and it was to be so interpreted by Washington in the dispute that erupted over the first apportionment bill. The provision would mean, for example, that a state with a representative population of three hundred and twenty-five thousand would be entitled to at most ten representatives.

Assigning to each member of a confederation a minimum number of seats, whatever its representative population, is a constraint that is found in many instances. In France each department receives at least two deputies. In Canada each province is guaranteed as many members of Parliament as it has senators, and the number of senators varies from province to province. The Convention adopted in 1975 to govern the apportionment of the newly constituted European Parliament included the principle of avoiding any reduction in the "present number of any State's representatives," implying that each of the four largest would receive at least thirty-six and the smallest, Luxembourg, at least six.[6] For proportional representation systems minima make little sense: splinter parties receiving only very few votes are normally discouraged.

The language of the Constitution thus identified four essential elements of apportionment: proportionality as the ideal, the basis of proportionality in a specially defined "representative population," periodic revisions to account for shifts in the relative populations of states, and top and bottom limitations that may override the pure ideal. These basic items are encountered in virtually every country that professes representative government.

The Constitution failed, however, to identify two other essential elements that were to become central to the congressional debates of later years. The *number of representatives* to be apportioned was left open. In fact, the size of the House has grown from 65 in 1790 to 435 today. In the 1950s, with the admission of Alaska and Hawaii as states, it temporarily grew to 437. The Constitution also failed to specify a definite *method* of apportionment. The lack of a clear rule has prolonged the debate on how to allocate seats down to the present day.

A particularly sensitive problem—common to many nations—addressed by the Constitutional Convention of 1787 was how to give to the large states their fair share of political power while at the same time assuring the small states a voice not drowned out by the large. The small states, afraid of being submerged by a proportional scheme, argued for a continuing federation in which each state would have an equal vote. The large stood with the philosophical ideal of the day. Some urged apportionment according to wealth. ''A vice in the Representation, like an error in the first concoction, must be followed by disease, convulsions, and finally death itself,''[7] exclaimed one member. The deadlock seemed unbreakable. Finally, the "great compromise," sponsored by Connecticut, won support for the idea of a legislature composed of two houses: one—the House of Representatives—apportioned to populations; the other—the Senate—apportioned equally among all states, each receiving two seats. The form of this compromise between large and small is common to many federal systems.

In the United States electoral system there is a unique feature: the indirect method of election of the president. This curiosity, born of a distrust of the masses, seems to have given to the small states a disproportionately large voice in the chief executive's election since the weight of each state is the number of its representatives plus the number of its senators. However, the current practice in which the winner in a state takes all of its electoral votes has a contrary effect. The reason for this is that a large block of votes (such as a sizable block of shares in a corporation) has a power beyond its numbers, and thus presidential contenders tend to invest campaign efforts in the large states that are more than proportional to their electoral votes.

Be that as it may, the fact is that both the power of a state in Congress and its influence in electing a president is determined by the method of apportionment that is chosen. The problem is: What method comes closest to meeting the ideal of proportionality?

CHAPTER 3

The Methods of Jefferson and Hamilton

Can you not take your draft of an apportionment law, and carefully revise it, till it shall be strictly & obviously just in all particulars, & then by an early & persistent effort get enough of the enemies men to enable you to pass it?

ABRAHAM LINCOLN

History attests to the mathematical inventiveness of politicians when seats in a legislature are at stake. In the United States the matter has concerned many of its greatest statesmen including George Washington, Alexander Hamilton, James Madison, John Quincy Adams, and Daniel Webster. Some of their proposals have turned out to be not merely ingenious solutions of the moment but practical and theoretically appealing approaches that are used in many nations to this day. The involvement of these eminent men, as well as many others, attests both to the complexity of the problem and to its profound political consequences. Indeed, some of the greatest contests over method have been over the disposition of a single seat.

The initial, somewhat arbitrary, distribution of seats in the United States House of Representatives was simply fixed by the Constitution until a census could be taken.[1] The results of the first census and the representative populations as defined by the Constitution were reported to Congress in 1791 (see Table 3.1).* No idea having been provided as to the rule of apportionment or the size of the House, the first contest over method immediately erupted. Out of this struggle, which pitted Jeffersonian Republicans against the Federalist forces led by Hamilton, emerged two methods that are still practiced in many federal and proportional representation systems.

The habit of thought in those days was not first to determine the total number of seats or *house size* and then to distribute them, but rather to fix

---

*Vermont and Kentucky had been admitted to the Union earlier in 1791, each with two seats. The census for South Carolina was delayed and the debates in Congress saw various assumptions about its representative population.

TABLE 3.1. 1791 Representative Populations

State	Representative Population
Connecticut	236,841
Delaware	55,540
Georgia	70,835
Kentucky	68,705
Maryland	278,514
Massachusetts	475,327
New Hampshire	141,822
New Jersey	179,570
New York	331,589
North Carolina	353,523
Pennsylvania	432,879
Rhode Island	68,446
South Carolina	206,236
Vermont	85,533
Virginia	630,560
Total	3,615,920

upon some "ratio of representation," that is to declare that there shall be "one representative for every x persons," and then allow the house size to fall where it may. Having fixed upon an agreeable ratio of representation x the next step was to divide this number into the representative populations to obtain *quotients*. Thereby, x came to be called a *divisor*. The results of using the divisor 30,000—the smallest permissible one, according to the Constitution[2]—are shown in Table 3.2. What should be done about the fractions or remainders? A prevalent view was to drop them, which leads to the apportionment of 112 seats, as shown in Table 3.2.

A multitude of divisors was offered for consideration, the favorites ranging between 30,000 and 40,000. Each concealed a calculated political logic. But the choice was not simple, for in nearly all their calculations the mathematicians of every state found that the gains for their own constituency entailed concessions to others they had no wish to strengthen.[3] The unseemly, self-serving nature of the chase for divisors was deplored by many: "Sir, it gave me pain to find these worthy members calculating and coldly applying rules of arithmetic to a subject beyond the power of numbers to express the degree of its importance to their fellow citizens."[4] On November 24, 1791, the House passed an apportionment bill with a divisor of 30,000, and so a House of 112 members (Table 3.2). Since constitutionally no smaller divisor could be

TABLE 3.2. House Apportionment Bill of 1792

State	Quotient (30,000)	Apportionment
Connecticut	7.895	7
Delaware	1.851	1
Georgia	2.361	2
Kentucky	2.290	2
Maryland	9.284	9
Massachusetts	15.844	15
New Hampshire	4.727	4
New Jersey	5.986	5
New York	11.053	11
North Carolina	11.784	11
Pennsylvania	14.429	14
Rhode Island	2.282	2
South Carolina	6.875	6
Vermont	2.851	2
Virginia	21.019	21
Total	120.531	112

TABLE 3.3. Senate Apportionment Bill of 1792

State	Quotient (33,000)	Apportionment
Connecticut	7.177	7
Delaware	1.683	1
Georgia	2.147	2
Kentucky	2.082	2
Maryland	8.440	8
Massachusetts	14.404	14
New Hampshire	4.298	4
New Jersey	5.442	5
New York	10.048	10
North Carolina	10.713	10
Pennsylvania	13.118	13
Rhode Island	2.074	2
South Carolina	6.250	6
Vermont	2.592	2
Virginia	19.108	19
Total	109.573	105

taken, no larger House could result with this approach. The Senate demurred on the choice of the divisor, raising it to 33,000 and so reducing the size of House to 105 members as in Table 3.3. Deadlock developed.

It had not escaped the notice of some congressional friends of Hamilton that Jefferson's idea of dropping fractions worked different effects on small and large states. "The injury arising from the unrepresented fractions of population is more severely felt by the smaller than by the larger States, as in the case of Delaware."[5] To see this, consider the House bill (Table 3.2). Delaware loses a fraction of .851 or 46% of its total quotient, whereas Massachusetts loses a fraction of .844, which is almost as large but is only some 5% of its total quotient. The result is that Delaware gets one seat for 55,540 persons and Massachusetts one seat for every 31,688 persons (475,327 divided by 15). Every representative in Massachusetts thus comes to stand for 43% fewer people than the representatives of Delaware. Put another way, every resident of Delaware has a 43% smaller share of representation in the House than a resident of Massachusetts. Ignoring fractions, therefore, tends to favor large states (in federal systems) or large parties (in proportional representation systems).

The contest over the division of seats arose from deep political divisions: the emerging conflict between North and South, between Republican and Federalist, between agricultural and industrial interests. A particular issue was the proper size of the House. At this time it consisted of a mere 65 seats. The Jeffersonians argued that so small a number would be an unsafe depository of the public trust. A larger House would not be "so easily corrupted as a small body"[6] and would assure government "founded on a broad bottom."[7] The fact was that nearly half the members held title to certificates of debt inherited from the Confederation whose value depended upon the vote of Congress. Second, they said, so small a number could not possess a proper knowledge of the local circumstances of their large constituencies. Third, they would invariably be chosen from a class of citizens likely to sacrifice the feelings of the many to the elevation of the few.[8] In short, there was a strong current in favor of a substantial increase in the size of the House and a continuing apprehension of the fragility of the democratic experiment.

At this juncture the group led by Alexander Hamilton, secretary of the treasury and the emerging major figure of the Washington administration, devised an entirely new proposal. They argued, correctly, that to find what a state really deserves, the total number of seats to be distributed must first be fixed, and then the proportional share of each state calculated.

Specifically, if 112 seats are to be apportioned, then Virginia's share should be 112 times its fraction of the total population, or 19.531 seats. The defenders of the Northern interests quite properly asked why the House bill gave Virginia 21 seats when she deserved only 19.531. "The whole number of Representatives being first fixed, they shall be apportioned to any state according to its census . . . the Rule of Three will show what part of the representation any State shall have . . . the number of Representatives will be one hundred twelve . . . Virginia having six hundred and thirty thousand persons . . . is entitled to nineteen members. The bill gives her twenty one. Is that right? . . . Are the Representatives, then, apportioned or disproportioned?''[9]

The "Rule of Three" means that the ideal share of representation for each state is found by dividing the state's population by the total population and then multiplying by the total number of representatives to be apportioned. This ideal share is the *quota* or *fair share*. Table 3.4 compares the states' quotas with the apportionment bills proposed by House and Senate. In the House bill, the large states of Virginia, New York, and Pennsylvania each get more than their fair shares, even though their fractions are relatively small, whereas Delaware and Vermont get less than their fair shares, even though their fractions are relatively large. In the Senate bill a similar phenomenon occurs with Virginia and Delaware. However, the

TABLE 3.4. Quotas for 1792 House and Senate Apportionment Bills

State	Quota (of 112)	House Bill	Quota (of 105)	Senate Bill
Connecticut	7.336	7	6.877	7
Delaware	1.720	1	1.613	1
Georgia	2.194	2	2.057	2
Kentucky	2.128	2	1.995	2
Maryland	8.627	9	8.088	8
Massachusetts	14.723	15	13.803	14
New Hampshire	4.393	4	4.118	4
New Jersey	5.562	5	5.214	5
New York	10.271	11	9.629	10
North Carolina	10.950	11	10.266	10
Pennsylvania	13.408	14	12.570	13
Rhode Island	2.120	2	1.988	2
South Carolina	6.388	6	5.989	6
Vermont	2.649	2	2.484	2
Virginia	19.531	21	18.310	19
Total	112.000	112	105.000	105

most glaring difference is Virginia's 21 seats when its fair share of 112 is only 19.531. Any apportionment that gives some state (or party) more than its fair share rounded up, or less than its fair share rounded down, *violates quota*; otherwise it *stays within the quota*.

To remedy the situation the Hamilton faction proposed, first, that the House be enlarged to 120 members. This number could be justified by construing the Constitutional statement, ''shall not exceed one for every thirty thousand,'' to mean that the *total* number of representatives was not to exceed one for every thirty thousand in the *total* population (3,615,920 divided by 30,000 is 120 plus a fraction). Second, they averred that some fractions should be represented—indeed *have to be* if the fractions are calculated correctly, because the quotas are the exact proportional shares due the states and so *must* add up to the total number of seats apportioned.

The compromise bill, which was passed by narrow majorities in both houses and presented on March 26, 1792, for Washington's signature, was the apportionment of 120 seats shown in Table 3.5. No specific rule was mentioned in the bill itself to support this choice, though one of its chief proponents, Alexander Hamilton, was soon to present a rule devised to justify it.

Prominent Southern representatives thought that the new bill was frankly motivated by Northeastern interests trying to tip the balance of power away from the South. James Madison confided his suspicions in a

TABLE 3.5. First Apportionment Bill Passed by Congress, 1792

State	Quota	Apportionment
Connecticut	7.860*	8
Delaware	1.843*	2
Georgia	2.351	2
Kentucky	2.280	2
Maryland	9.243	9
Massachusetts	15.774*	16
New Hampshire	4.707*	5
New Jersey	5.959*	6
New York	11.004	11
North Carolina	11.732*	12
Pennsylvania	14.366	14
Rhode Island	2.271	2
South Carolina	6.844*	7
Vermont	2.839*	3
Virginia	20.926*	21
Total	120.000	120

letter to his father dated March 15, 1792: "the secret of the business is that by these different rules the relative number of East.n & South.n members is varied. The number of 120 is made out by applying 1 for 30,000 to the aggregate population of the U.S. and allowing to *fractions* of certain amount an additional member."[10] Richard Henry Lee, representative from Virginia, was more explicit in a letter to his father dated ten days later: "six Eastern States have one apiece more than they ought, Jersey and Delaware the same, and North and South Carolina each one more than these States would have had, if the plain constitutional mode had been pursued of dividing the number of people in each *State Respectively* by the agreed ratio of 30,000. But by a certain arithmetico-political sophistry an arrangement of six to two against the South has been made of the eight members gained by this sophism."[11]

In fact the damage to the South because of the proposed change was slight. The Southern states—Delaware, Maryland, Kentucky, Virginia, the Carolinas, and Georgia—together had 46.0% of the representative population, and the compromise bill awarded them 55 out of 120 seats or 45.8% of the representation. In contrast they would have fared only slightly better with the House version of the bill receiving 46.4% of the representation. Perhaps more to the point was the fact that Virginia, primary spokesman for Southern interests, did not pick up *any* of the additional eight seats.

But Virginia had not fired its last shot. George Washington had until April 6, 1792 to decide whether to sign the bill. He sent for opinions from his cabinet. Hamilton—admitting he had not seen the bill—argued in favor, stating that it resulted from a logical process or "method" that could be applied to any apportionment situation. On April 4, 1792, he wrote to Washington:

> He now sends [his opinion] with his reasons but more imper-
> fectly stated than he could have wished—through want of time.
> He has never seen the bill, but . . . he takes it for granted that he
> cannot have misconceived its contents so as to cause any mate-
> rial error in the process of his reasoning. . . . It is inferred from
> the provision of the Act—that the following process has been
> pursued.
>
> I. The aggregate numbers of the United States, are divided by
> 30,000 which gives the total number of representatives, or 120.

II. This number is apportioned among the several states by the following rule—As the aggregate numbers of the *United States* are to the *total number* of representatives found as above, so are the *particular numbers* of *each state* to the number of representatives of such state. But

III. As this second process leaves a residue of Eight out of the 120 members unapportioned, these are distributed among those states which upon that second process have the largest fractions or remainders.[12]

Hamilton went on to give a more detailed support of the process he inferred had been followed, considering each pertinent clause of the Constitution in turn. The rule he set down may be stated simply as follows.

The Method of Hamilton. Choose the size of the house to be apportioned. Find the quotas and give to each state the whole number contained in its quota. Assign any seats which are as yet unapportioned to those states having the largest fractions or remainders

In Table 3.5 the sum of the whole numbers contained in the quotas is 111, so there remain 9 seats unapportioned.[13] These are assigned to the nine states having the largest fractions (marked *). The result is, as Hamilton said, the apportionment suggested in the bill passed by Congress. Hamilton's approach is simple and direct and so, not surprisingly, has emerged in many federal and proportional representation systems as the "method of largest remainders."

Precisely the same apportionment would have resulted if the rule had been to simply "round" the quotas in the usual way, that is, if any state with a fraction of above .5 had been rounded up and any with a fraction of below .5 had been rounded down. That Hamilton did not so describe his method suggests he was aware that it would not work in all cases. The difficulty is that *simple rounding* does not necessarily give a result that sums to the required number of seats. For example, if there are too many fractions that are less than .5 then simple rounding will result in too few seats, whereas if too many fractions are above .5 then simple rounding will give out too many seats. The phenomenon happens frequently, as may be seen in the historical apportionment problems in appendix B.

Hamilton's method seems reasonable and natural. It also justified a result he found politically palatable. Thomas Jefferson responded to Washington on the same day with equally cogent arguments against the bill:

> It will be said that, though, for taxes there may always be found a divisor which will apportion them among the States according to numbers exactly, without leaving any remainder, yet for *representatives* there can be no such common ratio, or divisor which, applied to the several numbers, will divide them exactly, without a remainder or fraction. I answer, then, that taxes must be divided *exactly* and representatives *as nearly* as the *nearest, ratio* will admit; and the fractions must be neglected because the Constitution calls absolutely that there be an *apportionment or common ratio,* and if any fractions result from the operation, it has left them unprovided for. In fact it could not but foresee that such fractions would result, and it meant to submit to them. It knew they would be in favor of one part of the Union at one time and of another at another, so as, in the end, to balance occasional irregularities. But instead of such a *single* common ratio, or uniform divisor, as prescribed by the Constitution, the bill has applied *two ratios*, at least to the different States. . . . And if *two* ratios be applied, then *fifteen* may, and the distribution becomes arbitrary. . . .
>
> 120 being once found, in order to apportion them, we must recur to the former rule which does it according to the numbers of the respective States; and we must take the nearest common divisor, as the ratio of distribution, that is to say, that divisor which applied to every State, gives to them such numbers as, added together, come nearest to 120.[14]

Jefferson then argued, using imaginative numerical examples, that his construction was superior to Hamilton's "difficult and inobvious doctrine of fractions." His rule, which was reinvented in 1878 by the Belgian lawyer Victor d'Hondt, may be stated briefly as follows.

> *The Method of Jefferson.* Choose the size of the house to be apportioned. Find a divisor x so that the whole numbers contained in the quotients of the states sum to the required total. Give to each state its whole number.

To apportion 120 seats by this method, 30,000 will not work as a divisor because, as we have seen (Table 3.2), the whole numbers that result from rounding down the quotients sum only to 112. A smaller divisor is needed; for example, 28,500 does the trick*, as shown in Table 3.6. Both the House and Senate bills were apportionments according to the method of Jefferson. The divisor 30,000 apportions 112 members by his formula, and 33,000 apportions 105 members. Despite the smaller size of house, Jefferson preferred either of these allocations to that of the bill supported by Hamilton.

The drama now moved rapidly toward its conclusion. Edmund Randolph, attorney general, concurred with his fellow Virginian, Jefferson. General Henry Knox of Massachusetts, secretary of war, "joined Hamilton in everything,"[15] and, indeed, he did so in this case. George Washington was becoming increasingly upset by the divisions within the administration. Jefferson reports that on April 5, with but one day left before the bill would automatically become law without presidential signature:

The President called me before breakfast and first introduced some other matters, then fell on the representn bill which he had

TABLE 3.6. Apportionment of 120 Seats by Jefferson's Method, 1791 Census

State	Quotient (28,500)	Jefferson Apportionment
Connecticut	8.310	8
Delaware	1.949	1
Georgia	2.485	2
Kentucky	2.411	2
Maryland	9.772	9
Massachusetts	16.678	16
New Hampshire	4.976	4
New Jersey	6.301	6
New York	11.635	11
North Carolina	12.404	12
Pennsylvania	15.189	15
Rhode Island	2.402	2
South Carolina	7.236	7
Vermont	3.001	3
Virginia	22.125	22
Total	126.874	120

*In fact any divisor between 28,356 and 28,511 will do.

now in his possn for the 10th day. I had before given him my opn
in writing that the method of apportionmt was contrary to the
Constn. He agreed that it was contrary to the common understanding of that instrument, & to what was understood at the time
by the makers of it: that yet it would bear the constn which the bill
put, & he observed that the vote for & against the bill was
perfectly geographical, a northern agt a southern vote, & he
feared he should be thought to be taking side with a southern
party. I admitted this motive of delicacy, but that it would not
induce him to do wrong: urged the dangers to which the scramble
for the fractionary members would always lead. He here expressed his fear that there would ere long, be a separation of the
Union; that the public mind seemed dissatisfied & tending to
this. He went home, sent for Randolph the Atty Genl. desired
him to get Mr. Madison immediately & come to me, & if we
three concurred in opn that he should negative the bill, he desired
to hear nothing more about it but that we would draw the
instrument for him to sign. They came. Our minds had been
before made up. We drew the instrument. Randolph carried it to
him & told him we all concurred in it. He walked with him to the
door, and as if he still wished to get off, he said, ''& you say you
approve of this yourself.'' ''Yes, Sir,'' says Randolph, ''I do
upon my honor.'' He sent it to the H. of Representatives
instantly.[16]

Washington's veto message read:

> Gentlemen of the House of Representatives: I have maturely
> considered the Act passed by the two Houses, intitled, ''An Act
> for an apportionment of Representatives among the several
> States according to the first enumeration,'' and I return it to your
> House, wherein it originated, with the following objections.

> First: The Constitution has prescribed that Representatives shall
> be apportioned among the several States, according to their
> respective Numbers: and there is no one proportion or division
> which, applied to the respective numbers of the States, will yield
> the number and allowment of Representatives proposed by the
> bill.

Second: The Constitution has also provided that the number of Representatives shall not exceed one for every thirty thousand: which restriction is, by the context, and by fair and obvious construction, to be applied to the separate and respective numbers of the States: and the bill has allotted to eight of the States more than one for thirty thousand.[17]

The first exercise of a presidential veto established, for some time to come, first, that the Constitution requires the use of some one divisor to apportion representatives; and second, that the clause "not exceed one for every thirty thousand" applies to each state separately. Jefferson, in his memoirs, described the general reaction: "A few of the hottest friends of the bill expressed passion, but the majority was satisfied, and both in and out of doors it gave pleasure to have, at length, an instance of the negative being exercised."[18]

The attempt to override the veto in the House failed: 28 for, 33 against. A scant two days sitting sufficed for the new bill, using the method of Jefferson with a divisor of 33,000, to pass in the House, despite a last-ditch Republican attempt to increase the total membership. The Senate agreed to its original proposal on the day the bill was laid before it. Washington signed the bill into law April 14, 1792. It contained the wording, "the House of Representatives shall be composed of members elected agreeably to a ratio of one member for every thirty-three thousand persons in each State." Jefferson had triumphed.

The struggle between Jefferson and Hamilton shows that the political competition over the disposition of as few as one or two seats can be fierce. This is no isolated eighteenth-century phenomenon. As late as 1941, the catalyst for a bitterly contested change in the apportionment law was the transfer of a single seat from Michigan to Arkansas. It shows, in addition, that to avoid the scramble over fractions and the self-indulgent calculations over extra members, some method must be decided upon in advance and then followed. Both Randolph and Jefferson had objected to the vetoed bill on the grounds that it merely announced an apportionment of 120 seats without stating any rule from which it followed, or which could be applied in other years. Jefferson had written to Washington:

The bill does not say that it has given the residuary representatives *to the greatest fractions*; though in fact it has done so. It seems to have avoided establishing that into a rule, lest it might not suit on another occasion. Perhaps it may be found the next time more convenient to distribute them *among the smaller States*; at another time *among the larger States*; at other times according to any other crochet which ingenuity may invent, and the combinations of the day give strength to carry; or they may do it arbitrarily by open bargains and cabal.[19]

But what method to use is not at all obvious. The skeptic who pretends it makes no difference is already answered: history shows that it does. Moreover, subsequent events would show that the methods of Jefferson and Hamilton both suffer from serious drawbacks that render their use questionable, at least in federal systems. In the coming decades many new methods would be proposed. The experience gained in applying them ultimately suggests the principles that should be used to choose among them.

CHAPTER 4

The Method of Webster

To apportion is to distribute by right measure, to set off in just parts, to assign in due and proper proportion.

DANIEL WEBSTER

Jefferson's method remained entrenched through the 1830s, even as enthusiasm for it waned. The country grew from fifteen states and a census population of 3,929,326 in 1790 to twenty-four states and 12,866,020 in 1830. The House of Representatives grew steadily as well, from 105 to 240 members, but proportionally not as fast: in 1790 the divisor had been 33,000; by 1830 it had climbed to 47,700. Through 1810 no state's number of representatives decreased; but by 1820 four of the immortal thirteen had suffered losses in the size of their delegations. Those regions fearing a loss of power searched for any new device to halt the erosion in their representation. New methods were proposed. Some were tried. Gradually, Congress began to feel its way toward the principles that should govern the distribution of its own members.

The evidence accumulated that Jefferson's method favors the larger states. In the five censuses from 1790 to 1830 Delaware had quotas of 1.61, 1.78, 1.95, 1.68, and 1.52, but in every case except 1810 it got only 1 seat. By contrast, New York received 10 seats with quota 9.63 in 1790, 17 with quota 16.66 in 1800, 27 with quota 26.20 in 1810, 34 with quota 32.50 in 1820 and 40 with quota 38.59 in 1830. The total fair share of Delaware over these five apportionments was 8.54 but it only got 6 seats, whereas the total share of New York was 123.58 and it got 128 seats.

In 1822 Representative William Lowndes of South Carolina introduced a genuinely new proposal—a variation of Hamilton's method—designed to remedy the manifest bias of Jefferson's method. Lowndes, a congressman from 1811 to 1822, had declined cabinet positions offered by both Madison and Monroe.

Determining on the number of representatives, the whole general population in representative numbers should be divided by this number—thus ascertaining the ratio of representation, and the number of representatives which each State would have, and then what would be the aggregate of the whole. . . . The complementary number—the number of members which should then be deficient of that first fixed upon, should then be divided among the States having the least representation in proportion to their respective number.[1]

The rule begins like Hamilton's, but differs in that the priority for getting an extra seat is determined, not by the size of the remainders, but rather by the average constituency that would result if no extra seat were assigned. The rationale is that a state with a larger average constituency is less well represented than a state with smaller average constituency, and so the extra seats should be given to those states which by this measure are the most disadvantaged by the initial allotment.

In 1820, twenty-four states were to share 213 seats. The representative population of Pennsylvania was 1,049,313 and its quota 24.917, while Illinois had a population of 54,843 and a quota of 1.302. In the first step Lowndes's method would, like Hamilton's, give Pennsylvania 24 seats and Illinois 1. Out of 213 seats this process would give out only 200 seats, leaving 13 unapportioned. To determine which states get the extra seats, divide the populations by the number of seats so far awarded to find the average constituencies. For Pennsylvania this constituency would be 1,049,313 divided by 24, or 43,721 whereas for Illinois it would be 54,845. Since the second number is the larger, Lowndes's method would give Illinois an extra seat before Pennsylvania. Hamilton's method would do the opposite, since Pennsylvania's remainder is larger than that of Illinois.

To compare the method more directly with Hamilton's, notice that the same priority list for the extras can be obtained by dividing the *quotas* (rather than the populations) by the initial allotment. This is because the quotas are precisely proportional to the populations. Pennsylvania's priority number would be 24.917 divided by 24, which is 1.038 whereas Illinois's is 1.302 divided by 1, which is 1.302. In fact the result will always be 1 plus a remainder; this new remainder is the state's original remainder divided by the whole number in its quota. Lowndes's method is therefore very similar to Hamilton's, except that the remainders are adjusted according to the size of the state.

The Method of Lowndes. Choose the size of the house to be apportioned. Find the quotas and give to each state the whole number contained in its quota. Adjust each state's remainder by dividing by the whole number in its quota. Assign any seats which are as yet unapportioned to those states having the largest adjusted remainders.

Regrettably, the method of Lowndes overcompensates for the large-state bias of Jefferson and gives an exaggerated handicap to the small states. Applied to the census of 1820, Lowndes's method would have given *all* of the extra seats to the *smallest* states: thus, Illinois with a quota of 1.302 would have reached 2 whereas Pennsylvania with a quota of 24.917 would have only gotten 24. The proposal died in Congress in the 1820s and was never revived. Jefferson's method, though admittedly biased, was resorted to once again.

In the 1830s the issue of bias finally came to a head. The concern of New England over its potential loss of seats was confirmed by an apportionment bill sponsored by James K. Polk of Tennessee. Polk, a protégé of Andrew Jackson, had gained renown for his bitter opposition to the policies of the Adams administration in the wake of the 1824 election. His star was rising: he would soon become Speaker of the House, then president.

Polk had originally reported a bill using Jefferson's method and a divisor of 48,000 which was later amended to 47,700 as that improved the lot of several key states.[2] There was no lack of other candidates, however. On February 15, 1832, alone, five weeks into the debate, the following nominees were discussed: 42,000; 44,300; 44,500; 44,999; 46,400; 46,500; 47,700; 48,500; 53,000; 57,000. Each divisor harbored its own political cunning. However, Polk's choice enjoyed a distinct advantage: he was chairman of the House committee on apportionment. The fact was not lost on the House. "We all know that if at a race a dozen nags are to start for the prize, fair play requires that they should start even. But, in this case, [Polk's nag] was on the course, bridled and saddled, and its rider mounted, and was to start before the others were started."[3]

The New England contingent was alarmed, but the forces of change could be brooked no longer: the tide of power was ebbing from New England—the bastion of Federalism—and rising fast in the newly opened West and South. With the divisor 47,700 the House would increase from 213 to 240 members, but Massachusetts would see her delegation decrease from 13 to 12, and New England's would drop from 39 to 38 (Table 4.1).

TABLE 4.1. Effect of Polk's Bill on New England, 1830

State	Population	Quotient of 47,700	Jefferson Appt.	Quota of 240
Massachusetts	610,408	12.797	12	12.279
Maine	399,454	8.374	8	8.035
Connecticut	297,665	6.240	6	5.988
Vermont	280,657	5.884	5	5.646
New Hampshire	269,326	5.646	5	5.418
Rhode Island	97,194	2.038	2	1.955
Total— New England	1,954,704	40.979	38	39.320

In fact New England, which had 25.7% of the total representative population in 1790, was down to 15.2% by 1830, and Massachusetts had declined from 13.1% to 5.1%. Even so the bill was not exactly kind to New England—its fair share of 240 was 39.320 seats but in Polk's bill it would only get 38. Its representatives saw the Polk bill as a direct attack. Evidently the only way to prevent a loss of seats would be to lower the divisor—or come up with some wholly new approach.

John Quincy Adams—then a representative from Massachusetts and former president—convened a meeting of his compatriots from both Houses of Congress, "to ascertain if we could not devise a means of obtaining some modification of this Apportionment bill."[4] An intellectual and high-principled New England aristocrat, out of touch with the rising spirit of democracy, Adams had lost to Andrew Jackson in the election of 1828. He feared New England's interests would be completely swamped. He recorded in his memoirs:

I passed an entirely sleepless night. The iniquity of the Apportionment bill, and the disreputable means by which so partial and unjust a distribution of the representation had been effected, agitated me so that I could not close my eyes. I was all night meditating in search of some device, if it were possible, to avert the heavy blow from the State of Massachusetts and from New England.[5]

He soon found the needed device, which he communicated by letter to his colleague Daniel Webster in the Senate.

Every word of these provisions [article I, section 2] imports the intention of the Constitution that the *whole* People shall be represented. Every apportionment therefore which leaves a portion of the People totally *unrepresented* fails to carry into effect the prescription of the Constitution. . . .

I submit to your consideration the following very simple plan for Representatives of the whole People, and which will be applicable to all future apportionment as well as the present.

It is to assume the ratio of 50,000 for the apportionment and then to add one member for the fraction of every State. The apportionment will give 226 members to which an addition of 24 members will make a House of 250 members. . . .

I have assumed the ratio of 50,000 only by way of illustration, and because it would be in the present instance, in my own opinion preferable to any other number—but the principle will adapt itself to any other number.[6]

The method is illustrated in Table 4.2. The rule is the mirror image of Jefferson's. Instead of giving to each state the largest whole number that is smaller than the quotient, it gives to each state the smallest whole number that is larger than the quotient. So, Massachusetts with quotient 12.208 receives 13 seats and New Hampshire with a quotient of 5.387 receives 6.

TABLE 4.2. Effect of Adams's Method on New England, 1830

State	Population	Adams Appt.	Quotient of 50,000	Quota of 250
Massachusetts	610,408	13	12.208	12.790
Maine	399,454	8	7.989	8.370
Connecticut	297,665	6	5.953	6.237
Vermont	280,657	6	5.613	5.881
New Hampshire	269,326	6	5.387	5.643
Rhode Island	97,194	2	1.944	2.037
Total— New England	1,954,704	41	39.094	40.959

The net result of Adams's device is that Massachusetts would be able to keep its 13 seats and New England's allotment would be 3 more than in the Polk bill.

> *The Method of John Quincy Adams.* Choose the size of the house to be apportioned. Find a divisor x so that the smallest whole numbers containing the quotients of the states sum to the required total. Give to each state its whole number.

By the time Adams had found his device it was too late to do anything in the House. "Many numbers, down to forty-two thousand and up to fifty-nine thousand were moved and rejected and lastly the number reported by the committee, forty-seven thousand seven hundred was adopted and the bill ordered to be engrossed for a third reading. I hung my harp upon the willow."[7] The torch passed to his colleague in the Senate, Daniel Webster.

By 1832 many regarded Webster as the greatest man in America. His eloquence and quality of mind were legendary. It was said that no man could be as great as Webster looked. His appetite for food, liquor, and money was gargantuan.[8] Many worshiped him, while others damned him. Some thought him godlike, others called him Black Dan.[9] An outstanding constitutional lawyer, he had won the celebrated Dartmouth College case, which laid the cornerstone for the property rights of corporations. First a representative, later senator from Massachusetts, he became one of the greatest defenders of the Union. His stirring call, "Liberty and Union, now and forever, one and inseparable," ended one of the greatest addresses ever made before a house of Congress. A perennial candidate for president, he served as secretary of state before returning to end his days in the Senate. Webster's gestures were always grand. On the morning of October 23, 1852, he announced his death for the coming evening, during the day enjoyed the sight of his favorite oxen brought to graze where he could see them from his window, and addressed the household on the existence of God. He died that night at 2:37 A.M.

In 1832 Webster was chairman of a Senate committee to study the apportionment problem. He received his friend Adams's proposal but did not act on it. From New England's standpoint it looked attractive enough, but what about the other states? Suppose that Adams's method had been applied with a divisor that apportions the same total number of seats as Polk's bill (240). Any divisor between 52,106 and 52,382 serves the purpose. The results are compared with Polk's bill for a selection of nine states in Table 4.3.

TABLE 4.3. Comparison of Adams and Jefferson Apportionments for Nine Selected States, 1830

State	Population	Quota	Adams Appt.	Jefferson Appt. (Polk Bill)
New York	1,918,578	38.593	37	40
Pennsylvania	1,348,072	27.117	26	28
Kentucky	621,832	12.509	12	13
Vermont	280,657	5.646	6	5
Louisiana	171,904	3.458	4	3
Illinois	157,147	3.161	4	3
Missouri	130,419	2.623	3	2
Mississippi	110,358	2.220	3	2
Delaware	75,432	1.517	2	1
U.S. Total	11,931,000	240	240	240

New York deserves 38.593 seats yet receives 37 under Adams's scheme. On the other hand Illinois deserves 3.161 but gets 4 and Mississippi's share is 2.220 but it gets 3. Adams appears to have a tendency to favor the smaller states, which mirrors Jefferson's tendency to favor the larger. Moreover, like Jefferson's method it does not necessarily stay within the quota: whereas Jefferson gives New York more than its quota rounded up, Adams gives it *less* than its quota rounded down. Indeed Adams's method is very similar to Jefferson's, save that instead of dropping fractions, it picks them up.

In the meantime, Webster had received another proposal from one James Dean, who was professor of astronomy and mathematics at the University of Vermont after having been a professor at Webster's alma mater, Dartmouth:

I cannot express my rule so densely and perspicuously as I could wish, but its meaning is, that each State shall have such a number of representatives, that the population for each shall be nearest possible, whether over or under, to [−].[10]

By [−] he meant a divisor x. Dean's proposal is easily explained by example. The 1830 representative population of Massachusetts was 610,408: if it received 12 seats its average constituency size would be 50,867 (610,408 divided by 12); if it received 13 it would be 46,954. So, if the divisor were 47,700 as Polk proposed, Massachusetts should receive 13 seats because 46,954 is closer to 47,700 than is 50,867.

The Method of Dean. Choose the size of the house to be apportioned. Find a divisor x so that the whole numbers which make the average constituencies of the states closest to x sum to the required total. Give to each state its whole number.

The method is illustrated in Table 4.4 for the 1830 example, using a divisor of 50,000, which apportions 240 seats. Compared to Adams's the method gives one more seat each to New York and Pennsylvania and one less each to Illinois and Mississippi (see Table 4.6). The result is an apportionment that seems less biased toward the smaller states. (Compare, however, New York and Louisiana.) In any event, Webster was apparently not persuaded by this suggestion either, though he did append it to the Senate Committee's Report.

On April 5, 1832, Webster addressed the Senate and lifted what had been a minor political squabble into a grave constitutional issue.

To apportion is to distribute by right measure, to set off in just parts, to assign in due and proper proportion. These clauses of the Constitution respect not only the portions of power, but the portions of the public burden, also, which should fall to the several States. . . . The end aimed at is, that representation and taxation should go hand in hand. . . . But between the apportionment of Representatives and the apportionment of taxes, there necessarily exists one essential difference. . . . (The) apportionment of taxes is capable of being made so exact, that the inequality becomes minute and invisible. But representation

TABLE 4.4. Dean's Method for Nine Selected States, 1830

State	Population	Quotient By 50,000	Constituency When Rounded Up	Constituency When Rounded Down	Dean Appt.	Quota
New York	1,918,578	38.372	49,194	50,489	38	38.593
Pennsylvania	1,348,072	26.961	49,929	51,849	27	27.117
Kentucky	621,832	12.437	47,833	51,819	12	12.509
Vermont	280,657	5.613	46,776	56,131	6	5.646
Louisiana	171,904	3.438	42,976	57,301	4	3.458
Illinois	157,147	3.143	39,287	52,382	3	3.161
Missouri	130,419	2.608	43,473	65,210	3	2.623
Mississippi	110,358	2.207	36,786	55,179	2	2.220
Delaware	75,432	1.509	37,716	75,432	2	1.517

cannot be thus divided. . . . It is quite obvious, therefore, that
the apportionment of representative power can never be precise
and perfect. . . .

The Constitution, therefore, must be understood, not as enjoin-
ing an absolute relative equality, because that would be demanding an impossibility, but as requiring of Congress to make the
apportionment of Representatives among the several States according to their respective numbers, *as near as may be*. That
which cannot be done perfectly must be done in a manner as near
perfection as can be. . . .

(The) Constitution prescribes no particular process by which this
apportionment is to be wrought out. It has plainly described the
end to be accomplished, namely, the nearest approach to relative
equality of representation among the States. . . .

(Whether) this end be attained best by one process or another,
becomes, when each process has been carried through, not
matter of opinion, but matter of mathematical certainty.[11]

Webster next asserted—as had Hamilton before him—that what should be
done for apportionment is analogous to what would naturally be done for
taxes: first decide the number of seats to be distributed, then compute the
exact share or quota deserved by each. The Polk bill passed by the House
gave 40 seats to New York with a quota 38.593, 28 to Pennsylvania with
quota 27.117, 5 to Vermont with quota 5.646, and 1 to Delaware with
quota 1.517.

Now two things are undeniably true: first, that to take away the
fortieth member from New York would bring her representation
nearer to her exact proportion than it stands by leaving her that
fortieth member; second, that giving the member thus taken from
New York to Vermont would bring her representation nearer to
her exact right than it is by the bill. And both these propositions
are equally true of a transfer to Delaware of the twenty-eighth
member assigned by the bill to Pennsylvania, and to Missouri of
the thirteenth member assigned to Kentucky.[12]

In three cases the transfer of a single seat from one to another state would
bring the apportionment of each state nearer to its quota (see Table 4.6).

How could it be said, Webster asked, that the House bill apportions *as near as may be*?

So, what should be done to achieve the intent of the Constitution? Webster suggested that when possible the most intuitive idea of all should be adopted: simply round the quotas to the nearest whole numbers. Unfortunately, this does not always work, since either too many or too few seats may be alloted. To remedy the difficulty, Webster found guidance on what to do in precedent. Washington's veto of the first apportionment bill in 1792, which used Hamilton's method, contained the objection that it was not based on any one common divisor. Webster therefore concluded:

> Let the rule be that the population of each State be divided by a common divisor, and, in addition to the number of members resulting from such division, a member shall be allowed to each State whose fraction exceeds a moiety of the divisor.[13]

The Method of Webster. Choose the size of the house to be apportioned. Find a divisor x so that the whole numbers nearest to the quotients of the states sum to the required total. Give to each state its whole number.

Applied to the populations of 1830, Webster's proposal apportions 240 seats using the divisor 49,800 (see Table 4.5), though any divisor between 49,747 and 49,833 will do as well. Webster had, in fact, reconciled the opposing points of view of Jefferson and Hamilton by using a common divisor—and so basing the method on proportionality—and yet

TABLE 4.5. Webster Apportionment for Nine Selected States, 1830

State	Population	Quotient (49,800)	Webster Appt.	Quota
New York	1,918,578	38.526	39	38.593
Pennsylvania	1,348,072	27.070	27	27.117
Kentucky	621,832	12.487	12	12.509
Vermont	280,657	5.636	6	5.646
Louisiana	171,904	3.452	3	3.458
Illinois	157,147	3.156	3	3.161
Missouri	130,419	2.619	3	2.623
Mississippi	110,358	2.216	2	2.220
Delaware	75,432	1.515	2	1.517
U.S. total	11,931,000	239.573	240	240

linking the computation more closely to the ideal shares or quotas of each state.

In presenting his brief, Webster was careful to anticipate the objections of the friends of Polk who would argue against giving seats to fractions. He pointed out that "unrepresented" fractions are mere chimera: every person, the whole of every state, is always represented. The real issue is that some states are represented more than adequately, some less than adequately. One need only contrast the apportionment with the quotas to see that. The fractions devolving from the method of Jefferson or any method that uses a divisor represent nothing real: they only result from the choice of the divisor. "What is a divisor? Not necessarily a simple number. It may be composed of a whole number and a fraction; it may itself be the result of a previous process; it may be anything, in short, which produces accurate and uniform division."[14]

By 1832 four different methods had been proposed that rested upon the choice of a single divisor. Each has its beguiling logic. Table 4.6 contrasts the solutions they wrought for nine of the twenty-four states in 1830. There is a clear tendency in going from left to right—from Adams to Dean to Webster to Jefferson—for the small states to lose advantage and the large states to gain advantage. Adams is kindest to the small, harshest on the large, and Jefferson the reverse. Between Dean and Webster there is less difference, though there is evidence that Dean favors the small more than Webster does. Which is fairest?

In 1832 Hamilton enthusiasts also entered the lists with Webster against the House bill. Prominent among them was Senator Dickerson of New Jersey, described as one of the soundest mathematicians in the

TABLE 4.6. Apportionments for Nine Selected States, 1830

State	Quota	Adams Appt.	Dean Appt.	Webster Appt.	Jefferson Appt.
New York	38.593	37	38	39	40
Pennsylvania	27.117	26	27	27	28
Kentucky	12.509	12	12	12	13
Vermont	5.646	6	6	6	5
Louisiana	3.458	4	4	3	3
Illinois	3.161	4	3	3	3
Missouri	2.623	3	3	3	2
Mississippi	2.220	3	2	2	2
Delaware	1.517	2	2	2	1
Subtotal	96.844	97	97	97	97

Congress. Dickerson pointed out that the fractions which result from Jefferson's method have no real meaning: in fact the quotients, including the fractions, add up to 250.13 seats whereas only 240 are given out. Dickerson challenged the supporters of the Polk bill to explain where the other 10 representatives had gone. In defense, a senator from Virginia sounded a warning to the Senate against those employing the abstruse principles of mathematics. Dickerson responded that it was rather the adherents of Jefferson's method who were being abstruse:

> He [the senator from Virginia] did distinctly insinuate his suspicion that I should resort to the differential calculus. . . . Now, I am entirely innocent of any such designs. . . . A knowledge of this calculus is by no means necessary to our purpose; common arithmetic, addition, subtraction, multiplication, and division, are sufficient to enable us to prove, beyond all doubt, that the bill deprives a part of the States of ten Representatives which fairly belong to them. . . . It is the Senator from Virginia who is endeavoring to avail himself of the principles of this calculus . . . by making use of ten fractional Representatives which he seems to consider as infinitesimal, evanescent quantities . . . then causing them to vanish. . . . These quasi-representatives, these infinitesimal, evanescent Representatives, these ideal Representatives, these ghosts of Representatives, after being counted in order to give the favored States their full proportion of a House of 250, are dismissed the service.[15]

For the moment these arguments went unheeded. The westward migration into the central states was in full swing. Their combined population had increased by more than 50% since 1820. Their members were not overly concerned with principles: they simply wanted a bigger share of the pie. Ultimately Polk's forces triumphed and Jefferson's method was adopted once again.

With time, however, the disenchantment with Jefferson's approach grew and the force of Webster's arguments began to be felt. In 1842 the debate on apportionment in the House began in the customary way with a jockeying for the choice of a divisor using Jefferson's method. On one day alone, 59 different motions to fix a divisor were made in a House containing but 242 members. The values ranged from 30,000 to 140,000, with more than half between 50,159 and 62,172. But the Senate had tired of this approach and proposed instead an apportionment of 223 members using

Webster's method. In the House, John Quincy Adams urged acceptance of the method but argued vehemently for enlarging the number of members, as New England's portion was steadily dwindling. In the end the House agreed to the smaller number. This was the one and only time in the course of congressional history that the number of members actually declined.[16]

The United States congressional debates of 1792 through 1832 were largely fired by sectional and political self-interest in the face of growth and of relative shifts in population. They produced the three methods most often used throughout the world: Webster's, Jefferson's, and Hamilton's. Webster's was later reinvented in other guises and is now alternatively known as the "method of odd numbers" or the "Sainte-Laguë" method. In contrast, neither Lowndes's nor Dean's seems ever to have been proposed elsewhere. In addition, the regular ten-year cycle of apportionment discussions steadily built up a collection of insights concerning what methods do in practice. Some stay within the quota, such as Hamilton's and Lowndes's, and some do not, such as Jefferson's and Adams's. Some methods, like Adams's, distinctly favor the smaller states; others like Jefferson's, favor the larger; while others, like Dean's and Webster's, seem to fall in between. These observations—decisive, it turned out, in the ultimate rejection of Jefferson's method for congressional apportionment—were soon to be complemented by the discovery of quite surprising anomalies in some of the other methods.

CHAPTER 5

Paradoxes

A most ingenious paradox!
We've quips and quibbles heard in flocks,
But none to beat this paradox!

W.S. GILBERT

The period 1850 to 1900 in the United States was characterized by growth, expansion, and industrialization. In these fifty years the population grew more than threefold, from some 23 million to 75 million. Fourteen new states were added. But in addition to the absolute increase in population and in states came important internal migrations from the Eastern seaboard to the newly opened West and from the country to the cities. The constitutional provision that asked for a census and reapportionment every ten years led to great shifts in political power between states and regions. New England declined from 12% to 7.5% of the population, the South from 32% to 25%, while the urban population increased from 15% to 40%. It was, of course, a time of intense sectional and social strife, and this was reflected in the apportionment debates of those years.

In this political environment the House grew from 234 members in 1852 to 386 in 1902. But not without objections:

> The greater the inefficiency of the House by reason of its unwieldy size, the greater advantage of the Senate in cases of collision. A body is not great by being big. Corpulence is not health or vigor. A wheezy adiposity is not necessarily a condition of mental alertness. Layers of lard and monstrosities of fat are not conducive to manhood. . . . Therefore, if we would strengthen the House, let us give the number most efficient, not the "wallowing, unwieldy" mass. Without being personal to myself, I go for the smaller body.[1]

These pressures subjected some of the known methods, such as Jefferson's and Hamilton's, to a variety of trials that revealed an anomalous and paradoxical behavior which ultimately led to their abandonment. With experience the method of Webster gradually emerged as the one that appeared both to avoid the paradoxes and to be the best suited on the basis of common sense.

Despite this, the method of Hamilton was the one enshrined in law during the entire period. This curious turn of events was due to a representative from Ohio, Samuel F. Vinton. In 1850, some two years before the habitual season, Representative Vinton rose to speak in favor of adopting a permanent apportionment act. He was no doubt seeking to prevent the wrangle between South and North that would almost inevitably occur if Congress waited until the numbers were actually reported. Vinton maintained that the Constitution had contemplated a permanent legal act—not a "disreputable contest about the unrepresented fractions" and a scramble for new divisors and new methods every ten years. It was recognized that the method he proposed bore a "striking similarity" to the one vetoed by Washington in 1792; nevertheless, "Vinton's Method of 1850" was enacted and remained formally on the books into the twentieth century, long after it had become apparent that it was unsatisfactory. It was nothing other than Hamilton's method.

In fact Vinton's Act was *never* strictly followed. It specified a fixed House size of 233 seats, but the apportionment of 1852 was of 234 seats (to give 2 seats rather than 1 to California, whose population was quickly climbing after Sutter's discovery of gold). At 234 ordinary rounding happens to work, so Webster would have given the same result.

In the 1860s and 1870s no real method was used, because the results of "Vinton's Method" were altered to satisfy the greed of certain states. In the 1860s, 233 seats were first meted out in accordance with the method, and then a pretext was found to give out 8 more seats—all of them to Northern states. A similar process was resorted to in the 1870s, but this time the results were more serious. A first apportionment of 283 seats—the number 283 chosen because the results of the methods of Hamilton and Webster would then agree—was supplemented by 9 additional seats several months later, and this definitive apportionment agreed with neither a Hamilton nor a Webster apportionment of 292 seats.[2] In the presidential election of 1876, Rutherford B. Hayes, governor of Ohio and the Republican candidate, received a popular vote of 4,036,298, whereas Samuel J. Tilden, former governor of New York and the Democratic candidate, received 4,300,590. Nevertheless, Hayes won by a margin of one in the electoral college, 185 to 184. Had Hamilton's method been followed as required by law, Tilden would have won instead.[3] This election is one of only two times in United States history that the electoral college gave a result contrary to the popular vote.*

In time, experience with Hamilton's—alias Vinton's—method brought to light a curious phenomenon. Based on the census of 1870 the Census Bureau had computed apportionments using Hamilton's method for all House sizes between 241 and 300. Inspecting the results a representative noticed the following strange fact:

> It appears . . . that allowing two hundred and seventy members to this house, the State of Rhode Island will have two members, but when the aggregate number of members of the House is increased to two hundred and eighty Rhode Island has . . . but one member. Whether it is a persuance of law matters not. We are not expounding the old law; we are seeking to establish a new law more in accordance with justice, with reason, and with wisdom.[4]

To remedy the situation he proposed the method of Webster; but his suggestion went largely unnoticed.

The phenomenon was observed again after the census of 1880 by C. W. Seaton, chief clerk of the Census Office. To provide the information needed by Congress, Seaton had computed apportionments using Hamilton's method for all House sizes between 275 and 350. In a letter to Congress dated October 25, 1881, he stated:

> While making these calculations I met with the so-called "Alabama" paradox where Alabama was allotted 8 Representatives out of a total of 299, receiving but 7 when the total became 300.

> Such a result as this is to me conclusive proof that the process employed in obtaining it is defective, and that it does not in fact "apportion Representatives among the States according to their respective numbers."

> This conclusion has been confirmed by the discovery of other anomalies, and the result of my study of this question is the

---

*In the election of 1888 Benjamin Harrison with 5,439,853 popular votes had 233 electoral votes against Grover Cleveland with 5,540,309 and 168.

strong conviction that an entirely different process should be employed.[5]

This time the Congress sat up and took notice.

How is it possible that Alabama can lose a seat when there are more to go around? The answer lies in the peculiar way in which Hamilton's method works. (Table 5.1) As the House increases from 299 to 300 the quotas of all states increase by the same proportion, but not by the same absolute amounts. By the census of 1880 Alabama's quota of 299 seats is 7.646, and it would be allotted 8 seats using Hamilton's method, but it is just at the dividing line: no state with smaller remainder would get an extra seat. In a House of 300 Alabama's quota is 7.671, an increase of .025 or .33%. The quotas of the larger states also increase by .33%, but being larger their remainders increase by more. Both Illinois and Texas run past Alabama and get extra seats, and since the House has only increased by 1 there are none left for Alabama.

In his letter, Seaton proposed a solution to the problem that he apparently thought was new, but which was simply a disguised version of Jefferson's method. Congress was quick to discover this, and greeted the proposal with derision:

> Now let us see this new method which we have here as a sort of new revelation in mathematics. I thought, Mr. Speaker, that mathematics was a divine science. I thought, that mathematics was the only science that spoke to inspiration and was infallible in its utterances. I have been taught always that it demonstrated the truth. I have been told that while in astronomy and philosophy and geometry and all other sciences, there was something left for speculation, that mathematics, like the voice of

TABLE 5.1. The Alabama Paradox under Hamilton's Method, 1880

State	Quota at 299	Quota at 300	% Increase	Absolute Increase
Alabama	7.646	7.671	.33	.025
Texas	9.640	9.672	.33	.032
Illinois	18.640	18.702	.33	.062

NOTE: We have used the representative populations as given in the 1880 census. In the tables he gave to Congress, Seaton used a slightly different set of representative populations. Presumably corrections were made after Seaton submitted his report.

Revelation, said when it spoke, "Thus saith the Lord." But here is a new system of mathematics that demonstrates the truth to be false.[6]

The earlier objections to the method were revived: it did not stay within the quota and it favored the larger states. In a House of 320 members, New York would have a quota of 32.94 and receive 34 seats and Pennsylvania a quota of 27.76 and receive 29; whereas Florida and Rhode Island would have quotas of 1.75 and 1.79 and receive only one seat each. One supporter of the method was accused of "committing a classic rape on a cloud of statistics right in the face of the House."[7]

The final outcome was a bill apportioning 325 seats. No method was specified, but 325 was specifically chosen because for that number the methods of Webster and Hamilton gave the same result. Thus, while Hamilton's method remained legally enshrined in Vinton's Act of 1850, a way was found to circumvent it—namely, by choosing the number of seats so that the Webster and Hamilton solutions agreed. The same compromise was resorted to again in the 1890s. In 1891 the House Select Committee on Apportionment investigated the Hamilton solutions for all house sizes between 332 and 375. They reported, "Trials were made until a number [356] was found that would give a ratio which in application would secure each State against any loss in its membership and in no instance lose a major fraction."[8]

The effect of Hamilton's method on the census returns for 1900 proved to be so upsetting to Congress, however, that compromise was no longer possible. In 1901 the Select Committee on the Twelfth Census, presided over by Representative Albert J. Hopkins of Illinois, submitted a report that contained tables giving apportionments for all House sizes between 350 and 400. Maine's delegation kept hopping up and down between 3 and 4 seats (see Table 5.2). Other states suffered similar anomalies. Colorado would get 3 seats in every instance except one: in a House of 357 members it would get 2. Colorado had Populist leanings and Hopkins was no friend of Populism. The bill reported by the Hopkins committee provided for a House of precisely 357 seats and furor erupted. Representative John E. Littlefield of Maine vented his righteous anger not

TABLE 5.2. Maine's Allotment by Hamilton's Method, 1900

House size	350–382	383–385	386	387–388	389–390	391–400
Maine seats	3	4	3	4	3	4

only against Hopkins's calculations but against the method that had led to this result:

> The gentleman [Mr. Hopkins] cannot stand here and deliver himself of his censorious criticism characterized by venom and spleen during a speech of an hour and a half and then rise on the floor and say that what he said was complimenting and eulogizing the State of Maine. . . . We submit that the bill of the Committee is not in accordance with any of the precedents since 1850. There never has been a reapportionment made since 1850 that does not give to every majority fraction a Representative in the House. . . . I do not say that the chairman of this Committee adopted the basis of 357, the only basis that would leave out Colorado above 350, because Populists happen to come from Colorado, as he sneeringly suggested. . . . I call attention to the remarkable fact, however. . . . Let me strike another paradox in connection with belabored and assaulted Maine. . . . Maine loses on 382. She loses again with 386, and does not lose with 387 or 388. Then she loses again on 389 and 390, and then ceases to lose. Not only is Maine subjected to the assaults of the chairman of this Committee, but it does seem as though mathematics and science had combined to make a shuttlecock and battledore of the State of Maine in connection with the scientific basis upon which this bill is presented. . . . In Maine comes and out Maine goes. . . . God help the State of Maine when mathematics reach for her and undertake to strike her down.[9]

The tone of the debate was malicious and partisan. Hopkins referred to the curse of Bryanism and Populism, then attacked Littlefield:

> It is true that under the majority bill Maine is entitled to only three Representatives, and, if Dame Rumor is to be credited, the seat of the gentleman who addressed the House on Saturday last is the one in danger. In making this statement he takes a modest way to tell the House and the country how dependent the State of Maine is upon him. How delightfully encouraging it must be to his colleagues of that State to know the esteem in which they are held by him. Maine crippled! Maine, the State of Hannibal Hamlin, William Pitt Fessenden, of James G. Blaine. . . . That

great State crippled by the loss of LITTLEFIELD! Why, Mr. Speaker, if the gentleman's statement be true that Maine is to be crippled by this loss, then I can see much force in the prayer he uttered here when he said "God help the State of Maine."[10]

The results produced by Hamilton's method proved to be more than Congress could accept. Hopkins's bill failed, and Hamilton's method was finally abandoned altogether—three decades after the phenomenon of the Alabama paradox had first come to the attention of Congress. Instead, Webster's method was applied to a House enlarged to 386 members. At 386 no state would lose a seat.[11]

The debate of 1901, and the deliberate choice of Webster's method over Hamilton's, seems to have established the precedent that no method which admits the Alabama paradox can be considered for Congressional apportionment. Moreover, Congress arrived at this conclusion not because of some particular numerical outcome that was overturned for political reasons, but because it saw that qualitatively Hamilton's method gave results that were contrary to common sense. No apportionment method is reasonable that gives some state fewer seats when there are more seats to go around.

This was not the first time that Congress had rejected a method on the basis of principle: ultimately Jefferson's method had been abandoned because it frequently gave some states more than their quotas rounded up and was systematically more generous to the large states than to the small. In federal systems like the United States, where strict proportionality and adherence to one-man, one-vote are the overriding considerations, methods exhibiting such favoritism must be considered unacceptable.

Congress detected the Alabama paradox in practice because of the changing House size, but it appears to have missed an even graver paradox of Hamilton's method that occurs when populations change. As the populations of states shift relative to one another it is natural to expect that their apportionments will change accordingly. If in the period between two censuses some state A grows larger relative to state B, then it is absurd to suppose that state A would lose seats to state B. Yet this can happen with Hamilton's method—and would have been noticed in this decade if the Census Bureau had systematically applied the method as the populations changed.[12]

Suppose that to stay abreast of the rapid shifts in population reapportionment were deemed necessary every year. From the compound annual growth rate of each state in the period between the censuses of 1900 and

1910 the states' populations in the intermediate years may be interpolated. In 1900 the method of Hamilton would give 10 seats to Virginia and 3 to Maine, whereas in 1901 it would give 9 to Virginia and 4 to Maine. But Virginia was growing faster than Maine. In 1900 Virginia's population was 1,854,184 compared to Maine's 694,466, or 2.67 times as large, whereas by 1901 it was 1,873,951 compared to 699,114 or 2.68 times as large. Yet by Hamilton's method Virginia loses a seat to Maine!

The reason the method suffers from this *population paradox* is easy to see by studying the quotas. In 1900 Virginia's fair share of 386 seats was 9.599 and Hamilton rounded it up, whereas Maine's fair share of 3.595 was rounded down. Virginia was growing at the rate of 1.07% per year and Maine by .67% per year but the nation as a whole was growing at the faster pace of 2.02% per year. This implies that by 1901 the shares of Virginia and Maine had both declined to 9.509 and 3.548 respectively. In absolute terms Virginia's share had declined more because it was larger and so, even though Virginia was growing larger relative to Maine, the two states changed places in the race of remainders and Maine would receive the last of the "extra" seats.

The population paradox violates the fundamental idea that changes in apportionments ought to reflect correctly changes in population. Between 1900 and 1901 Virginia was not just growing much faster than Maine—in absolute numbers Virginia increased by 19,767 and Maine by 4,648—but her rate of growth relative to Maine's was almost 60% greater. Virginia became proportionally larger than Maine, but the method of Hamilton would translate this into taking one seat from Virginia to give it to Maine. This in itself would seem to rule out the use of Hamilton's method. However, still another, albeit related, anomaly of the method arises when states join—or secede from—the Union.

Oklahoma became a state in 1907. Prior to its entry the House was composed of 386 members apportioned according to the census of 1900, when the total representative population was counted as 74,562,608, so each member of the House represented some 193,167 persons. Oklahoma's representative population at the time of entry was about 1 million, so it should have been entitled to about 5 seats. In fact, it received this number, bringing the total in the House to 391 members. One would certainly assume that the previous apportionment of 386 seats plus 5 for Oklahoma would have given a just allocation of 391 seats—that no tampering with the distribution to the other states would have been necessary—but with Hamilton's method this is not so. Applied to 391 seats it gives Oklahoma 5 seats, Maine 4, and New York 37. But without Oklahoma it apportions the original 386 seats differently: New York gets 38 and Maine only 3. In other words when Oklahoma entered the Union with its fair share of seats, Hamilton's method would have forced New York to give up a seat to Maine, even though there was no change in the populations of New York and Maine or any of the other states. By the same token, if Oklahoma had dropped out of the Union taking its 5 seats with it, Hamilton's method would have required Maine to hand over 1 seat to New York. This *new states paradox* occurs for much the same reason as the population paradox. When Oklahoma enters, the quotas of all the other states decrease proportionally by a small amount. But in absolute terms New York's fraction decreases faster than Maine's, so their priorities for receiving an extra seat are reversed (see Table 5.3)

Intrinsic to the idea of fair division is that it stand up under comparisons. If an estate is divided up fairly among heirs, then there should be no reason for them to want to trade afterward. Anyone should be able to compare his share with anyone else's and remain satisfied. Any group should be able to conclude that the share it gets is fairly divided among its own members. In short, any part of a fair division should be fair. If New York and Maine share 41 seats then 37 and 4 cannot be the fair shares when Oklahoma is in the Union whereas 38 and 3 are the fair shares when Oklahoma is out. In both cases 41 seats are shared, in both cases the claims are the same, and in both cases they should be shared in the same way.

What is the explanation for these paradoxes? In each case it is the Hamilton method's use of the remainders to determine the priority for "extra" seats. The use of remainders is not an idea rooted in proportionality because the relative sizes of the states are ignored. Intuitively, the objection Washington had raised, at Jefferson's prompting, in his 1792 veto of Hamilton's apportionment, is correct: "there is no one proportion or division which applied to the respective numbers of the States, will yield

TABLE 5.3. The New States Paradox

State	Without Oklahoma			With Oklahoma		
	Population	Quota	Hamilton Appt.	Population	Quota	Hamilton Appt.
Maine	694,466	3.595	3	694,466	3.594	4
New York	7,264,183	37.606	38	7,264,183	37.589	37
Oklahoma	—	—	—	1,000,000	5.175	5
U.S. totals	74,562,608	386	386	75,562,608	391	391

the number and allowment of Representatives proposed by the bill.'' The challenge—destined to nourish many more years of United States congressional debates—is to find a satisfactory method that escapes from the population, new states, and Alabama paradoxes.

CHAPTER 6

The Controversy over Bias

A man may be very sincere in good principles without having good practice.
SAMUEL JOHNSON

In the twentieth century the choice of a method of apportionment engrossed not only members of Congress but also the scientific and academic communities. The focus of the argument was the treatment of the smaller as against the larger states. The reason is simple: continuing immigration together with the migration from the country to the cities threatened the rural states with a further erosion of power. This was so strikingly revealed by the census of 1920 that the entrenched rural interests put a stop to any reapportionment for the decade. The resulting inequity in representation made reapportionment a burning issue in Congress and focused attention on it nationwide.

For the first time, apportionment had begun to be studied systematically as a mathematical problem. The impetus for this development came from the Census Office itself, which as early as 1899 had established a program to involve scholars from leading universities in the work of the Office. Among these was Walter F. Willcox, then a young professor in the philosophy department at Cornell. Willcox had helped prepare the tables for the apportionment of 1900, which began an involvement in the problem that was to last for more than a half century.

Willcox was a pioneer in the study of public opinion and the application of the new science of statistics to demography, public health, and the law. He served at different times as president of the American Economic Association, the American Statistical Association, and the American Sociological Association. Despite his academic prominence he was a man of strongly practical bent. He emphasized careful attention to empirical data and the application of straightforward statistical procedures. He lived to be 103, and had remained professionally active well into his nineties. Among other accomplishments, he was renowned as a great walker, and is reported to have remarked: "Unfortunately there is some danger that I will be remembered more for my feet than for my head."[1]

By 1910 Willcox had become the first serious student of apportionment. He concluded, based on a study of examples as well as congressional debates, that Webster's method—which he called the method of "major fractions"—was the correct approach. In December 1910 he communicated his opinion to the chairman of the House Committee on the Census:

> The history of reports, debates, and votes upon apportionment seems to show a settled conviction in Congress that every major fraction gives a valid claim to an additional Representative. This conviction has controlled the final apportionment, I believe, on every occasion since and including the apportionment based on the census of 1840. It has been followed even when to follow it has entailed some departure from the method on which the computations were based.[2]

With this opinion he attached tables showing the result of Webster's method applied to the census of 1910 for every size of House between 390 and 440. Based on these tables, Congress passed a bill in the spring of 1911 apportioning 433 seats, together with the provision that the territories of Arizona and New Mexico receive one seat each, should they be admitted as states before the next census. The number 433 was chosen because it was "the lowest number that will prevent any State from losing a Representative."[3] Thus Webster's method was unequivocally adopted, and the heritage of Vinton's bill, and so of Hamilton's method, was finally discarded.

In the meantime, however, another method had been advanced. In a letter to the chairman of the House Committee on the Census, Joseph A. Hill, chief statistician of the Division of Revision and Results, Bureau of the Census, described a new approach and attached tables showing its results for the same House sizes given by Willcox:

> The principle here followed is that the ratios of the number of inhabitants per Representative should be as nearly uniform as possible, because it is assumed that in this way the nearest possible approach is made to an apportionment conforming to the population of the several States. . . . The only question (is) how we shall measure these divergences so as to determine that they are in fact the smallest that are possible. . . .

We might subtract one ratio from the other, measuring the divergence by the resulting arithmetical difference; or we might consider how many times greater one ratio is than the other, measuring the divergence on a percentage basis, and expressing it as a percentage or relative difference instead of an arithmetical or absolute difference.

This (latter) is believed to be the correct method.[4]

Why should the relative difference in representation be the proper measure of inequality? Hill observed that if a state has average constituency 100,000, and another 50,000, their absolute inequality is 50,000; whereas, if one has 75,000 and another 25,000, their absolute inequality is again 50,000, or the same. And yet the inequality in representation seems to be worse in the second case than in the first. For in the first case the state with 50,000 per representative is 100% better off, and in the second case the state with 25,000 per representative is 200% better off. Measuring in this manner, Hill believed, the injustice to the small states as compared with the large states would be redressed.

The Method of Hill. Choose the size of the house to be apportioned. Give to each state a number of seats so that no transfer of any one seat can reduce the percentage difference in representation between those states.

The subtlety of the method may be seen by comparing its results with those of Dean's method for the 1910 census and 425 seats. The two methods would have differed in two states: Massachusetts and Florida (see Table 6.1). By Dean's method Florida is advantaged and Massachusetts disadvantaged. Hill's approach is to ask *how many times* better off Florida is than Massachusetts, and then check whether the discrepancy can be reduced by a transfer. By Dean's solution Massachusetts would have one representative for every 224,428 persons, whereas Florida would have one for every 188,155. The ratio of 224,428 to 188,155 is 1.193 which means that Florida is 19.3% better represented than is Massachusetts. Suppose one seat is taken from Florida and given to Massachusetts. The average constituency of Florida would then be 250,873 and of Massachusetts 210,401, so now Massachusetts is better off. But since the ratio of 250,873 to 210,401 is 1.192, Massachusetts is only 19.2% better off relative to Florida. Since 19.2% is a slightly smaller percentage than 19.3%, by Hill's reasoning the second apportionment is to be preferred to the first.

TABLE 6.1. Hill versus Dean Solution for 425 Seats, 1910

State	Population	Quota	Dean Appt.	Constituency	Diff. Rel. %	Diff. Abs.
Massachusetts	3,366,316	15.710	15	224,428		
					19.3	36,273
Florida	752,619	3.512	4	188,155		

State	Population	Quota	Hill Appt.	Constituency	Diff. Rel. %	Diff. Abs.
Massachusetts			16	210,401		
					19.2	40,472
Florida			3	250,873		

Hill's method—as compared with Dean's—favors the larger state over the smaller. But it is the Dean solution that minimizes the inequality between states, if inequality is measured in terms of the *absolute difference* in persons per representative (an idea mentioned but rejected by Hill). This is because Dean's method finds a common divisor x (in this case 217,500) and an assignment of seats to each state which makes the number of persons per representative closest to x. A transfer of a seat between two states will therefore move the number of persons per representative further away from x in both states, and so will increase their absolute difference. Dean's method can therefore also be described as the one that makes the inequality between any two states as small as possible if inequality is measured as the absolute difference in persons per representative. In contrast, Hill's method uses the relative difference to measure inequality. The analogy also suggests a practical way to calculate Hill's method that he had not noticed: find a common divisor x and assign that number of seats to each state which makes the number of persons per representative closest to x in relative terms, then adjust x until the seats assigned sum to the required total.

In 1921 Edward V. Huntington, professor of mechanics and mathematics at Harvard, made his appearance on the stage of apportionment. During the war Huntington had gone to Washington, where he was associated with the Bureau of the Census. He was noted for his axiomatic work in algebra and was greatly admired as a teacher. He was affable, courteous, enjoyed a good sense of humor, and was most adept in giving testimony in Congress, as subsequent events were to prove.

Huntington had been a classmate of Hill at Harvard. In renewing their aquaintance, he naturally learned of Hill's idea that an apportionment should minimize the relative difference in representation between every pair of states. Unfortunately, Hill, after stating his idea perfectly succinctly, had gone on to suggest a method for computing solutions that does not always give a result which agrees with his idea.[5] Hill had called his approach the "method of alternate ratios." Huntington showed how to find apportionments correctly by Hill's method and cleverly renamed it the "method of equal proportions." Henceforth he was to regard it as his own invention.

Between 1910 and 1920 two new states—Arizona and New Mexico—had joined the Union, each with one seat. This brought the total to 435 seats and completed the addition of new states for the immediate future. Based on the experiences of 1900 and 1910, there was every reason to expect that the 1920 apportionment would again be done by Webster's method. In an effort to head off this possibility, Huntington addressed a letter to the chairman of the House Committee on the Census in January 1921, which ran in part as follows: "Within the last few days . . . I have finished the formal exposition of my method and its application to the 1920 Census . . . statistical experts in the university who have examined my plan have pronounced it the only scientific method and have given me permission to state so."[6] He then compared the results of "his" method with Webster's for the 1920 census and 435 seats. They differed in six states, as shown in Table 6.2.

A cursory comparison of the two solutions suggests that Hill's method favors the small states more than Webster's does, since in each case where a difference exists Hill's method gives more to the small states

TABLE 6.2. Differences between Hill and Webster Apportionments, 1920

State	Population	Quota	Hill Appt.	No. Reps. per Million	Webster Appt.	No. Reps. per Million
New York	10,380,589	42.919	42	4.046	43	4.142
North Carolina	2,559,123	10.581	10	3.908	11	4.298
Virginia	2,309,187	9.547	9	3.897	10	4.331
Rhode Island	604,397	2.499	3	4.964	2	3.309
New Mexico	353,428	1.461	2	5.659	1	2.829
Vermont	352,428	1.457	2	5.675	1	2.837
Total U.S.	105,210,729	435	435		435	

and less to the large states. There is a reason for this: the relative-difference idea in effect ascribes more weight to the fractions of small states than to those of large states. The idea behind using the relative difference may seem attractive but are the results fair? Compared with the quotas, the Webster solution for 1920 seems more natural. Huntington chose to omit this comparison by not giving the quotas in his letter.

However, events were moving in a different direction. Before Huntington's letter had been received the House Committee had reported a bill apportioning 483 seats using the method of Webster. The logic of 483 was the time-honored one that assured no loss to any state. The bill passed the House but died in the Senate: 435 was tried and failed. These were the first in a series of apportionment bills in the 1920s, all of which came to naught. In the end the 1911 apportionment stood for the entire decade and there was to be no apportionment based on the 1920 census—in direct violation of the Constitution.

The reason was rural reaction to the enormous gains in population being made by the cities. Rapid industrialization, the first World War, and the increasing mechanization of agriculture had all combined to accelerate migration from the rural to the urban states during the preceding decade. The census of 1920 showed an overall increase of some 14 million persons, but the rural population had actually declined by 5 million and the cities had swelled by 19 million. If the 435 seats of the House had been reapportioned by Webster's method in 1920, ten rural states would have lost 11 seats, California would have gained 3, and Michigan and Ohio 2. Altogether, nineteen states would have been affected.

But the agricultural states still had the votes—particularly in the Senate—and grasped at any means to prevent or delay the inevitable erosion in their power. The arguments were advanced that during the war many people had left the farms temporarily to seek work in the cities, and that the rural areas had been grossly undercounted because the census had been taken in the middle of an unusually severe winter. The underlying cause of the failure to reapportion was not only one of numbers but also one of social and economic issues, as was succinctly put by Emmanuel Celler of New York:

> The issue and the struggle underlying reapportionment is between the large States with large cities on one side and the rural and agricultural States on the other side. That thread of controversy runs through all the political struggles evidenced in this House. That thread runs through immigration, prohibition, in-

come tax, tariff. It is the city versus the country. The issue grows more and more menacing.[7]

During this hiatus in reapportionment, the controversy over method had been warming up. The chief protagonists were Willcox and Huntington. Willcox contended that Webster's method is not only the most natural and has the weight of precedence on its side, but that it meets the fundamental constitutional objective of being evenhanded in the treatment of small and large states. By contrast, he said, Hill's method is biased in favor of the small states and for this reason must be rejected. He had enunciated his position as early as 1915 in his presidential address to the American Economic Association.

> We have, then, two criteria of a just and constitutional apportionment: first, the ratio in each state must be as near as may be to the standard ratio, and, secondly, the method must hold the scales even between the large and the small states.

> . . . The use of [Hill's method] has recently been advocated. To use it, however, not merely would run counter to the unvarying conviction of Congress that every major fraction gives a valid claim to another seat, it would also result in defeating the main object of the Constitution, which is to hold the scales even between the small and the large states. For the use of [it] inevitably favors the small state.

> . . . the method of major fractions [Webster's] is the correct and constitutional method of apportionment.[8]

Huntington argued even more vehemently that the method of Hill, rather than that of Webster, was the unbiased one and was more natural. These claims were founded on an interesting mathematical discovery. Huntington noticed that five of the historical methods—Jefferson's, Dean's, Hill's, Webster's and Adams's—could all be understood as variations on a single theme. Moreover, it was presumably no accident that these five methods had been cast up by history, since Huntington showed further that within his framework they were the *only possible* methods that could arise. The essential idea for his framework is a simple extension of Hill's proposal: the object of apportionment should be to minimize the inequality in representation between every two states. Huntington's contribution was to show that, depending on how this inequality is measured, exactly these five methods result and no others.

In an ideal or perfect apportionment the constituency size—the number of persons per representative—would be exactly the same in every state. Likewise the per capita representation—the number of representatives per million persons—would be the same in every state. The ratio of the populations of every two states would be the same as the ratio of their apportionments, and so forth. In practice, however, this ideal cannot be met. Therefore one should try to come as close to the ideal as possible. The principle should be to allocate "the seats among the several states in such a way that any transfer of a seat from any state to any other state will be found to increase, rather than decrease, the disparity between the two states."[9] In other words, a good apportionment is one that cannot be improved by the transfer of any seat. The only question is how this "disparity" should be measured.

Hill had proposed that the relative or percentage difference in constituency size is the most appropriate measure. At the same time he had rejected using the absolute difference in constituency size, which we know leads to Dean's method. Another possibility would be to consider the differences in per capita representation between states. Indeed this criterion is perhaps the most natural one to consider when interpreting the Supreme Court's dictum that "as nearly as practicable one man's vote in a Congressional election is to be as worth as much as another's."[10] If the relative or percentage difference in per capita representation is used, this gives Hill's method again, because the relative difference in constituency size is the same as the relative difference in per capita representation. On the other hand, if the absolute difference in per capita representation is used, then Webster's method is obtained.[11]

The change in the outcome between taking the relative versus the absolute difference may be seen in the 1920 apportionment problem (Table 6.2). In the Hill apportionment New York has a population of 10,380,589 and gets 42 representatives, or 4.046 representatives per million, whereas New Mexico has a population of 353,428 and gets 2 representatives, which is 5.659 representatives per million. New Mexico is favored relative to New York because New Mexico's per capita representation is larger: in absolute terms New Mexico gets 1.613 representatives per million more than New York. Suppose one seat were shifted from New Mexico to New York to try to redress the inequality between them. Then New York's per capita representation would be 4.142 whereas New Mexico's would be only 2.829, a difference of 1.313. Therefore the transfer reduces the absolute difference in per capita representation between the two states. If the same reasoning is applied to all pairs of states and the indicated transfers are made, the result is a Webster apportionment. Thus Webster's method may also be interpreted as minimizing the inequality between states, provided the criterion of inequality is the absolute difference in per capita representation.

By considering other ways of expressing the ideal of proportionality between a state's population and the number of seats it gets, Huntington showed that the methods of Jefferson and Adams could also be interpreted as minimizing inequality by suitably chosen, albeit less natural, measures.[12] Moreover all of the other measures of inequality that Huntington investigated either give no outcome at all or else result in one of the five historical methods. This led Huntington to conclude that only these five methods need to be considered.

The question that remained was which measure of inequality to choose. Huntington saw no difficulty, because "it is clearly the relative or percentage difference, rather than the mere absolute difference, which is significant."[13] Why "clearly" or "mere" is not explained: he seems to have preferred it. He did, however, point out that no matter which of many absolute measures of inequality is used, the same measure interpreted as a percentage or relative difference is always the same, and leads to Hill's method.

The centerpiece of Huntington's argument for the method of Hill, however, was that it—and not Webster's—is the only one that is evenhanded in its treatment of large and small states. He reached this conclusion with the following line of reasoning. Of the five methods, Adams's clearly favors the small most, whereas Jefferson's favors the large most. Of the remaining three, Dean's method tends to favor the small states somewhat more than Hill's, and Webster's method favors the large states somewhat more. Therefore, said Huntington, Hill's method favors neither the small nor the large states:

> The method of [Webster] has a distinct bias in favor of the larger states, while the method of [Dean] has a similar bias in favor of the smaller states. Between these two methods stands the method of [Hill] which has been mathematically shown to have no bias in favor of either the larger or the smaller states.[14]

Walter Willcox did not agree. The controversy began in earnest in House hearings[15] of 1927 and 1928, then raged in a series of written

exchanges published in the pages of the prestigious journal *Science*.[16]
Willcox, it must be remembered, was not a mathematician, but a pioneer
social scientist. He believed that "the only test by which Congress judges a
method is its results."[17] So he studied the numbers. He prepared tables and
diagrams showing how the small and the medium and the large states fared
individually, and how they fared as groups, under each of the five
methods. He concluded that "if the main purpose is, as it probably was in
the Constitutional Convention of 1787, to hold the balance even between
the large and the small States as groups, that end is best secured by the
method of [Webster]."[18]

Understandably, Congress was confused by these rival claims, which
dragged on through 1927, 1928, and into 1929. As the debate wore on,
Huntington's attacks became increasingly personal and his claims more
exaggerated. Webster's method, he said, was "unscientific," "an obso-
lete method which had failed to secure the approval of any scientific
body." By contrast equal proportions was a method "which in point of
simplicity, directness, and intelligibility leaves nothing to be desired."[19]
Taking the superior stance of the theoretician he pounced on relatively
minor logical inaccuracies in Willcox's statements, accused him of "crass
misstatements of mathematical facts" and "evasive and misleading arguments," and challenged him to publish his findings in "some regular
journal." For the most part Willcox simply ignored these attacks, stating it
was his purpose to be of help to Congress and that he had no interest in
justifying his doing so to his academic colleagues.

Faced with this confrontation of men and disciplines, the members of
Congress most sensibly sought advice. At the formal request of the
Speaker of the House, Nicholas Longworth, the National Academy nomi-
nated a committee of four prominent mathematicians to review the problem. Their report gave the official seal of approval to Huntington's
position:

> In the present state of knowledge your committee regards [the
> five methods] as the only methods of apportionment avoiding the
> so-called Alabama paradox which require consideration at this
> time. . . .

> The method of [Dean] and the method of [Webster] are symmet-
> rically situated on the list. Mathematically there is no reason for
> choosing between them. A similar symmetry exists for the
> methods of [Adams] and [Jefferson] for which the defining

discrepancies seem, however, more artificial than those for any one of the other three methods.

The method of [Hill] is preferred by the committee because it satisfies the [relative difference] test . . . when applied either to sizes of congressional districts or to numbers of Representative per person, and because it occupies mathematically a neutral position with respect to emphasis on larger and smaller States.[20]

Huntington was gleeful: "All controversy concerning the mathematical aspects of the problem of reapportionment in Congress should be regarded as closed by the recent authoritative report of the National Academy of Sciences signed by Professors G. A. Bliss, E. W. Brown, L. P. Eisenhart, and Raymond Pearl. . . . The appearance of this statement from the National Academy which confirms authoritatively the established mathematical theory is particularly timely, since Congress has been in serious danger of being confused and misled by an erroneous theory."[21]

Throughout this monumental academic dispute the number of seats held by the states remained those determined on the basis of the census of 1910. All attempts to reapportion in the 1920s failed. As the years went by, the clamour had risen steadily: State legislatures sent protests; newspapers published editorials. People worried that, since the 1930 census would show a still more radical loss of seats for the rural areas, reapportionment might well be even more difficult than it was already.

The man who set his sights on rectifying this situation was the junior senator from Michigan, Arthur H. Vandenberg. Vandenberg was to have a long and distinguished career in the Senate, where he served from 1928 until his death in 1951. His first major effort in Congress was to fight for permanent apportionment legislation that would avoid a recurrence of the deplorable siutation then prevailing. Detroit, which had mushroomed with the advent of the automobile, suffered particularly. Altogether by 1929 Michigan was estimated to have three congressional districts with constituencies of about 800,000, whereas some states had districts as small as 160,000. California and Kentucky had the same electoral vote, but California's population was estimated to be 4.4 million and Kentucky's only 2.5 million. Other equally bad situations existed.

In the spring of 1929, Vandenberg introduced a bill in the Senate that provided for an automatic reapportionment of the House if the Congress failed to act within a specified period. The president was charged with transmitting to Congress an apportionment of the existing number of seats based on the method used in the last preceding apportionment—Webster's method. If the Congress did not act within the current session to determine some apportionment of its own, then the former would automatically become law.

Faced with the political reality of a sure loss of representation, the rural interests sought any pretext to torpedo permanent legislation. They were led by Senator Hugo Black of Alabama, the future Supreme Court justice. He raised the specter of the bill concentrating yet more power in the hands of the executive and demanded "an enumeration of aliens lawfully in the United States and aliens unlawfully in the United States."[22] But his major argument was the National Academy's report that he said had "closed" the scientific controversy over method. The "unholy, unrighteous and unjust" method of Webster was perhaps good for the larger states like Michigan and California, but "manifestly unfair" to Alabama, and every other state of "reasonable size." "It seems as though the overwhelming majority will run us down under the wheels, crush us by the system of major fractions, yielding not one jot or tittle, but exercising the power they have, ruthlessly and without mercy."[23] But Black's tactics failed and the Vandenberg bill passed the Senate. In the House the usual points were raised and accusations hurled as to who was responsible for the failure to reapportion. "When it comes to complaints and lamentations the Prophet Jeremiah had nothing on the Michigan delegation and a few of the crêpe hangers from California."[24] There was some comfort in sticking with precedent and the method of Webster, but in deference to lingering doubts, changes were brought to the bill after extensive negotiation in a joint House-Senate committee.

The bill that was finally passed in the summer of 1929 provided that the president would send to Congress the representative populations of the states as ascertained by the census, as well as apportionments of the existing number of representatives using (1) the method used in the preceding apportionment, (2) the method of Webster (referred to as "major fractions"), and (3) the method of Hill (referred to as "equal proportions"). If the Congress, which received the message, did not apportion itself, then the apportionment was to be found by the method last used. It happened that for the census of 1930 the methods of Webster and Hill agreed, leaving no immediate grounds for further dispute.

Ten years later the numbers were less kind. On January 8, 1941, President Franklin D. Roosevelt transmitted to Congress the Webster and Hill apportionments based on the 1940 census.[25] The two allocations were identical except for two states, Arkansas and Michigan (see Table 6.3).

TABLE 6.3. Hill and Webster Apportionments, 1940

State	Population	Hill Appt.	Webster Appt.	Quota
Arkansas	1,949,387	7	6	6.473
Michigan	5,256,106	17	18	17.453
U.S. total	131,006,184	435	435	435

Representative Ezekiel C. Gathings of Arkansas promptly moved H. R. 2665, "An Act To Provide for Apportioning Representatives in Congress among the Several States by the equal proportions method," and the issue was joined again. The political motives were only too apparent. Arkansas was a safe Democratic state, Michigan's normal leanings were Republican. Every Democrat, except those from Michigan, voted for Gathings's bill, and every Republican voted against. A representative of Michigan declared, "One Democrat is quoted—perhaps erroneously—as having stated that there was no partisanship in this bill; that it was merely a measure to give the Democratic Party a Congressman and a Presidential elector which they could not otherwise be certain of securing."[26]

The Senate convened new hearings and the old arguments were once again presented by their protagonists. The central issue was to determine which method was unbiased. But in the end, most of the representatives and senators of Congress remained unconvinced as to the relative merits of the different methods. "Every single one of these formulas . . . is arbitrary in one respect . . . every advocate of a formula comes with a particular interest. He can sit down with his slide rule and squirrel cage . . . and do what [he] wants done with it."[27]

Political expediency decided the issue instead: the possibility of an extra seat in the House for a Democrat could not be resisted. Public Law 291, signed by Roosevelt on November 15, 1941, designates the method of Hill, and it has been used to apportion every Congress since then.[28]

The merits of the case that gave the Congress the excuse to choose Hill's method are not clear. Not one of the participants in the controversy over bias had made precise what is meant by saying that a method is biased or unbiased. The evidence of history that was presented was discarded in favor of the argument claiming Hill's method is in "the middle" and so that it is "unbiased." This conclusion, it turns out, is false.

Arthur Vandenberg, the champion of permanent legislation, was farsighted in the choice of the language for his bill. It provided that any change in the method used by Congress would set a precedent and therefore leave untouched the permanency so desirable for the sensitive problem of apportionment. For, as he explained in presenting it to the Senate:

> To identify any one method in this permanent act—whether the method of major fractions or equal proportions—would be to assume that science itself has traversed the subject with finality. Science is not thus static. . . . The last word by no means has been spoken. Scientists themselves will be among the first to recognize this fact, and, like the National Academy, scrupulously confess themselves limited to "the present state of knowledge." A permanent ministerial apportionment act should be susceptible of accommodation to the progressive state of knowledge.[29]

CHAPTER 7

Overview of Methods

If time permitted I could prove that there are not only the five methods but as many as there are fractions between zero and one.

WALTER WILLCOX

History has handed down a rich collection of recipes for solving a problem with deceptively simple ingredients: a house of representatives to be divided proportionally to state populations or party vote totals. Each of the historical methods is based on a precise formula, and each gives a clear-cut outcome for any situation. Which of them best captures the spirit of proportionality?

It is useless to try to argue the pros and cons of different methods by appealing merely to the formulas on which they are based. Each formula has its own seductive logic. Yet none seems completely compelling. To date seven methods have appeared in the historical narrative: Hamilton's, Lowndes's, Jefferson's, Adams's, Dean's, Webster's, and Hill's. Are there no more, or are these only the tip of the iceberg?

The issue is further complicated because certain formulas and procedures that *seem* different actually give the same result in every case and so represent the same method in disguise. Jefferson's method was rediscovered in a different form by Seaton in the 1880s and in 1878 by d'Hondt for proportional representation. Webster's method was proposed independently by Sainte-Lagüe in 1910 in an entirely different guise.

The purpose of this chapter is to provide a framework in which all of the historical methods can be understood as variations on several computational themes. It then becomes clear why there are actually an infinite number of possible methods that must be considered. One category includes the methods of Hamilton and Lowndes; a second category consists of "divisor methods," which includes the remaining five. We also discuss the possibility of using lotteries.

The Hamilton-type methods take quota as their cue. Each of them begins by computing the quotas and then giving to each state the whole number contained in its quota. The seats left over are then distributed, one to a state, according to some priority list until all have been allotted. Hamilton's method itself gives priority to the states having the largest remainders. Lowndes's method adjusts the priorities by dividing each state's remainder by the whole number in its quota, thereby discounting fractions more for the larger states.[1]

The logic of this approach is clear: it guarantees a result that stays within the quota. No state's allotment strays from its quota by as much as one seat; each state gets either its quota rounded down or its quota rounded up. But it is equally clear that there are countless ways to construct a method that stays within the quota. Why not instead distribute the left-over seats according to the remainders divided by the quota rounded up, or divided by the quota itself, or perhaps multiplied by the quota . . . or, as Jefferson put it, "according to any other crotchet which ingenuity may invent and the combinations of the day give strength to carry."[2] How can we judge which, if any, of these innumerable variations best answers the intent of apportionment according to numbers?

A second broad category of methods is that based on a common divisor. Jefferson's, Webster's, and Adams's are examples of these *divisor methods*. The essential idea is to choose as a target some *ratio* of population to representatives, and then divide this ratio or "divisor" x into the populations of the states to obtain quotients. The quotients are rounded up or down to a neighboring whole number according to a rule that depends on the particular method. The whole numbers so obtained must sum to the required number of seats: if the sum is too large the divisor is adjusted upward, if it is too small the divisor is adjusted downward, until the correct sum results.[3]

What distinguishes these methods is their treatment of fractions. Jefferson's rule is to drop all fractions; Adams gives an extra seat for every fraction. Webster rounds in the usual way: a fraction greater than one-half qualifies for an extra seat, a fraction less than one-half does not. The methods of Hill and Dean turn out to be divisor methods as well, but the criteria for deciding when a fraction qualifies for an extra seat are more complicated.

Recall that Dean's method is calculated by choosing a common divisor x and giving to each state that number of seats which brings its number of persons per representative closest to x. The same result can be obtained by dividing each state population by x, and then giving the state either its quotient rounded-up or rounded-down, depending on whether or not the quotient exceeds the "harmonic mean" of these two choices.[4] The harmonic mean of two numbers is their *product* divided by their *average*.[5] Thus the harmonic mean of 1 and 2 is 2 divided by 1.5, or 1.33. Hence if a state's quotient is 1.39 it would get 2 seats. The harmonic mean of 2 and 3 is 2.40, of 3 and 4 is 3.43, and so forth. The harmonic mean of any two consecutive numbers is always less than their average or arithmetic mean. So Dean's method is a divisor method, like Webster's except that it rounds up certain quotients that Webster's method would round down. Of course, the common divisor x must be adjusted in each case so that the results add up to the required total number of seats. Typically, the divisor will be larger for Dean's method than for Webster's.

Hill's method is also a divisor method in disguise. Hill's original formulation involved minimizing the relative differences in constituency sizes between any two states. The same result can be obtained by introducing a divisor x and giving to each state that number of seats which brings its constituency size (i.e., the number of persons per representative) closest to x in *relative* terms. A convenient way to calculate it is to divide x into each population to obtain a quotient, and then give a state either its quotient rounded up or rounded down, depending on whether or not the quotient exceeds the "geometric mean" of these two choices.[6] The "geometric mean" of two numbers is simply the square root of their product.[7] Thus the geometric mean of 1 and 2 is the square root of 2 or about 1.41, so a state with quotient 1.39 would by Hill's method get 1 seat, whereas if it had a quotient of 1.42 it would get 2 seats. The geometric mean of 2 and 3 is the square root of 6, or 2.45, of 3 and 4 is the square root of 12, or 3.46. In fact, the geometric mean always lies between the harmonic mean and the arithmetic mean, and so a divisor that works for Hill's method will always be between ones that give Dean and Webster solutions.

The upshot is that five of the historical methods—Adams's, Dean's, Hill's, Webster's, and Jefferson's—are all of the same type, even though they were in some cases described in very different forms by their originators. In each of these methods a common divisor is divided into the populations to determine a quotient for each state. The only difference is in the choice of thresholds for determining when a quotient gets rounded up rather than rounded down. Any method that works like this is called a "divisor method."

A useful way to think about divisor methods is to imagine a road marked periodically with signposts. There is one signpost in the first mile, one in the second, one in the third, and so forth. Each state occupies a position along the road that corresponds to the size of its quotient. Figure 7.1 shows the placement of the signs for the method of Dean. The number

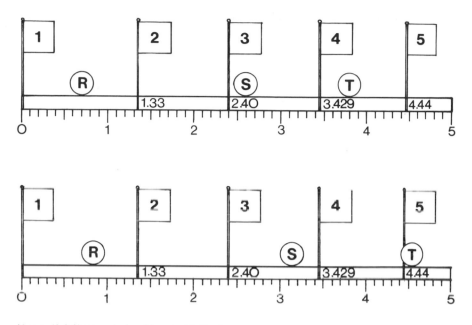

Figure 7.1 Signposts for Dean's Method

of seats due any state is the number of signs it has passed. In the example state R would receive one seat, state S three seats, and state T four seats. If nine seats instead of eight were to be distributed, then the divisor would have to be adjusted downward, causing all the quotients to increase—and so all the states to roll forward. State T, being the largest, moves fastest and passes a new signpost before either of the other states do, so the new distribution would be one to R, three to S, and five to T.

Each divisor method places the signposts differently. The arrangement of signposts for the five traditional methods is illustrated in Figure 7.2. Ranked from top to bottom, Adams is the most liberal in giving an extra seat for a fraction. Dean is next, then Hill, then Webster, and Jefferson is as far right as possible. The Webster signposts are always exactly halfway between the milestones, whereas the Hill and Dean markers are always less than halfway, although they get closer and closer to Webster further down the road.[8]

It is plain to see that there are not just five divisor methods but literally untold numbers of them. Each different placement of the signposts results in a different method, so they may be manufactured at will. One was proposed in 1792 by the great French political theorist and mathematician Condorcet in his plan for a new French Constitution. It would give an extra seat for every fraction of .400 or more.[9]

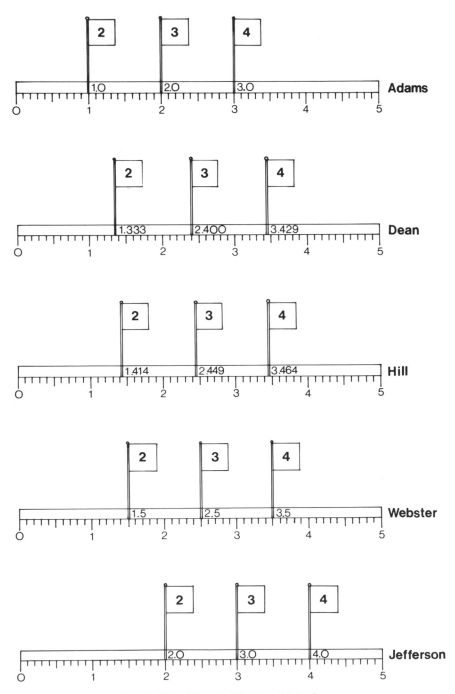

Figure 7.2 Signposts for the Five Historical Divisor Methods
NOTE: With a minimum requirement of 1 the first signpost would be placed at 0 in every case.

Figure 7.3 The Golden Section: $a+b$ is to b as b is to a

A more bizarre example is obtained from another discovery of the ancient Greeks: the "golden mean," the most famous of all the proportions. It was revered by the Order of Pythagoreans and was used to construct the five-pointed star, which served as a badge of this secret brotherhood. The golden mean is found by dividing a line segment into two unequal parts in such a way that the ratio of the whole segment to its large part is the same as the ratio of the larger part to the smaller part. This suggests an entirely new divisor method—the "golden method"—in which the threshold for getting the extra seat is the golden mean of each marked mile segment of the road. By this method any fraction above .382 would merit an extra seat since 1 is to .618 as .618 is to .382.

On the other hand, the mirror image of Figure 7.3 is just as pleasing, which suggests a divisor method that allots an extra seat to all fractions greater than .618—the "golden mirror method." Obviously the same device could be used to produce the mirror images of Dean's and Hill's methods as well. The reader will no doubt be able to dream up other entertaining proposals.

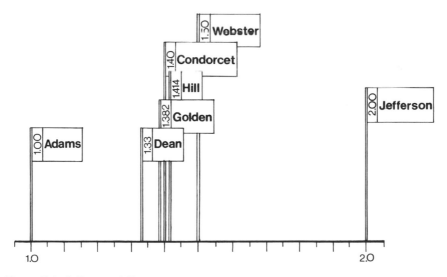

Figure 7.4 A Forest of Signposts

Another category of methods may appeal to the gambling man. As one example, construct a roulette wheel divided into fifty slots, one for each state, the size of each slot being exactly proportional to the population of the state. Spin the wheel and drop a small ball onto it: the state at which it comes to rest "wins" and is awarded one seat. Do this 435 times consecutively and the house is apportioned. The method is perfectly unbiased: every state is treated fairly; none can complain that the method discriminates against it.

An alternative and perhaps preferable scheme is to compare the quotas of the states and first give to each the whole number in its quota; then use a roulette wheel, with each slot proportional to a state's remainder, to distribute the seats left over.

Which of all possible methods is *fairest*? To answer this question, standards or principles must be formulated by which methods can be evaluated. History itself points to such principles. What are the methods that avoid the population paradox, the Alabama paradox, the new states paradox? What are the methods that always stay within the quota? What are the methods that systematically favor neither the large states at the expense of the small nor the small at the expense of the large? Or, for proportional representation systems, which methods discourage the splintering of large parties into smaller ones?

Each of these questions captures a *principle* of apportionment. They have repeatedly been used in history to judge the merits of competing proposals. In a word, they are the guides to those methods that feel right, that are fair, that are indeed proportional.

CHAPTER 8

Resolving the Paradoxes

For the best and safest method of philosophizing seems to be first diligently to investigate the properties of things, and establish them by experiment, and then seek hypotheses to explain them.

ISAAC NEWTON

Instead of combing through the haystack of arithmetical schemes one by one, we now reverse the process of search: the principles are used as sieves to separate the chaff of methods that do not meet the standards from the grains that do. Of all the methods that exist—of all the methods that could possibly be dreamed up—some will exclude the possibility of the population paradox, such as Hill's, and some will not, such as Hamilton's. Rather than test each method in turn, our approach is to use each principle in turn as a sieve, and "shake" them to find what methods are let through that live up to the standards established by common sense and history. Together, the sieves constitute a *theory of apportionment*.

A distribution of seats exactly proportional to the populations of the states is, of course, the ideal solution. Perfect proportionality can really never be achieved, but in the unlikely event that the quotas of the states are *all* very close to being whole numbers (or all actually are whole numbers!), then these should surely be the apportionment that is chosen. Any worthy method must guarantee this result. Of course, if the size of the house were large enough—if, for example, every citizen were a representative, as every citizen can be in town meetings—then there would be no problem. But the membership of the House of Representatives is not "large enough," since by its very nature a deliberative body must be restrained in size. Still, the larger the house the closer a method should come to the ideal of allocating seats in proportion to numbers.

All of the historical methods that have been discussed so far satisfy this elementary principle. But the lottery methods do not. A basic problem with a betting man's method is that, although it may be "fair" over the long run, the immediate outcome is almost sure to be unfair. And, as a rule, politicians and voters tend to be more interested in the political power of today than of tomorrow.

Proportionality is what the apportionment problem is all about; this means that only the relative sizes of the states matter. A state with three times the population of another should get three times the representation: it does not matter whether the first has 27 million and the second 9 million or the first has 2,100,000 and the second 700,000; only their proportions count. Had the number of states and size of house stayed the same from 1792 to the present day, and had all the states grown at exactly the same rate, then there would be no reason for the apportionment to be altered at all, because the relative sizes of the states would not have changed.

The true state of affairs is far different. The number of seats, the number of states, and especially the relative sizes of the states have changed frequently in the past and will do so in the future. In proportional representation systems the number of parties and their vote totals are in constant flux. It is essential that a method of apportionment should respond to these changes in a consistent way: they must at least avoid the kinds of paradoxes and anomalies exhibited by Hamilton's method.

No method can be considered acceptable for either proportional representation or federal systems that forces one state to give up seats to another that has become proportionally smaller, i.e. that suffers from the population paradox. With a method that did admit the paradox one political party could give away some of its votes and thereby *gain* seats. In federal systems, a state could deliberately undercount its population or encourage emigration to obtain an increase in its representation. Incredibly, Hamilton's method—and indeed all Hamilton-type methods—admit this possibility, as we have observed in the decade 1900–1910. This turns out to be no isolated quirk of the method. If Congress had been reapportioned in each of the 180 years from 1791 to 1970, the population paradox would have occurred 10 times.[1]

A striking and recent instance occurs in the decade 1960 to 1970. The total representative population grew from 178,559,219 to 204,053,325 implying an average annual growth rate of 1.34% for the nation as a whole. In this same period some states grew considerably faster, some slower. California grew at an annual rate of 2.49%, while Pennsylvania had a rate of growth of only .49%, and North Dakota at −.13% actually shrank. If Hamilton's method had been used to apportion in 1960 and again in 1961 there would have been changes in four states (Table 8.1). North Dakota gets 2 seats in 1961 as opposed to 1 in 1960 in spite of the fact that it is shrinking in size. Meanwhile Pennsylvania and Illinois each get *one less* seat than before even though they are growing. North Dakota loses

TABLE 8.1. The Population Paradox 1960–1961, Hamilton's Method

State	Population 1960	Population 1961	Growth Rate	Quota 1960	Quota 1961	Appt. 1960	Appt. 1961
California	15,717,204	16,108,493	2.49%	38.290	38.733	38	39
Illinois	10,081,158	10,186,391	1.04%	24.559	24.493	25	24
Pennsylvania	11,319,366	11,374,631	.49%	27.576	27.350	28	27
North Dakota	632,446	631,615	−.13%	1.541	1.519	1	2
Total U.S.	178,559,219	180,912,144	1.32%	435	435	435	435

831 people and gains a seat, whereas Pennsylvania gains 55,265 people yet loses a seat.

The reason for it is easily explained. In 1960 the quotas of North Dakota and Pennsylvania were 1.541 and 27.576. Pennsylvania, having the larger remainder, gets priority over North Dakota for the extra seat. Moreover North Dakota is low enough on the priority list so that all the extra seats are given out before its turn comes up. However, in 1961, Pennsylvania has a quota of only 27.350—its share of the total has gone down because it is growing more slowly than the nation as a whole. Of course, North Dakota's share has also decreased, but because it is small, the *size* of its remainder has not decreased as much as the remainder of Pennsylvania. Pennsylvania's quota decreased by .226 whereas North Dakota's decreased by only .022 to 1.519. *As a percentage* North Dakota's share shrinks more than Pennsylvania's: .022 is 1.4% of 1.541, whereas .226 is only 0.8% of 27.350. But Hamilton's method does not take account of this percentage change; it looks only at the remainders. And according to the remainders, the priorities for getting an extra seat have switched: in 1961 North Dakota gets one of the extras, while Pennsylvania does not. Similar arguments apply to North Dakota vis-à-vis Illinois.

The population paradox—and the related new states paradox—occur because at bottom the use of remainders to determine priority is simply not a proportional device. It does not adequately reflect the *relative* sizes of the states. It is of course obvious that no lottery method can possibly escape the population paradox.

One is tempted to ask whether the method of Hamilton can be doctored so as to avoid the paradox. Lowndes's proposal may be viewed as one attempt, but the imagination is open to countless other possibilities. The fact is that any attempt is doomed to failure. The method of Hamilton and *any* of its innumberable variations stumble on the population paradox.

It can be shown that to avoid the population paradox it is necessary to use a divisor method. (The proof is given in appendix A.)

Divisor methods are the only methods that avoid the population paradox.

It is easy to see why all divisor methods are immune from the population paradox. Suppose that one state increases *relative* to another, and that the slower-growing state gains at least one seat. Then it must have passed some signposts. But since the first state has grown *relative* to the other, it must also have moved forward and so in no case could possibly have lost seats. So the population paradox cannot have occurred. Why the divisor methods are the only ones that avoid the paradox is not so obvious. But that is the part played by mathematics. For our analysis it is only necessary to know the fact. But more is true:

All divisor methods avoid the Alabama paradox.

In other words, all methods that avoid the population paradox *also* avoid the Alabama paradox. The reason is this. The number of signposts a state has passed is the number of seats it gets. If the total number of seats to be apportioned is to increase, then the common divisor x must be made smaller. As the divisor decreases, the quotient of every state moves forward, and each time a quotient passes a signpost its state has a right to one more seat. Since no state's quotient can possibly move backward, no state can lose a seat. Therefore the Alabama paradox cannot occur.

What about avoiding the new states paradox? That comes for free too.

All divisor methods avoid the new states paradox.

Again it is easy to see why. Once the common divisor x is fixed, the number of seats each state gets can be determined by looking at that state's quotient *alone*. So, if several states drop out and take their seats with them, the remaining states will have exactly the same quotients as before and therefore get the same number of seats as before.

To sum up, all divisor methods avoid the population paradox, and they are the only ones that do so. Furthermore, they all avoid the Alabama and new states paradoxes. In summary, all the paradoxes can be done away with by using a divisor method, and no other method will do. In particular all Hamilton-type methods and all roulette-type methods are eliminated.

The question that remains is: *Which* of the multitude of possible divisor methods are best for federal and proportional representation systems?

CHAPTER 9

Eliminating Bias

The great and Small States must be brought as near together as possible: and I am not without Hopes, that this may be done to the tolerable Satisfaction of both.
JOHN ADAMS

Concern over bias is a thread that runs through many of the historical debates on apportionment. It was noted early in the game that some methods—like Jefferson's—seem to favor the larger states, while others—like Adams's—appear to favor the smaller. The use of Jefferson's method in the United States was discontinued in the 1840s precisely because it exhibited bias toward large states. If each person's vote is supposed to count equally, then systematic bias—a tendency for a method to give citizens living in large states proportionally more voice than those living in small (or vice versa)—cannot be countenanced. This seems to be an essential principle in federal systems and in many proportional representation systems—although, in the latter case it may sometimes be considered more desirable to give a deliberate advantage to large parties so as to discourage political fragmentation (see Chapter 12).

Is there any method that is completely unbiased? In the United States, the long and bitter contest between Willcox and Huntington in the 1920s, 1930s, and 1940s finally resulted in a victory for Hill's method over Webster's, but political expediency had a heavier hand in the outcome. In fact, the question never received a scientifically satisfactory answer.

To begin with, what precisely is meant by ''bias,'' and how is it to be measured? In essence, it means a systematic tendency to favor some states. Favoritism may be described in absolute or in relative terms. A state is favored absolutely in an apportionment if it is assigned more seats than its fair share or quota. A state is favored relative to another if it receives more representatives per capita than the other. As a practical matter any single apportionment favors some states and puts others at a disadvantage because some states necessarily get more than their quotas and others less. In practice, no two states can ever be expected to have exactly the same ratio of representation to population, so for any pair of states one will always be favored relative to the other.

In the 1970 apportionment, California had a representative population of 20,098,863, a quota of 42.847, and got 43 seats; whereas Delaware had a representative population of 551,928, a quota of 1.177, and got 1 seat. California received more than it deserved, Delaware less, so California is favored over Delaware. This can also be seen since one representative from Delaware speaks for 551,928 persons, whereas on average each representative from California speaks only for 467,415 persons. Put another way, Delaware has 1.812 representatives per million whereas California has 2.139 representatives per million. This is a large difference, and it shows that by the 1970 apportionment California was significantly better off than Delaware.

However, this one comparison does not show that the *method* used in 1970 was biased toward larger states; it only shows that the outcome happened to favor California over Delaware. In the same apportionment Illinois, with a population of 11,184,320 and a quota of 23.843, got 24 seats, whereas Hawaii, with a population of 784,901 and a quota of 1.673, got 2 seats. Both received more than their quotas, but the small state Hawaii, is favored *relative to* the large state, Illinois, because Hawaii got 2.548 seats per million of population whereas Illinois only got 2.146 per million of population.

Bias in a method emerges only when a systematic *pattern* of favoritism is detected. Some methods are patently biased: for example, a method that assured the original states 50% of the representation; or a method that used two different divisors, one for the South and one for the North. Methods like these are obviously unsatisfactory because they do not apportion representation "according to numbers" only. Methods must be blind to all but the head counts, so that over the long run—as the populations of states ebb and flow relative to each other—there cannot be any reason to expect that one region is systematically favored more than another.

As the historical record shows, however, methods that otherwise seem reasonable can harbor a more insidious form of bias according to the *size* of states. Compare, for example, the methods of Adams and Jefferson for the 1970 census results (see Appendix B). Overall they differ in the disposition of 18 seats. The states to which Jefferson gives more than Adams are the nine largest states, as may be seen in Table 9.1. Those states to which Adams gives more seats than Jefferson are comparatively small. Some of the differences are startling: the New York delegation changes by

TABLE 9.1. Differences between Adams and Jefferson Solutions,
1970: Nine Largest States

State	Quota	Adams	Jefferson
California	42.847	41	44
New York	39.093	37	41
Pennsylvania	25.335	24	26
Texas	24.087	23	25
Illinois	23.843	23	25
Ohio	22.875	22	24
Michigan	19.052	19	20
New Jersey	15.366	15	16
Florida	14.615	14	15

4 seats or about 10%. Adams, it seems, would rob the large to pay the small, whereas Jefferson would be of the opposite persuasion.

Every large state is not, however, favored by the Jefferson solution, nor is every small state favored by the Adams solution. Indiana, the tenth largest state, deserves 11.145 but gets 11 seats by Jefferson; Nevada, the fourth smallest, deserves 1.050 but Adams only gives it 1 seat. On balance however, the Jefferson solution favors the large states, not only relative to Adams, but absolutely; and the Adams solution favors the small, absolutely as well. To see this, divide the states into three approximately equal classes: the large, the middling, and the small. The sixteen smallest states have a combined quota or fair share of 25.45 seats. Adams gives them 33, a bonus of 7.55 seats. Jefferson gives them 22, a deficit of 3.45 seats. The situation is reversed for the sixteen largest states; Jefferson gives them 309 seats, Adams 291, whereas their combined fair share is 300.79. Jefferson hands them a gift of 8.21 seats, Adams expropriates 9.79 seats. The net result is that the amount of representation per capita in the small states is 34% greater than in the large states by Adams's solution, whereas by Jefferson's the large states have a nearly 19% greater per capita representation than do the small.

The evident bias of Jefferson's method toward the large states would be even greater than this if the requirement of at least one seat per state were not imposed. This stricture tilts the solutions slightly toward the small. If this minimum requirement were not imposed, then in the 1970 example the Jefferson solution would give no seats to either Wyoming or Alaska, and the bias would be 32% in favor of the large.

Of course, the results of one year do not prove that a method is biased. But the example of 1970, together with the observation of many other

years, raise strong suspicions. To show that a method is biased, a tendency
to favor small or large over many problems must be established. Even a
perfectly unbiased method will show some favoritism in a particular
problem, because exact proportionality can practically never be achieved.
What characterizes an unbiased method is that it sometimes favors the large
states and sometimes favors the small, but over many problems these
advantages balance out. If there is a better than 50% chance that a method
will favor the small states, then it does not treat small and large even-
handedly and is biased toward the small, whereas if the chance is better
than 50% that a method will favor the large, then it is biased toward the
large. A method is *unbiased* if the class of large states has the same chance
of being favored as the class of small states. The roulette methods—albeit
unacceptable on other grounds—are perfectly unbiased.

A brief look at the data of United States history shows convincingly
that Jefferson's and Adams's methods are grossly biased. In *every one* of
the nineteen congressional apportionment problems Jefferson's method
would have favored the class of large states whereas Adams's method
would have favored the class of small states. This is true of Jefferson's
despite the built-in bias toward the small that comes from the minimum
requirement of one seat. In contrast, the method of Hill favors the small 15
of 19 times, and the method of Webster 11 of 19 times.

To correct for the built-in bias caused by the guarantee of one seat to
any state, however small, the 19 apportionments of history were also
analyzed after setting aside all states whose quotas were less than ½ seat. In
this case the method of Adams would have favored the small every time,
Dean's would have favored the small 14 times, Hill's 12 times, and
Webster's 7 times. Jefferson's would have always favored the large.
Figure 9.1 shows the accumulated average bias that would have resulted
from using each of the five traditional methods over the 19 apportionment
years of United States history. For example, the average bias of the method
of Hill over the 13 apportionments up to and including 1910 would have
been 2.1% in favor of the small and that of Webster would have been 0.4%
in favor of the large. The average bias of each of the five methods over the
entire course of the 19 problems may be read off from the right-most point
of each of the corresponding curves.

The historical statistics come to have significance only as they ac-
cumulate over time—after the particular happenstance of one or another
problem comes to be averaged with the rest—so it is the overall directions
of the curves that are of importance. The methods of Dean and of Hill seem
to be tending toward favoring the small more, whereas the method of

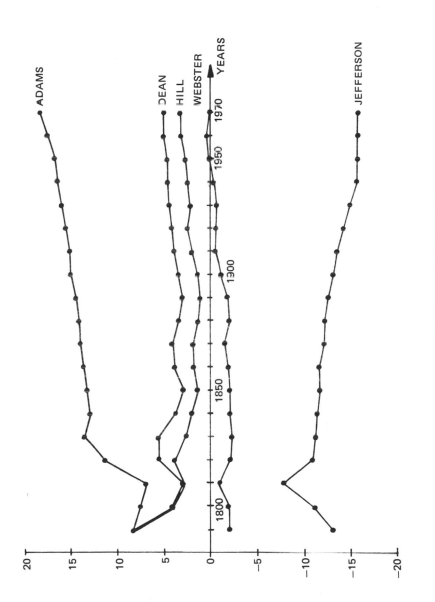

Figure 9.1 Cumulative Average Bias of Five Traditional Methods, 19 U.S. Censuses

NOTE: On each curve the point at any census year is the average of the percentage biases of the corresponding method up to and including that year. The number of seats allocated is the actual number that was apportioned. Any state with quota less than .5 is ignored. The remaining states are divided into thirds: large, middle, and small, the "middle" third being slightly larger if the number of states is not divisible by three. The bias percentage is the relative difference between the large states' and the small states' total number of seats divided by their fair shares or total quotas.

Webster appears to hover closer to evenhanded treatment of large and small. It is a fact that in every one of the nineteen historical problems the Webster solutions would have given the smallest bias of the five.

The historical evidence points very strongly to the conclusion that, of the five historical divisor methods, Webster's is the fairest in its treatment of smaller and larger states. Two questions now present themselves. Is this conclusion only an accident of history, and would data from a different source (or from a longer series) lead to a different conclusion? Second, are there other methods not yet discussed that are even less biased than Webster's?

To answer the second question it seems entirely reasonable to restrict attention to divisor methods, because, as shown in the preceding chapter, divisor methods are the only ones that are free of paradox. This still leaves an infinite number of possibilities. But mathematical analysis shows that of all the divisor methods Webster's is the *only* one that is perfectly unbiased.

Webster's method is the one and only unbiased divisor method.

There is an intuitive reason why this is so. If we divide a state's population by a common divisor to find its quotient, the fractional part of the quotient may be expected to be above one-half just as often as it is below one-half. This is true for each state no matter what its size. Since the Webster method rounds fractions above one-half up and below one-half down, each state will be advantaged or disadvantaged the same number of times on average. By contrast, some divisor methods—such as Dean's and Hill's—round up quotients having fractional parts less than one-half, which tends to favor the smaller states; others—such as Jefferson's—round down quotients having fractional parts greater than one-half, which tends to favor the larger states.

Imposing minimum requirements tends to favor the small states no matter what method is used. But Webster's method is unbiased even in this case—provided attention is restricted to just those states that get more seats than they are required to have. The intuitive reason is exactly the same as in the case of no requirements, and again it is the only divisor method with this property.

It is possible to estimate the probability that a method favors the larger or smaller states, and by how much. The idea is to pick some distribution of seats, for example that of 1970, and to look at all possible populations of the states that would lead to this distribution by the method under investigation. For Hill's method the actual 1970 census populations obviously yield

TABLE 9.2. Bias Estimates (Minus sign means the bias in favor of the large.)

	Adams	Dean	Hill	Webster	Jefferson
Chance to favor small (%)	100.0	93.9	78.5	50.0	0.0
Expected bias toward small (%)	28.2	7.0	3.5	0.0	−20.8

NOTE: The calculation of these estimates is based on the 1970 apportionment. It is explained in appendix A, section 5.

the apportionment of 1970 but many other distributions of populations that are close to the 1970 census results also give the same solution. For some, the solution favors the smaller states, for others it favors the larger states. Assuming that all of these small variations in population are equally likely, one can evaluate what percentage of the time the smaller states are favored, and by how much. The results depend on the initial distribution of seats chosen—that is, on the number of seats, the number of states, and their approximate distribution in size.

Under these assumptions Webster's method is perfectly unbiased for any distribution of seats. The chance that it will favor the small states or the large states—or any class of states—is an even bet. The estimates in Table 9.2 give a good idea of the bias of each method for distributions of seats similar to that of 1970. The estimated bias for Hill's method is significant: the chances are almost 4 to 1 that the Hill solution favors the small, and the expected percentage by which the small states' per capita representation exceeds that in the large states is about 3.5%. The actual bias percentages recorded over the nineteen United States censuses for each of the five methods support the theoretical estimates (Table 9.3). Since the theoretical estimates were made on the assumption of 50 states and 435 seats, whereas for much of United States history there were fewer of both, the historical figures tend to be somewhat smaller than the estimates.

The conclusion from both empirical observation and theory is inescapable: Webster's is the unique unbiased divisor method. It seems amazing therefore that Hill's method could have been chosen in 1941 on precisely the ground that it was *the* unbiased method, and that Webster's method was discarded. A peculiar combination of professional rivalry, scientific error, and political accident seems to have decided the issue.

A 1929 report of the United States National Academy of Sciences supported the choice of Hill's method because "it occupies mathematically a neutral position with respect to emphasis on larger and smaller

TABLE 9.3. Historical Average Percentage Biases in Favor of Small
            States

Adams	Dean	Hill	Webster	Jefferson
18.3	5.2	3.4	0.3	−15.7

NOTE: These actual averages over the nineteen censuses are as explained in note to figure 9.1.

states."[1] The reasoning was repeated in a report prepared for the president of the National Academy of Sciences at the request of Congress in 1948. Three of the most distinguished mathematicians of the day, John von Neumann, Marston Morse, and Luther Eisenhart, concurred with the earlier brief and concluded that the method of Hill is indicated since it "stands in a middle position as compared with the other methods."[2] One can but remark that for this logic it was fortunate that the number of methods under consideration was odd.

Apparently Huntington and his mathematical colleagues ignored the possibility of other divisor methods. This error in judgment might easily have been rectified by looking at and comparing the actual apportionments of history, although lacking computers and pocket calculators, the job would admittedly have been tedious. This did not deter Willcox, who had a healthy respect for data. A former student of his remarked in 1965, "My wrist still aches from cranking the hand computer on that problem in 1925."[3]

Willcox had the insight but, unfortunately, not the mathematical arguments to prove his point. In the end, Huntington's claims bolstered by the muddle over "middle," provided the scientific excuse, and straight party-line interests provided the votes.

CHAPTER 10

Staying within the Quota

Finality is death. Perfection is finality. Nothing is perfect. There are lumps in it.
JAMES STEPHENS

Little mention has been made of one of the most appealing and natural apportionment ideas: staying within the quota. Surely no state should get more than its quota rounded up nor less than its quota rounded down. This concept motivated the methods of Hamilton and Lowndes, and it was very much in Webster's mind when he argued for his method. The discovery that Jefferson's method frequently gives large states more than their quotas rounded up contributed to its abandonment by Congress in the 1840s. E. V. Huntington expressed the contrary view that "it is a common misconception that in a good apportionment the actual assignment should not differ from the exact quota by more than one whole unit,"[1] no doubt because he realized that his method (Hill's) did not invariably stay within the quota. In fact, neither does Webster's method.

Table 10.1 shows how this can happen: it seems that state D should get 26 instead of 25 seats. The trouble is that one seat must then be taken from another state, all of which have large remainders. Which should it be? Hamilton's method would take it from state A. But state A is the smallest and so would suffer most by losing one seat. Other examples can be invented for which a large state appears to get too many seats.

The question immediately arises whether there is *any* divisor method that always stays within the quota. Unfortunately, the answer is no.

There is no method that avoids the population paradox and always stays within the quota.

This is a disturbing discovery, a paradox in itself. How can it be? The root of the problem is that forcing all states to stay within one seat of their quotas operates very unequally on small and large states. For a state with a

TABLE 10.1. Example of Webster's and Hill's Methods Not Staying within the Quota

State	Population	Quota	W and H Appt.
A	70,653	1.552	2
B	117,404	2.579	3
C	210,923	4.633	5
D	1,194,456	26.236	25
Total	1,593,436	35	35

quota between 1 and 2, one seat more or less represents a much greater shift in proportion to its size than it does for a state with quota between 41 and 42. In a word, staying within the quota is not really compatible with the idea of proportionality at all, since it allows a much greater leeway in the per capita representation of small states than it does for large states.

The example in Table 10.1 illustrates this point. Suppose that staying within the quota is insisted on, so that state D gets 26 seats, and suppose that it is taken from state B, which then gets only 2. Now let states B and D lose part of their populations to the other two states, so that the new populations and quotas are as shown in Table 10.2. The obvious solution, with which Webster and Hill agree, is the one shown in Table 10.2 in which B gets 3 seats and D gets 25. But this would imply the population paradox, because state B decreased by 3.0% whereas state D decreased by 2.8% so it is now relatively larger than state B but gave up one seat to it.

Similar examples can be invented to show that the population paradox occurs no matter which of the first three states in Table 10.1 is forced to give up a seat in order to bring state D within quota. Other examples show that staying within the quota leads unavoidably to the new states paradox.

TABLE 10.2. How Staying within the Quota Leads to the Population Paradox

State	Population	Quota	W and H Appt.
A	86,228	1.894	2
B	113,908	2.502	3
C	232,778	5.113	5
D	1,160,522	25.491	25
Total	1,593,436	35	35

Do all methods that stay within the quota also admit the Alabama paradox? This is true of all the Hamilton-type methods; nevertheless it is possible to construct methods that both avoid the Alabama paradox and stay within the quota. Unfortunately they are rather complicated methods and have little appeal because they suffer from the population and new states paradoxes (see section 6, appendix A).

Thus we are confronted with a dilemma: *There is no perfect method.* Some compromise must be made. Either the principle of staying within the quota must be abandoned, or the possibility of the population and new states paradoxes must be accepted. On the whole, achieving apportionments that accurately reflect relative changes in populations seems more important than always staying within the quota. The preceding examples cast doubt on the validity of the quota principle in the first place. So if compromise there must be, it seems best to stay with methods that avoid the paradoxes—in other words, with divisor methods.

Fortunately the "price" of doing so turns out to be small. After all, the example of Table 10.1 is a pure invention. How likely is it in practice that a specific divisor method will produce apportionments that violate the quota? Some methods are very prone to quota violations, but with others a violation is so improbable that it may be considered a virtual impossibility. Theoretical estimates have been made of the probability of violating quota for each of the five historical divisor methods (see Table 10.3). For a relatively large number of states with significantly different populations and a large number of seats (as in the United States), the methods of Adams and Jefferson can be expected to violate quota virtually all of the time. Webster's method, by contrast, almost never violates it—the probability under present conditions in the United States is only about 1 in 1,600 apportionments, or once in every 16,000 years.

TABLE 10.3. The Chance of Violating Quota in the U.S.

	Adams	Dean	Hill	Webster	Jefferson
Expected number per 1,000 problems	1,000	15.40	2.86	.61	1,000

NOTE: These estimates assume fifty states and a fixed apportionment of 435 seats (the 1970 U.S. apportionment). All populations that produce this apportionment using a fixed divisor were assumed to be equally likely, and the number of instances was counted in which some state violated quota by Monte Carlo simulation.

Of all divisor methods Webster's is the least likely to violate quota.

The table shows that Hill's method is about five times as likely to violate quota as Webster's, and Dean's is about twenty-five times as likely.

The conclusion that Webster's method is very unlikely to violate quota is supported by empirical evidence. In each of the 19 United States historical problems, and each of the 180 problems that would have resulted if the House had been reapportioned every year from 1791 to 1970, Webster's method *never* violated quota. In contrast, were Hamilton's method adopted in order to guarantee staying within the quota, the population paradox would occur frequently—as often as 1 time in 18, as we have seen.

There is a natural reason why Webster's method comes closest to satisfying quota. Webster himself never actually argued that a method must always stay within the quota. Rather, he proposed a closely related, but more workable, idea: in a good apportionment it should not be possible to take a seat away from one state and give it to another and simultaneously bring *both* of them nearer to their true quotas. This is called "staying near the quota."[2] Referring back to Table 10.1, notice that to transfer one seat to state D would bring it nearer to its quota, but taking one away from any other state would move it further away from its quota. In the 1920 Hill solution (see Table 6.2), three transfers are necessary to obtain the Webster solution, and each brings *both* states nearer to their quotas.

Most important, these differences do not depend on precisely how "nearness" to quota is defined. Instead of the absolute difference between a state's allocation and its quota, we could consider the relative or percentage difference between the allocation and the quota. The result is the same: in the 1920 example the Webster solution brings six states relatively nearer to their quotas than does the Hill solution. For example Virginia, with a quota of 9.547, is 4.7% above its quota if it gets 10 seats and 5.7% below its quota if it gets 9, so it is relatively (and absolutely) nearer its quota if it gets 10. There is no effective difference between the two measures because the relative and absolute differences amount to the same thing when measured with respect to the fixed standard of what a state deserves—its quota.

It is a remarkable fact that even though Webster's method does not stay within the quota all of the time, it does stay near the quota all of the time, whether measured in absolute or relative terms. Furthermore it is the *only* divisor method that does so (see section 6, appendix A).

Webster's is the one and only divisor method that stays near the quota.

Without minimum requirements the ideal standard by which to judge apportionments is the quotas. With requirements the standard must be modified, since if the minima cause some states to get *more* than their quotas, other states must perforce get less. To find the fair shares of the states in the presence of minima, reduce the quotas of all states by the same proportion until the reduced shares (or the minimum requirements when they are larger), summed over all states, equals the number of seats to be apportioned. This *modified quota* of a state is its reduced share or requirement, whichever is bigger. By this definition, proportionality remains the ideal for all states except for any whose quota is less than its minimum guarantee.

For example, in 1970 there were three states with quotas less than 1: Alaska, Vermont, and Wyoming. Their modified quotas are each exactly 1, and the quotas of the remaining states are reduced by 0.16% so that the sum over all states is 435 seats. This means that California's quota is 42.847, but its modified quota is 42.779; South Carolina's quota is 5.580, and its modified quota is 5.571.

Modified quotas represent the ideal standard of comparison in the presence of minimum requirements. This suggests that the traditional way of applying Hamilton's method (which gives all states their requirements, and then uses the *old* quotas to distribute the remaining seats) should be changed. The *modified Hamilton method* works like Hamilton's except that it is applied to the modified quotas in place of the quotas. For 1970, the modified Hamilton solution differs from the Hamilton solution by transferring one seat from Oregon to Montana. Surprisingly, the methods also give different solutions in 1870, 1880, 1900, 1910, and 1960.[2] The modified method has the virtue of being unbiased, whereas the traditional way of applying Hamilton's method is slightly biased towards the large states.[3] Unfortunately, the modified method is subject to all the paradoxes of its parent.

The ideas of staying within the quota and staying near the quota carry over to the modified quotas and the basic facts remain the same. There is no divisor method that satisfies modified quota. Webster's method is the only divisor method that stays near the modified quota—indeed is the only one that stays near the quota whether or not minima are imposed.

To conclude, while it is not possible to satisfy all of the principles all of the time, it is possible to satisfy all of them *almost* all of the time.

CHAPTER 11

The Choice for Federal Systems

Nature is pleased with simplicity, and affects not the pomp of superfluous causes.
ISAAC NEWTON

History reveals that there is no obvious answer to the intent of finding representation proportional to populations. The issue is at once complex and sensitive since it concerns the very substance of political power.

In the United States great struggles over methods have been provoked over the disposition of a single seat. A matter of one seat in 1791 prompted the first presidential veto and the discovery of the methods of Jefferson and Hamilton. To protect Massachusetts and the whole of New England from the loss of but one seat in 1830, John Quincy Adams began the search for a device that would ward off the blow. From that resulted three new methods: Adams's, Dean's, and Webster's. To increase the delegation of the then "safe" Democratic state of Arkansas by 1 is what motivated the adoption of the method used since 1941.

The theoretical and political debates of 180 years, however, go deeper than mere bickering over numbers. They have established the principles that should be used to guide the search for solutions.

The essence of fair representation is that the apportionment of seats should correctly reflect relative changes in the populations of states or provinces. It is for precisely this reason that revisions in solutions are made periodically. Therefore, an acceptable method must avoid the population and new states paradoxes. The erratic behavior of the method of Hamilton following the census of 1900—with Maine's delegation oscillating between 3 and 4 as the House grew—has taught that no method which admits the Alabama paradox is politically acceptable either. Mathematical analysis proves that the *only* methods which avoid these three paradoxes are the divisor methods: neither Hamilton-type methods nor lottery schemes, nor *any* other rule that might be proposed will do.

Staying within the quota is another desirable criterion that has naturally been advanced in the political debates on apportionment: no state's allocation should differ from its true quota by more than one seat. But there is no method that avoids the three paradoxes and invariably stays within the quota. Some compromise is necessary. Webster proposed the principle that at least solutions should be near to the quota: it should not be possible to transfer a seat from one state to another and bring both nearer to their true quotas. Mathematical analysis proves that the only divisor method that meets this requirement is Webster's. At the same time Webster's is the divisor method that is *least likely* to violate the quota. Indeed, when the number of seats and states are reasonably large, as in the United States, Webster's method violates quota so seldom that for all practical purposes it may be considered actually to stay within the quota too. This remains true when modified quota is taken as the benchmark.

For federal systems it is of paramount importance that a method should not tend to favor one state rather than another. One person's vote should carry as much weight as another's irrespective of the state in which he happens to reside. In other words, a method should be unbiased. Both analysis and empirical observation support the conclusion that the only divisor method that is perfectly unbiased—which fully satisfies the principle of one-man, one-vote—is Webster's.

In the United States the case for choosing an unbiased method is particularly clear. The great compromise that reconciled the small and large states at the 1787 Convention established two chambers: the Senate, in which all states are equally represented; and the House, in which the ideal is representation in proportion to population. Proportionality was further altered to protect the small by allowing to each state, however small, at least one seat in the House. The effect of these departures from proportionality—a necessary step to the establishment of a federation of independent states—is a strong, built-in bias that favors the representation of the small states. Setting these Constitutional obligations to the side, Congress has expressed an unwavering resolve to choose a method of apportionment that favors neither the small nor the large states. The rule of Jefferson was discarded when its bias in favor of the large became apparent. The principle upon which the argument for the choice of Hill's method was based was the avoidance of bias. The claim was made that it alone of the methods known was balanced in its treatment of small and large. That claim, we know, is false.

The case is made even stronger by recent United States Supreme Court decisions in redistricting cases. In *Wesberry* v. *Sanders* in 1964 the

Court ruled that districts should be determined so that "as nearly as is practicable one man's vote in a congressional election is to be worth as much as another's."[1] In 1969 the Court stated further that "the 'as nearly as practical' standard requires that the state make a good-faith effort to achieve precise mathematical equality. Unless population variances among congressional districts are shown to have resulted despite such effort, the State must justify each variance, no matter how small."[2] And in 1973 the Court overturned a Texas district plan because the maximum deviation of a district from the ideal was 2.4%.[3] These standards concern deviations between electoral districts *within* states. Apportionment determines the deviation between the ideal district sizes *among* states. Had Hill's method been applied to the first 19 United States censuses, the cumulative bias in favor of the small states would have been worse—about 3.3%. By contrast the method of Webster—the one most often used by Congress—would have shown a bias of less than 0.3%, a statistically negligible amount.

The conclusion is that Webster's method is to be preferred for federal systems, and in particular for the United States. In the end it is also the most natural method.[4] Plain common sense points to simple rounding when it works. Webster's method is just a natural device for making this idea work in all cases. By introducing a common divisor Webster synthesized the best elements of Hamilton's and Jefferson's approaches.

The development of a theory of apportionment has, in effect, shown us *why* the simplest and most intuitively appealing method of all *is* the best one. It alone meets all of the principles: it avoids the paradoxes, it is unbiased, and in practice it stays within the quota. It is hard not to agree with a representative in 1882 who declared (with pardonable exaggeration):

> Since the world began there has been but one way of proportioning numbers, namely, by using a common divisor, by running the "remainders" into decimals, by taking fractions above .5, and dropping those below .5; nor can there be any other method. This process is purely arithmetical. . . . If a hundred men were being torn limb from limb, or a thousand babes were being crushed, this process would have no more feeling in the matter than would an iceberg; because the science of mathematics has no more bowels of mercy than has a cast-iron dog.[5]

CHAPTER 12

The Choice for Proportional Representation Systems

But real equality of representation is not obtained unless any set of electors amounting to the average number of a constituency, wherever in the country they happen to reside, have the power of combining with one another to return a representative.

JOHN STUART MILL

How to apportion representation in the United States—and by implication in other federal systems—is resolved by the theory developed in the preceding chapters. Yet the nations of the world present a bewildering array of electoral systems involving federalism, proportional representation, and various combinations thereof.[1] Each has developed in an historical context carrying its own political legitimacy. The purpose of this chapter is to show how the theory can be applied to the design of more complex systems of representation.

A federal system with a ''first past the post'' or simple plurality vote within each single-member constituency seems to be peculiarly well adapted to the United States and other relatively homogeneous societies. It has been claimed, however, that this same electoral system would be the surest way to kill the very idea of democracy in heterogeneous societies encompassing traditionally hostile groups because minorities might go without any representation at all.[2]

The fact is that federal, majoritarian systems place high obstacles in the way of small parties. Their votes being scattered among many regions means that they obtain a less than proportional voice nationally. Proportional representation (PR) systems were devised to overcome this defect by making political parties, rather than geographical districts, the units of representation.

In a ''pure'' PR system voters cast a single vote for a party or party list in a multimember district. This idea was first introduced in ethnically heterogeneous countries such as Denmark (1855), Switzerland (1891), Belgium (1899), and Finland (1906). However, very few nations have a ''pure'' PR system in which the country forms one large multimember electoral district. Among the few examples are the Netherlands' Second Chamber and the Israeli Knesset.

Proportional representation has provoked conflicts over territorial versus party affiliation and on where to set the thresholds of representation—the percentage of the vote necessary for a party to obtain at least one seat. These struggles have occupied political forces in many nations and have led to a wide variety of electoral arrangements that seek to balance the competing needs for regional as against party representation.[3]

Most nations that use PR are divided into a number of multimember electoral districts with each district electing a specified number of representatives by pure PR. One example is the 155 seats of the Norwegian Storting in which each of 19 districts elects from 11 to 13 representatives depending upon its population. Another is the 200 seats of the Swiss National Council, where each of 17 cantons and 3 half-cantons fills from 2 to 35 seats, depending upon its population. There are many others that use pure PR by district for at least one House, including (as of 1976) Argentina, Austria, Belgium, Brazil, Costa Rica, Italy, and the Netherlands (First Chamber).[4] In each such case *two problems* must be solved: the first is how to apportion seats to districts according to their populations; the second is how to apportion the seats of each district to the parties according to their vote totals.

There are still other, more involved, combinations of PR and federalism. In the Federal Republic of Germany each voter disposes of two votes: the first is cast to elect an individual by plurality within each of 248 single-member districts; the second is cast for a party and is used to fill 248 additional seats so that the final allocation of the 496 seats is made "proportional" to the national vote totals. Sweden's system is similarly motivated: 310 seats of its single House are apportioned among 28 districts, and a pure PR system is used within each one of them. Then, an additional 40 seats are awarded to parties so that the final allocation is made "proportional" to the national party vote totals.

The apportionment of seats to districts and of seats to parties raises one and the same formal, mathematical problem. On the face of it the only change is in the basis of apportionment, from populations to vote totals. In reality there are essential differences between the two problems. A key one is the treatment of small parties. In his extensive survey of the political consequences of electoral laws, Rae concluded that "the prejudice of electoral laws in favor of strong elective parties and against weak ones is a very nearly universal fact of life."[5] Of course this prejudice may help promote more effective government, since it prevents fragmentation and helps to simplify legislative processes. Rae observed that federal systems with single member districts tend to be associated with a two-party system, whereas a pure PR system with no territorial representation tends to lead to a proliferation of parties.

Many nations set explicit percentage thresholds of the total vote below which a party obtains no seat at all in order to exclude small extremist groups from the political process.[6] In Israel electoral law denies any representation to a party receiving less than 1% of the national vote. In Sweden, to qualify for seats in any district a party must have at least 4% of the votes in the nation as a whole, or 12% in the district itself. In a federal system the concern is just the opposite: it is to assure every district, however small, some minimum number of seats. For American states this minimum is 1, for French departments it is 2, and for Canadian provinces it is the number of their senators. This special feature of PR systems can be accommodated by simply excluding those parties having less than the required minimum percentage, and then applying one of the previously discussed methods to the parties that remain.

A second important difference between PR and federal systems is that in the latter the number of districts—of states, departments, or provinces—does not change very frequently, whereas in PR systems the number of parties does. Some parties fade away while others form; some merge, some splinter. This fluidity may give rise to political instability; it argues for a method of apportioning seats that is robust under a changing composition of parties, and that does not encourage fragmentation. If one party increases its vote total relative to another in two successive elections it is inconceivable that the first should lose seats to the second. In other words, just as for federal systems, the population paradox must be avoided. This is particularly necessary in PR systems since otherwise it would be possible for a party to misrepresent part of its vote by giving it to a rival party and thereby gain seats. The only way to avoid this paradox is, as we have already seen, to choose a divisor method.

It is also important to ask whether the method influences parties to merge or to splinter. The way in which a method allocates seats may create subtle institutional incentives for larger or smaller parties to evolve, depending upon whether the merger of parties tends to result in a net gain of seats or in a net loss of seats. This question is independent of any coalitions or schisms that might occur in a parliament after an election. Rather it forms an underlying structural incentive for larger or smaller parties to form before elections. This type of incentive is institutional rather than psychological and cannot be expected to be observable or measurable in any one election. Nevertheless, it may be detectable over many elections and it does constitute a normative basis for the choice of method in PR systems.

For political stability it would seem desirable to have a method that encourages parties to merge by assuring that this would never result in a loss of seats. Specifically, a method "encourages coalitions" if the merger of two parties realized by pooling all their votes into one total assures the coalition *at least* as many seats as the two partners would obtain separately, and perhaps more. It is a mathematical fact that among all possible divisor methods, Jefferson's is the only one that invariably encourages coalitions. If this principle is considered of paramount importance, and the paradoxes are to be avoided, then Jefferson's method must be chosen for the PR part of the problem.

Jefferson's is the one method that encourages coalitions and avoids the population paradox.

Although this conclusion must be established by a rigorous argument, it can be explained intuitively. Of all the divisor methods Jefferson's is the one that most favors the larger parties: the larger a party the better it is treated, so mergers can hardly be harmful. That it actually does encourage coalitions is also easy to see. To obtain a Jefferson solution after a coalition is formed, begin by using the same common divisor x that was used to obtain a solution before the coalition formed. The quotient of the coalition is simply the sum of the two parties' respective quotients, and either their remainders sum to less than 1 or to at least 1. If less than 1, the coalition receives the total of what the two parties received before, and all other parties receive the same number of seats as before. If the remainders sum to at least 1, then the coalition has been awarded one extra seat, but one too many seats have been apportioned. So the common divisor must be increased—thereby decreasing all the quotients—until the quotient of some party passes a whole number (a Jefferson signpost) and it loses a seat. This may be the coalition party or it may be another party, but in any case the coalition cannot receive less than what its two partners had before.

That Jefferson's is the *only* method encouraging coalitions is less easy to establish and requires a rigorous argument (see section 9, appendix A). However, it is not difficult to devise examples for which a method other than Jefferson's, e.g. Dean's or Webster's, would give to a coalition fewer seats than its partners got separately. Adams's method is particularly perverse in that it always "encourages schisms." This means that if a party splits up, the parts are bound to get at least as many seats as the whole party did formerly—and perhaps more. Adams's method can be characterized as the one and only divisor method that encourages schisms.

Viewed from the perspective of coalition formation, the Jefferson method presents strong credentials for being adopted in a pure PR system. Another fact strengthens the argument. The essential idea of PR as versus federal systems is to give small parties their due (except for the possible exclusion of very small parties by thresholds). Jefferson's method favors the large parties the most of any divisor method, yet it also guarantees to every party at least its fair quota rounded down. To see why this is so, compute the quotas of all parties by taking the ideal number of votes per seat as the common divisor. Applying Jefferson's rule results in apportioning too few seats and so the divisor must be decreased, causing the quotients to increase. Therefore, by Jefferson's method, no party can obtain less than the whole number contained in its quota. Remarkably, Jefferson's is the *only* divisor method that guarantees the whole number in each party's quota (or modified quota in the case of minimum requirements). Combining the preceding results yields the following conclusion.

The only method that encourages coalitions, guarantees each party the whole number in its quota, and avoids the population paradox is Jefferson's.

If the goal of national policy is to favor the larger parties, encourage coalitions, and yet give all small (qualifying) parties their due, then Jefferson's method seems compelling—at least for "pure" PR systems, such as Israel's or Holland's.

But most PR systems are not pure. In a mixed system, the use of a method that favors large parties, like Jefferson's, tends to penalize the smaller parties district by district, so that nationwide the bias against them can be greatly magnified. Nationwide, the small parties may get very much less than their due. One very reasonable choice for these systems is Webster's method, since as has been demonstrated it is the only divisor method that is perfectly evenhanded in its treatment of larger and smaller parties. It can also be shown that it encourages neither coalitions nor schisms, but is approximately neutral: most of the time a coalition will get exactly what its partners would have received separately; otherwise the coalition has just as much chance of gaining a seat as losing one (and it will never gain or lose more than *one* seat).

The methods most used in practice are Hamilton's, Jefferson's, and Webster's. Thus, with the exception of Hamilton's method, usage seems to conform well with the dictates of reason. Hamilton's method is used for the pure PR part in each of Costa Rica's provinces and the Swiss National Council, and for the federal parts of Sweden's one House. It is usually referred to as the method of "greatest remainders."

Jefferson's method is used in many countries and goes by almost as many different names. This is because seemingly different arithmetic rules actually give identical results.[7] The PR component of the National Councils in Austria and Switzerland is found by the "Hagenbach-Bischoff method," which is the same as Jefferson's. The Netherlands and Israel use "d'Hondt's method" for their pure PR systems, which is again Jefferson's. D'Hondt, a Belgian lawyer active in the proportional representation movement, had reinvented the method in 1878 using almost exactly the same language as Jefferson.[8] Belgium uses it for the pure PR part of the election of each of its houses. Brazil uses the "method of highest averages" to allocate seats in its Chamber of Deputies to parties in each of its twenty-two Federal States: this is again Jefferson's method. Liechtenstein, Finland, and West Germany also use it under one of these various names, with or without specified thresholds, as part of their electoral systems.

The method of Webster also has several aliases: it is alternately referred to as "Saint-Lagüe's method" and as the "method of odd numbers." It is used for pure PR in Denmark, Sweden, and Norway, in some cases with a threshold. In Norway the method is slightly altered to make it more difficult for a party to gain its first seat by moving the first signpost forward from .5 to .7.

The application of the theory as a normative guide to the choice of methods for PR systems leads to the following conclusions. For the apportionment of seats to parties in proportion to their votes within a district, there are two reasonable choices: Jefferson's or Webster's, either with or without minimum thresholds. Jefferson's method is a good choice for a pure PR system, but the greater the number of districts in a mixed PR system the more all but the largest parties are penalized, thus denying the very goal of PR. Webster's method is also a good choice for a pure PR system and should definitely be considered for mixed systems having many districts.

There are also systems in which one part of the seats is apportioned to regions on the basis of populations and the remainder is allocated to parties on the basis of national vote totals. Examples are Sweden and the Federal Republic of Germany. A good solution in such cases is: First, apportion the seats to regions by the method of Webster (with minima of one or more). Second, in a specific election the number of districts captured by each national party establishes its minimum allocation, and the parties' total allocations are found by applying either Webster's or Jefferson's method with these minima.

The ultimate choice in any nation must, of course, depend upon its political, social, and legal heritage. The role of our analysis has been to show how the choice among methods can be reduced to a choice among principles.

APPENDIX A

The Theory of Apportionment

1. THE PROBLEM

A widely held ideal of fair representation is representation in proportion to some numerical criterion. In the United States, each state receives seats in the House of Representatives proportionally to its population but in any case is assured of at least 1 seat. In France, each department is given a number of deputies in like manner but is assured of at least 2. In the European Parliament, each country is also accorded representation in proportion to its population but is assured a minimum number of seats that ranges between 6 and 36, depending upon the country in question.

A specific *problem of apportionment* is given by a vector of "populations" $\mathbf{p} = (p_1,\ldots,p_s)$, an integer "size of house" $h \geqq 0$, and a vector of "minimum requirements" $\mathbf{r} = (r_1,\ldots,r_s) \geqq 0$. The p_i are positive integers and the r_i nonnegative integers. Usually the minimum requirements are a common number r. For the United States $r = 1$ and for France $r = 2$. However, Canada and the European Parliament are instances where minimum requirements differ. Occasionally, maximum limits may also be imposed on the number of seats allowed to each state, as for example the United States Constitution's stated limit of one per thirty thousand, though this is not an issue today. An *apportionment of* h *among* s is, therefore, a vector $\mathbf{a} = (a_1,\ldots,a_s)$ of nonnegative integers $a_i \geqq r_i$ that sum to h. In the sequel we will explicitly treat $\mathbf{r} = \mathbf{0}$ and for the most part leave as propositions for the reader the verification of the general cases.

The question that we address is, What is a fair method for determining apportionments? This is done in the framework and the language of allocating representation among geographical regions. However, many other problems have the same form. In proportional representation the problem is to allocate seats proportionally to party vote totals (Cotteret and Emeri, 1970). In manpower planning a problem is to allocate jobs in proportion to certain characteristics of the labor pool (Mayberry, 1978b). Service facilities—courts, judges, or hospitals—may need to be allotted to areas in proportion to the numbers of people to be served. In reporting statistical findings there is the problem of making tables of rounded percentages add up to 100% (Diaconis and Freedman, 1978). Any problem in which h objects are to be allocated in non-negative integers proportionally to some numerical criterion belongs to this class, and the theory below applies to it. Some of the principles we discuss are particularly relevant to the regional representation problem while other principles may be more telling for other applications (Balinski and Young, 1978b, 1979a).

EXAMPLE 1.1. Consider the apportionment problem with populations $\mathbf{p}$ = (27,744; 25,178; 19,951; 14,610; 9,225; 3,292) and h = 36. Let q_i = $p_i h/(\Sigma_j p_j)$ be the *quota* of state i, so that $\mathbf{q}$ = (9.988, 9.064, 7.182, 5.260, 3.321, 1.185) represents the vector of "fair shares." What integer apportionment *should* each state receive?

EXAMPLE 1.2. Members of the European Parliament are now elected by direct universal suffrage in each of the nine countries that constitute the European Economic Community (E.E.C.). The apportionment of seats was decided upon in April 1976 after a period of intense negotiation. By previously agreed-upon convention, the apportionment was to be proportional to the populations of the respective countries and yet assure each country at least the number of seats it held in the previous Parliament. The populations of the nine countries were estimated to be (in thousands): Germany 62,041; United Kingdom 56,056; Italy 55,361; France 53,780; Netherlands 13,450; Belgium 9,772; Denmark 5,052; Ireland 3,086; and Luxembourg 357. The total population was 258,955,000. The vector of minimum requirements was $\mathbf{r}$ = (36, 36, 36, 36, 14, 14, 10, 10, 6). The negotiation produced the apportionment $\mathbf{a}$ = (81, 81, 81, 81, 25, 24, 16, 15, 6). Compare this solution with the quotas.

2. ELEMENTARY PRINCIPLES

We seek a method of apportionment, that is, a rule that for every s-vector $\mathbf{p} > 0$ and integer $h \geqq 0$ gives an apportionment of h among s. A single-valued function does not suffice as the concept for a method. For suppose two states with identical populations are to share an odd number of seats $2a + 1$. There are only two natural solutions, $(a, a + 1)$ and $(a + 1, a)$, but there is no basis in terms of the proportional ideal for preferring one to the other. Any method that is fair must admit both possibilities as solutions.

Formally, then, define a *method* to be a multiple-valued function M, consisting of a set of apportionments of h among s for each s-vector $\mathbf{p} > 0$ and integer $h \geqq 0$. A *particular* M-*solution* is a single-valued function f with $f(\mathbf{p}, h) = \mathbf{a} \in M(\mathbf{p}, h)$. A particular M-solution breaks every "tie" in some arbitrary fashion, e.g., it might choose $(a, a + 1)$ in the case of two equal states sharing $2a + 1$ seats. Ties can also arise in more interesting ways that depend on the logic of the particular method used.

The ideal of proportionality immediately imposes several elementary properties that a method should enjoy. If all populations change by the same proportion then, since there is no change in the proportional shares of the states, there should be no change in the set of apportionments. Specifically, M is *homogeneous* if the M-apportionments for $\mathbf{p}$ and h are the same as the M-apportionments for $\lambda\mathbf{p}$ and h, for any positive rational number λ. This means that any positive s-vector of rational numbers may be considered as "populations."

Proportionality concerns the size of populations, not their names or other characteristics. Therefore, permuting the populations to obtain a "new" problem should only result in apportionments that are permuted in the same way. Methods with this property are called *symmetric*.

Proportionality means that whenever a problem can be solved perfectly in integers, then it must be. M is *weakly proportional* if whenever an apportionment $\mathbf{a}$ is proportional to $\mathbf{p}$, then $\mathbf{a}$ is the unique M-apportionment for $\mathbf{p} > 0$ when $h = \Sigma\ a_i$. Moreover, as the house size grows solutions should increasingly approach the ideal of proportionality. So if $\mathbf{b}'$ is an M-apportionment for $\mathbf{p} > 0$ and $\mathbf{b}$ is integer and proportional to $\mathbf{b}'$ with $\Sigma\ b_i < \Sigma\ b_i'$ then $\mathbf{b}$ should be the unique apportionment in $M(\mathbf{p}, \Sigma b_i)$. This means that if M splits 6 seats between two states 3 and 3, then it must split 4 seats between the same two in no way other than 2 and 2. A method that satisfies this condition and is also weakly proportional is called *proportional*. Although all reasonable methods are proportional, much of the theory is developed using the weaker notion.

Ties—where a method gives several different apportionments for the same problem—arise naturally not only from considerations of symmetry but also from changing populations. One expects that as populations change more and more in some direction, a point (i.e. an s-vector $\mathbf{p}^*$) is eventually reached where the method changes apportionments, otherwise the ideal of proportionality could not be met. These natural tie points depend, of course, upon the method that is used. One way of describing a tie point $\mathbf{p}^*$ is to say that arbitrarily small perturbations about it can produce different apportionments: a slight increase in one state's population relative to another's may result in one apportionment, while a slight decrease may result in another apportionment. Such tie points $\mathbf{p}^*$ may involve irrational numbers. Hence it is important to extend the concept of method to all real populations $\mathbf{p} \in \mathbf{R}^s$, $\mathbf{p} > \mathbf{0}$. We say that a method is *complete* if whenever $\mathbf{p}^n \to \mathbf{p} > \mathbf{0}$ and $\mathbf{a} \in M(\mathbf{p}^n, h)$ for every n, then $\mathbf{a} \in M(\mathbf{p}, h)$. A method M is *completed* by letting $\mathbf{a} \in M(\mathbf{p})$ for $\mathbf{p} \in \mathbf{R}^s$ if and only if there is a sequence of rational s-vectors $\mathbf{p}^n$ converging to $\mathbf{p}$ such that $\mathbf{a} \in M(\mathbf{p}^n)$ for all n. Any natural view of proportional allocation carries with it the idea of completeness; however some consequences of the theory also hold for methods that are not complete.

In the presence of minimum requirements—or of minimum and maximum requirements—it is natural to generalize symmetry by attaching the requirements to the particular states (e.g., recall the European Parliament). Thus a method is *symmetric* if permuting the populations results in permuting the apportionments in the same way, provided the requirements remain satisfied. Homogeneity and completeness hold in the case of minimum requirements without any further modification. It can be shown that weak proportionality and proportionality can be modified by simply imposing the requirements as constraints.

From this point on, methods of apportionment will always be assumed to be homogeneous, symmetric, weakly proportional, and complete, unless stated otherwise. These are the rock-bottom requirements that must be satisfied by any method that is worthy of consideration.

PROPOSITION 2.1. *The methods of Hamilton, Jefferson, Lowndes, Webster, Adams, Dean, and Hill are homogeneous, symmetric, proportional, and complete.*

PROPOSITION 2.2. *The completion of a method is complete, and inherits the properties of homogeneity, symmetry, and proportionality.*

3. TRADITIONAL APPROACHES

This section reviews the different types of methods that have traditionally been followed. The claims for these methods have typically been based on the computational procedures they employ, in other words on *ad hoc* considerations. Moreover, it often happens that these differing computational approaches represent the same method in different guises.

A most natural approach is to compute the quotas and *round* in the usual way. But this does not always work (e.g., the example of section 1). Hamilton's method is one way around the difficulty. Another is to choose an ideal district size or *divisor x*, to compute the *quotients* of each state $q_i^x = p_i/x$, and to round these according to some rule. The proposal of Webster was to round these in the usual way: remainders above one-half are rounded up, remainders below one-half are rounded down, and a remainder of exactly one-half may be rounded either up or down—it is a natural tie point. In general, for any real number z, let $[z]$ denote the integer closest to z. If the fractional part of z is one-half, then $[z]$ has two possible values. The *method of Webster* is

$$W(\mathbf{p},h) = \left\{ \mathbf{a} : a_i = [p_i/x], \quad \sum_i a_i = h \quad \text{for some choice of } x \right\}.$$

If there are states having quotients with a remainder of one-half, then all possible values of $[p_i/x]$ are admitted that sum to h.

Instead of "ordinary" rounding, the same approach may be used with rounding of quotients taken at other points, as was for example proposed by Jefferson and Adams. In general, any rounding procedure may be described by specifying a dividing point $d(a)$ in each interval of quotients $[a, a + 1]$ for each nonnegative integer a.

For any positive real number z a *d-rounding* of z, $[z]_d$, is an integer a such that $d(a - 1) \leq z \leq d(a)$, which is unique unless $z = d(a)$, in which case it takes on either of the values a or $a + 1$. To avoid more than two-way ties it is required that $d(a) < d(a + 1)$. Any monotone increasing $d(a)$ defined for all integers $a \geq 0$ and satisfying $a \leq d(a) \leq a + 1$ is called a *divisor criterion*. The *divisor method based on d* is

$$M(\mathbf{p},h) = \left\{ \mathbf{a} : a_i = [p_i/x]_d \quad \text{and} \quad \sum_i a_i = h \quad \text{for some } x \right\}.$$

In case $d(0) = 0$ and $0 < h < s$ we adopt the convention that the h largest states each get 1 seat. The five traditional divisor methods are described as divisor methods in Table A3.1.

TABLE A3.1   The Five Traditional Divisor Methods

Method :	Adams	Dean	Hill	Webster	Jefferson
$d(a)$:	a	$a(a+1) \Big/ \left(a + \dfrac{1}{2}\right)$	$\sqrt{a(a+1)}$	$a + \dfrac{1}{2}$	$a + 1$

An alternative but equivalent description is that **a** is an M-apportionment if and only if there exists an x such that for all $a_i > 0$, $p_i/d(a_i - 1)$ $\geq x \geq p_i/d(a_i)$ and for all $a_i = 0$, $x \geq p_i/d(a_i)$. So the divisor method based on d can also be described in terms of a min-max inequality:

$$M(\mathbf{p},h) = \{\mathbf{a} : \min_{a_i > 0} p_i/d(a_i - 1) \geq \max_{a_j \geq 0} p_j/d(a_j), \Sigma\, a_i = h\}.$$

Throughout $p/0$ is defined, and $p_i > p_j$ implies $p_i/0 > p_j/0$.

PROPOSITION 3.1. *Each of the traditional five divisor methods gives a different apportionment for the problem of example 1.1.*

PROPOSITION 3.2. *Every divisor method M has particular solutions that avoid the Alabama paradox.*

PROPOSITION 3.3. *The divisor method M based on* d *may also be described recursively as follows*: (i) $M(\mathbf{p}, 0) = \mathbf{0}$, (ii) *if* $\mathbf{a} \in M(\mathbf{p},h)$ *and k satisfies* $p_k/d(a_k) = \max_i p_i/d(a_i)$, *then* $\mathbf{b} \in M(\mathbf{p}, h + 1)$, *with* $b_k = a_k + 1$ *and* $b_i = a_i$ *for* $i \neq k$.

PROPOSITION 3.4. *A divisor method M based on* d *for problems with both minimum and maximum requirements* $\mathbf{r} \leq \mathbf{r}^+$ *may be described as follows:*

$$M(\mathbf{p}, h) = \left\{ \mathbf{a} : a_i = mid\, \{r_i, r_i^+, [p_i/x]_d\} \quad and \quad \sum_i a_i = h \quad for\ some\ x \right\}$$

where mid $\{u,v,w\}$ *is the middle in value of the three numbers* u, v, w. *Corresponding min-max and recursive descriptions may be derived.*

There are an infinite number of different divisor methods. How is one to choose among them? An ingenious approach to this question, first suggested by Joseph Hill (1911) and fully carried out by E. V. Huntington (1921, 1928, 1940), was to make *pairwise comparisons* of states' representations. "Between any two states, there will practically always be a certain inequality which gives one of the states a slight advantage over the other. A transfer of one representative from the more favored state to the less favored state will ordinarily reverse the *sign* of this inequality, so that the more favored state now becomes the less favored, and vice versa. Whether such a transfer should be made or not depends on whether the 'amount of inequality' between the two states after the transfer is less or greater than it was before; if the 'amount of inequality' is reduced by the transfer, it is obvious that the transfer should be made. The fundamental question therefore at once presents itself, as to how the 'amount of inequality' between two states is to be measured'' (Huntington, 1928).

Let states i and j, having populations p_i and p_j, be apportioned a_i and a_j seats respectively. It is unambiguous to say that i *is favored relative to* j if and only if $a_i/p_i > a_j/p_j$. One natural measure of the inequality between i and j is therefore $|a_i/p_i - a_j/p_j|$.

Huntington's argument is that if this inequality can be reduced by a transfer of seats between i and j, then such a transfer should be made. In particular, if $|(a_i - 1)/p_i - (a_j + 1)/p_j| < |a_i/p_i - a_j/p_j|$, then i should give up one seat to j. Of course it is quite conceivable that *every* apportionment is *unstable*, i.e. admits such transfers. Remarkably enough, this is not the case. An apportionment admits *no* such transfers if for all pairs i and j with $a_i/p_i \geq a_j/p_j$

$$a_i/p_i - a_j/p_j \leq (a_j + 1)/p_j - (a_i - 1)/p_i$$

or

$$p_i \bigg/ \left(a_i - \frac{1}{2}\right) \geq p_j \bigg/ \left(a_j + \frac{1}{2}\right) \qquad (3.1)$$

Therefore such an **a** must be a Webster method apportionment. Conversely, every Webster method apportionment satisfies (3.1), hence satisfies the transfer test. In particular this pairwise comparison approach has produced a house monotone method!

Unfortunately for this logic, the statement that i is favored relative to j can be expressed in many different ways. The inequality $a_i/p_i > a_j/p_j$ can be rearranged by cross-multiplication in $2^4 = 16$ different ways. Hence to measure the inequality between states i and j it would be equally valid to consider the inequalities between the numbers p_i/a_i and p_j/a_j, or between a_i and $a_j p_i/p_j$, or p_i and $p_j a_i/a_j$, or $p_i a_j/p_j a_i$ and 1, or p_i/p_j and a_i/a_j, etc.

Not every measure of inequality gives stable apportionments: for some measures there exist problems for which every apportionment can be improved upon by some transfer. Huntington showed that, except for four such ''unworkable'' measures, all others resulted in the methods of either Adams, Dean, Hill, Webster, or Jefferson. Examples of tests that lead to these methods are given in Table A3.2. Huntington argued that it is not the absolute difference that should be used in measuring the inequality between two numbers y and z, but the relative difference $|y - z|/\min(y, z)$, and he observed that the relative differences in all 16 cases are the same: $a_i p_j / a_j p_i - 1$. All relative differences yield the method of Hill, or what Huntington called the "method of equal proportions." This is a neat argument, yet it boils down to a question of preference for one among several competing tests of inequality.

> PROPOSITION 3.5. *The test* $|a_i/a_j - p_i/p_j|$ *does not always yield stable apportionments. The three state example with* $\mathbf{p} = (762,534,304)$ *and* $h = 16$ *has no stable solution.*

> PROPOSITION 3.6. *The pairwise comparison approach may be modified to accommodate minimum and maximum requirements.*

TABLE A3.2   Pairwise Comparison Tests for Five Traditional Methods

Method :	Adams	Dean	Hill	Webster	Jefferson
Test : (for $a_i/p_i \geq a_j/p_j$)	$a_i - a_j(p_i/p_j)$	$p_j/a_j - p_i/a_i$	$\dfrac{a_i/p_i}{a_j/p_j} - 1$	$a_i/p_i - a_j/p_j$	$a_i(p_j/p_i) - a_j$

A favorite approach of operations research analysts is *constrained optimization*. Not surprisingly it has been advocated for apportionment. The variables in the problem are $\mathbf{a} = (a_1,\ldots,a_s)$ and the constraints are that $\mathbf{a}$ be nonnegative and integer with $\Sigma_i a_i = h$. The question that remains is: what function should be optimized?

Ideally one would like to have the a_i "close to" the quotas $q_i = p_i h/p$, where $p = \Sigma_i p_i$ is the total population. One plausible choice is to minimize $\Sigma_i |a_i - q_i|$, or perhaps instead $\Sigma_i (a_i - q_i)^2$. In either case the *method of Hamilton* solves the problem: first, give every state its *lower quota** $\lfloor q_i \rfloor$; second, give the remaining $\Sigma_i(q_i - \lfloor q_i \rfloor)$ seats one each to states having the largest remainders, $q_i - \lfloor q_i \rfloor$.

The "error" inherent in a trial apportionment can, of course, be measured in other ways. $a_i \neq q_i$ means that the average district size in state i, p_i/a_i, is different from the average national district size, p/h. So, perhaps, it might be reasonable to minimize $\Sigma_i |p_i/a_i - p/h|$ or $\Sigma_i(p_i/a_i - p/h)^2$. These

---

*$\lfloor z \rfloor$ is the largest integer less than or equal to z.

yield two different methods, neither of which is Hamilton's. Alternatively, and just as reasonably, one might choose to minimize $\Sigma_i |a_i/p_i - h/p|$ or $\Sigma_i (a_i/p_i - h/p)^2$, or other variations on the theme.

In 1910 Sainte-Lagüe argued—as did F. W. Owens in 1921—that if individuals are considered the basic elements whose shares are to be made as nearly equal as possible, then the error should be measured by $\Sigma_i p_i (a_i/p_i - h/p)^2$. The method of Webster, it turns out, minimizes this function. To see this, note that

$$\Sigma\, p_i (a_i/p_i - h/p)^2 = \Sigma\, a_i^2/p_i - (2h/p)\,\Sigma\, a_i + (h^2/p^2)\,\Sigma\, p_i$$
$$= \Sigma\, a_i^2/p_i - h^2/p.$$

Thus, the constrained optimization problem is equivalent to minimizing $\Sigma\, a_i^2/p_i$ when $\Sigma\, a_i = h$, $a_i \geq 0$ integer. If $\mathbf{a}$ is optimal then for all a_i, a_j, with $i \neq j$ and $a_i > 0$, a transfer from i to j cannot improve the objective, that is,

$$(a_i - 1)^2/p_i + (a_j + 1)^2/p_j \geq a_i^2/p_i + a_j^2/p_j$$

which is the same as

$$p_i \Big/ \Big(a_i - \frac{1}{2}\Big) \geq p_j \Big/ \Big(a_j + \frac{1}{2}\Big).$$

Therefore, $\mathbf{a}$ optimal implies

$$\min_{a_i>0} p_i \Big/ \Big(a_i - \frac{1}{2}\Big) \geq \max_{a_j \geq 0} p_j \Big/ \Big(a_j + \frac{1}{2}\Big),$$

which is the min-max inequality that characterizes Webster apportionments.

Conversely, suppose that $\mathbf{a}$ satisfies the Webster min-max inequality or, what is the same thing,

$$(2a_i + 1)/p_i \geq (2a_j - 1)/p_j \quad \text{for all } a_i \geq 0 \quad \text{and } a_j > 0.$$

If $\mathbf{b}$ is some apportionment different from $\mathbf{a}$, let $S^+ = \{i : b_i > a_i\}$, $S^- = \{j : b_j < a_j\}$ and let $b_i = a_i + \delta_i$ for $i \in S^+$, $b_j = a_j - \lambda_j$ for $j \in S^-$. Then $\Sigma_{S^+}\delta_i = \Sigma_{S^-}\lambda_j = \alpha > 0$ and, by the above inequalities,

$$(2a_i + \delta_i)/p_i \geqq (2a_j - \lambda_j)/p_j \quad \text{for all } i \in S^+ \text{ and } j \in S^-. \tag{3.2}$$

Now we can see that

$$\sum_i b_i^2/p_i - \sum_i a_i^2/p_i = \sum_{S^+} (2a_i + \delta_i)\delta_i/p_i - \sum_{S^-} (2a_j - \lambda_j)\lambda_j/p_j \geqq 0$$

since the last term is simply the sum of α differences between the left and right hand sides of (3.2). Therefore **b** gives to the objective function a value that can be no smaller than that of **a**, showing that **a** must be a minimizing solution.

If instead the average district sizes are taken as the basic elements to be made as equal as possible, the natural measure of statistical error to minimize would be $\Sigma_i a_i(p_i/a_i - p/h)^2$. Sainte-Lagüe (1910) suggested this possibility and cryptically remarked, "one is led to a more complex rule"; this rule turns out to be Hill's method, as Huntington (1928) later showed.

The total error inherent in an apportionment could be small, while the error for some particular state might be unreasonably large. The objective might therefore be formulated in terms of making the worst error for any state as small as possible. There are, again, many different ways of realizing this idea. One such approach, advocated by Burt and Harris (1963) is the objective $\min_a \max_{i,j} |p_i/a_i - p_j/a_j|$. Why not then take instead $\min_a \max_{i,j} |a_i/p_i - a_j/p_j|$? In a slightly different spirit one might choose $\min_a \max_i |a_i - q_i|$, or $\min_a \max_i |p_i/a_i - p/h|$.

A still different point of view is to consider a state's situation by itself, comparing it neither to another state nor to any fixed standard. $\text{Min}_a \max_i$ p_i/a_i makes the least advantaged state as advantaged as possible. It is solved by the method of Adams. $\text{Min}_a \max_i a_i/p_i$ makes the most advantaged state as little advantaged as possible. It is solved by the method of Jefferson.

The moral of this tale is that one cannot choose objective functions with impunity, despite current practices in applied mathematics. The choice of an objective is, by and large an *ad hoc* affair. The same is true of the other traditional approaches that have been used: Why advocate one divisor $d(a)$ rather than another? Why adopt one measure of pairwise inequality rather than another? Why choose one objective function rather than another? Of much deeper significance than the formulas that are used are the *properties* they enjoy.

PROPOSITION 3.7. *(Birkhoff, 1976). Hamilton apportionments minimize* $\Sigma|a_i - q_i|$, $\Sigma(a_i - q_i)^2$ *and, actually, any ℓ_p norm of* **a** $-$ **q**.

PROPOSITION 3.8. *Hill apportionments minimize* $\Sigma a_i (p_i/a_i - p/h)^2$.

PROPOSITION 3.9. *The methods defined by* $min_a\ max_{i,j}\ |p_i/a_i - p_j/a_j|$ *and* $min_a\ max_i\ |a_i - q_i|$ *both admit the Alabama paradox.*

PROPOSITION 3.10. *Jefferson apportionments solve* $min_a\ max_i\ a_i/p_i$ *and Adams apportionments solve* $min_a\ max_i\ p_i/a_i$.

PROPOSITION 3.11. *The constrained optimization approach can be modified to accommodate both minimum requirements and maximum requirements by incorporating them as constraints. These modifications lead to solutions that are consistent with the previous approaches.*

4. PRINCIPLES: POPULATION MONOTONICITY

History and common sense have provided the principles we need to sift through the vast number of different numerical apportionment schemes and determine which are appropriate to the problem. A few fundamental principles suffice: consistency with changes in populations, avoiding the Alabama paradox, lack of bias, and staying within the quota. The interplay of these four simple ideas provides a logical framework with which to judge the merits of different methods.

What methods should be seriously considered? The view of the National Academy of Sciences Committees was that "there are only five methods that require consideration at this time"—namely the five traditional divisor methods that have kept recurring throughout the two-hundred-year history of the problem and were shown by Huntington to be variations on the single theme of pairwise comparisons. The single most important criterion applied by the Academy Committees to judge between these five methods was bias. Their conclusion was that Hill's method was the least biased. But a careful analysis of historical data shows that this conclusion is wrong: Hill's method is consistently biased toward the small states, whereas Webster's method is apparently unbiased and is the only one of the five that is so. In other words, a straightforward empirical analysis of a historically important class of methods points to Webster's as the preferred one, and little or no theory is needed to reach this conclusion.

The foregoing argument is simple but limited in scope. What about other methods? In particular, what about the divisor methods, of which the five are but special examples? To study this infinite class with respect to bias requires theoretical models that are treated in the next section. The conclusion, however, is the same: different models of bias all point to Webster's as the only method in the class that is unbiased.

But why should the analysis be restricted to divisor methods? After all, they represent but one computational approach out of many. The reason lies not in their computational attractiveness—many methods, including Hamilton's, could be said to be more attractive computationally. The reason is more fundamental: they are the only methods that are consistent with changing data. This section is devoted to establishing this result.

Of the various parameters affecting apportionment—populations, house size, and number of states—the former is constantly in flux, whereas the last two typically change less frequently. It is essential that a method be consistent with changes in all three of these parameters, and most particularly with changes in populations. If over the short term both the house size h and number of states s are assumed to be fixed, then it suffices to have a *partial method* $M^*(\mathbf{p})$, which gives a set of apportionments of h for every s-vector $\mathbf{p} > \mathbf{0}$. M^* should behave monotonically in populations: roughly speaking, states that increase in size should get more, while those that decrease should get less. Formally, this desire can be interpreted in several different ways.

One approach to population monotonicity would be the usual mathematical definition:

> *If p_i increases and all $p_j (j \neq i)$ remain the same,*   (4.1)
> *then i's apportionment does not decrease.*

This notion was proposed as early as 1907 by Erlang and has been studied by Hylland (1975, 1978). The difficulty with this definition is that it is not relevant to the problem in an applied sense, since such comparisons scarcely ever occur in practice. Populations change dynamically, and any useful definition of population monotonicity must reflect this fact.

An alternative definition that seems more appealing at first sight and that takes dynamic changes into account is the following.

> *If a state's quota increases then its apportionment*   (4.2)
> *does not decrease.*

This notion is called *strong population monotonicity*. Unfortunately it is too strong.

THEOREM 4.1. *For* s $\geq$ 3 *and* h $\neq$ 0, h $\neq$ s, *no partial method satisfies strong population monotonicity.*

Given M^*, the minimum number of seats a state ever gets over all populations **p** is denoted by $\bar{a}$, the maximum number by $\bar{\bar{a}}$. For many (but not all) methods $\bar{a} = 0$ and $\bar{\bar{a}} = h$ (see Proposition 4.2 below).

PROOF OF THEOREM 4.1. Fix $s \geq 3$ and h different from 0 and s and suppose that M^* is strongly population monotone. By homogeneity it suffices to restrict $M^*(\mathbf{p})$ to the set $\bar{P}$ of populations **p** whose sum is h, i.e. to the quotas.

If $h = 1$, $(1, 0, \ldots, 0)$ is an apportionment for $(1/s, 1/s, \ldots, 1/s)$. It follows that whenever $p_i > 1/s$ then $a_i \geq 1$. But then for any small enough $\varepsilon > 0$ $\mathbf{p} = ((1 + \varepsilon)/s,(1 + \varepsilon)/s,(1 - 2\varepsilon)/s,1/s,\ldots,1/s) \in \bar{P}$ and for any apportionment $\mathbf{a} \in M^*(\mathbf{p})$ $a_1 \geq 1$, $a_2 \geq 1$ which implies $h \geq 2$, a contradiction.

Next suppose that $1 < h < s$. Consider any $\mathbf{p} \in \bar{P}$ such that $p_1 > p_2 > \ldots > p_s$ and $h/s < p_i < h/(s - 1)$ for $i = 1, \ldots, h - 1$ while $p_h < h/s$. Every apportionment $\mathbf{a} \subset M^*(\mathbf{p})$ must satisfy $a_1 \geq a_2 \geq \quad \geq a_s$.

Choose rational $\varepsilon > 0$ small enough such that $p_1 + \varepsilon < h/(s - 1)$ and let $\mathbf{p}' = (p_1 + \varepsilon, \ldots, p_1 + \varepsilon, p_s') \in \bar{P}$ where $p_s' < h/s$. Each of the first $s - 1$ states gets at least a_1 seats for any apportionment $\mathbf{b} \in M^*(\mathbf{p}')$. Thus $h = \Sigma\, b_i \geq a_1(s - 1)$, which is a contradiction unless $h = s - 1$ and $a_1 - 1$. We may conclude that $a_1 - 1$ whenever $\bar{p}_1$ is arbitrarily close to $h/(s - 1) = 1$ and $a_s = 0$ whenever $\bar{p}_s$ is arbitrarily close to h/s. But then $(1 - (s - 1)\varepsilon, (h - 1)/(s - 1) + \varepsilon, \ldots, (h - 1)/s \quad 1 + \varepsilon)$ has apportionment $(1,0,\ldots,0)$ which sums to $1 < h$, a contradiction.

Finally consider the case $h > s$. By weak proportionality, $\bar{a} = 0$ or 1, and $\bar{\bar{a}} \geq h - s + 1 \geq 2$. Define the sets

$$P_{\bar{a}} = \{p \in (0,h) : a_1 = \bar{a} \quad \text{whenever } \mathbf{a} \in M^*(\mathbf{p}) \quad \text{and } p_1 = p\},$$
$$P_{\bar{\bar{a}}} = \{p \in (0,h) : a_1 = \bar{\bar{a}} \quad \text{whenever } \mathbf{a} \in M^*(\mathbf{p}) \quad \text{and } p_1 = p\}.$$

By definition of $\bar{a}$ there is a $\mathbf{p} \in \bar{P}$ and $\mathbf{a} \in M^*(\mathbf{p})$ with $a_1 = \bar{a}$ hence $p \in P_{\bar{a}}$ for every $0 < p < p_1$. Moreover for any $p \in P_{\bar{a}}$ and $0 < p' < p$, $p' \in P_{\bar{a}}$. Therefore $P_{\bar{a}}$ is an interval such that $g\ell b(P_{\bar{a}}) = 0$, lub $(P_{\bar{a}}) = \bar{q} > 0$. Similarly $P_{\bar{\bar{a}}}$ is an interval with $g\ell b(P_{\bar{\bar{a}}}) = \bar{\bar{q}} < h$, lub $(P_{\bar{\bar{a}}}) = h$.

Choose rational $\varepsilon > 0$ such that $\varepsilon < \bar{q}$ and $(s - 1)\varepsilon + \bar{\bar{q}} < h$. By definition of $\bar{q}$ and $\bar{\bar{q}}$, $\mathbf{p}' = (h - (s - 1)\varepsilon,\varepsilon,\varepsilon,\ldots,\varepsilon)$ has the unique apportionment $(\bar{\bar{a}},\bar{a},\bar{a},\ldots,\bar{a})$. Hence $\bar{\bar{a}} + (s - 1)\bar{a} = h$. Letting ε approach $\bar{q}$ from below, the inequality $(s - 1)\varepsilon + \bar{q}' \leq h$ must always be satisfied, since otherwise state 1 would receive fewer than $\bar{a}$ seats while all the others receive $\bar{a}$. Therefore $(s - 1)\bar{q} + \bar{q}' \leq h$. Hence $(\bar{q}' + \gamma, \bar{q}, \ldots, \bar{q}) \in \bar{P}$ for some $\gamma \geq 0$. Define $\mathbf{p}'' = (\bar{q}' + \gamma + (s - 2)\delta/2, \bar{q} + (s - 2)\delta/2, \bar{q} - \delta, \ldots, \bar{q} - \delta) \in \bar{P}$. $\mathbf{p}''$ has apportionment $\mathbf{a} = (\bar{a}, a_2, \bar{a}, \ldots, \bar{a})$ where $a_2 > \bar{a}$, a contradiction since then $\Sigma\, a_i > h.\square$

PROPOSITION 4.1. *There exist counterexamples to the theorem when* h = 0 *and* h = s.

PROPOSITION 4.2. *Weak proportionality implies* ā = 0 *or* 1.

A more satisfactory approach to population monotonicity is this: if state i's population increases and j's decreases, then i should not get fewer seats and j more (unless there is a tie). By homogeneity, the same conclusion holds whenever i's population increases *relative* to j's. More exactly, a partial method M^* is *population monotone* if for every two s-vectors $\mathbf{p}$, $\mathbf{p}' > \mathbf{0}$ and corresponding M^*-apportionments $\mathbf{a}$ and $\mathbf{a}'$, and for all $i < j$,

$$p'_i/p'_j \geq p_i/p_j \quad \text{implies} \quad \begin{cases} a'_i \geq a_i \quad \text{or} \quad a'_j \leq a_j, \\ \text{or} \\ p'_i/p'_j = p_i/p_j, \quad \text{and} \quad a'_i, a'_j \\ \text{can be substituted for } a_i, a_j \text{ in } \mathbf{a}. \end{cases} \quad (4.3)$$

A partial method M^* is a *partial divisor method* if for some monotone increasing function $d(a)$

$$M^*(\mathbf{p}) = \{\mathbf{a} \geq \mathbf{0} : \Sigma\, a_i = h, \min_{a_i > 0} p_i/d(a_i - 1) \geq \max_{a_i \geq 0} p_i/d(a_i)\}. \quad (4.4)$$

Note that $d(a)$ may not be a divisor criterion in the strict sense, since it is not assumed to satisfy $a \leq d(a) \leq a + 1$.

THEOREM 4.2. *Let* h ≥ s ≥ 2, s ≠ 3. *The partial method* M* *is a population monotone method if and only if it is a partial divisor method.*

PROPOSITION 4.3. *Every partial divisor method is population monotone, even when* s = 3.

The proof of the converse in the case $s = 2$ is relatively simple and intuitive. Fix $h \geq s = 2$. Given a population monotone method M^* we shall show the existence of a monotone increasing function $d(a)$ such that for every $\mathbf{p} = (p_1, p_2) > 0$, $\mathbf{a} = (a_1, a_2) \in M^*(\mathbf{p})$ if and only if $a_1, a_2 \geq 0$, $a_1 + a_2 = h$, and

$$\min_{a_i > 0} p_i/d(a_i - 1) \geq \max_{a_i \geq 0} p_i/d(a_i).$$

Equivalently,

$$d(a_1 - 1)/d(a_2) \leq p_1/p_2 \leq d(a_1)/d(a_2 - 1) \quad \text{if } a_1, a_2 > 0, \quad (4.5)$$

$$p_1/p_2 \leq d(0)/d(h - 1) \quad \text{if } a_1 = 0, \quad a_2 = h, \quad (4.6)$$

and

$$d(h - 1)/d(0) \leq p_1/p_2 \quad \text{if } a_1 = h, \quad a_2 = 0. \quad (4.7)$$

Let $\bar{P}$ be the set of *normalized* populations $\bar{P} = \{\mathbf{p} > 0 : p_1 + p_2 = h\}$, and for each $a_1, a_2 \geq 0$, $a_1 + a_2 = h$, let $\bar{P}(\mathbf{a})$ be the set of populations $\mathbf{p} \in \bar{P}$ such that $\mathbf{a} \in M^*(\mathbf{p})$. By population monotonicity, each $\bar{P}(\mathbf{a})$ is an *interval* of the line $\bar{P}$. By weak proportionality, $\mathbf{a} \in \bar{P}(\mathbf{a})$ whenever $\mathbf{a} > 0$. Moreover, since $\mathbf{a}$ is the *unique* apportionment when $\mathbf{p} = \mathbf{a} > 0$, completeness implies that $\mathbf{a}$ is in the *interior* of the interval $\bar{P}(\mathbf{a})$. Completeness also implies that $P(\mathbf{a})$ is a *closed* interval whenever $\mathbf{a} > 1$; the intervals $P(1,h - 1)$ and $\bar{P}(h - 1,1)$ are either closed or half-open; whereas $\bar{P}(0,h)$ and $\bar{P}(h,0)$ are either half-open (since zero populations are not admitted) or empty. Finally, the intervals can overlap only at their endpoints, since otherwise population monotonicity would be violated. Thus the situation is like that shown in Figure A4.1 for the case $h = 6$.

To define the divisor criterion $d(a)$, simply let $(d(a_1 - 1), d(a_2))$ be the left-hand endpoint of the interval $\bar{P}(a_1, a_2)$ and $(d(a_1), d(a_2 - 1))$ the right-hand endpoint, for all $a_1 \geq a_2 > 0$, $a_1 + a_2 = h$. This defines $d(a)$ for $0 \leq a \leq h$, and $d(a)$ is evidently monotone increasing in a. In fact $d(a)$ also satisfies $a \leq d(a) \leq a + 1$.

For the case $s = 3$ the result does not hold, as will be shown presently by a counterexample.

For the case $s \geq 4$, several definitions and lemmas are needed. For every $\mathbf{a} \geq 0$, $\Sigma a_i = h$, let $P(\mathbf{a}) = \{\mathbf{p} > 0 : \mathbf{a} \in M^*(\mathbf{p})\}$.

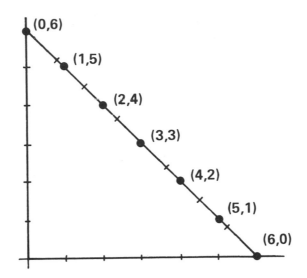

Figure A4.1   Intervals Defining a Population Monotone Partial Method on Two
               States

LEMMA 4.1.   P(**a**) *is convex.*

PROOF. Let **p**, **p**' $\in P$ (**a**) but suppose that $\bar{\mathbf{p}} = \lambda\mathbf{p} + (1 - \lambda)\mathbf{p}' \notin$ $P(\mathbf{a})$ for some λ, $0 < \lambda < 1$. Let $\bar{\mathbf{a}} \in M^*(\bar{\mathbf{p}})$ differ from **a** in a *minimal number of coordinates.* By hypothesis $\bar{\mathbf{a}} \neq \mathbf{a}$, so choose $i \neq j$ with $a_i < \bar{a}_i$, $a_j > \bar{a}_j$. By population monotonicity $p_i/p_j < \bar{p}_i/\bar{p}_j$; the inequality is strict since otherwise a_i, a_j could be substituted into $\bar{\mathbf{a}}$ for $\bar{a}_i$, $\bar{a}_j$, contradicting minimality.

Similarly, $p_i'/p_j' < \bar{p}_i/\bar{p}_j$. Thus

$$\lambda p_i < \lambda(\bar{p}_i/\bar{p}_j)p_j,$$

$$(1 - \lambda)p_i' < (1 - \lambda)(\bar{p}_i/\bar{p}_j)p_j',$$

so

$$\bar{p}_i = \lambda p_i + (1 - \lambda)p_i' < \bar{p}_i/\bar{p}_j(\lambda p_j + (1 - \lambda)p_j') = \bar{p}_i,$$

a contradiction. Hence $P(\mathbf{a})$ is convex. $\square$

As before let $\bar{a}$ be the minimum number of seats any state receives and $\bar{a}$ the maximum number over all populations **p** and $\mathbf{a} \in M^*(\mathbf{p})$.

LEMMA 4.2. *There exists* $\mathbf{p}^* > \mathbf{0}$ *such that* $\mathbf{p}^*$ *has an M*-apportionment of form* $(\bar{a},\bar{\bar{a}},a_3,\ldots,a_s)$.

PROOF. Choose some $\mathbf{p}'$ having an M^*-apportionment of form $\mathbf{a} = (\bar{a},a_2,\ldots,a_s)$ and $\mathbf{p}''$ having an M^*-apportionment of form $\mathbf{b} = (b_1,\bar{a}, b_3,\ldots,b_s)$. Choose α sufficiently large that $\alpha p_2'/p_j' > p_2''/p_j''$ for $1 \leq j \leq s$ and let $\mathbf{p}^* = (p_1',\alpha p_2',\ldots,p_s')$. For every $\mathbf{c} \in M^*(\mathbf{p}^*)$ population monotonicity implies that $c_2 \geq a_2$, $c_1 = \bar{a}$ and $c_j \leq a_j$ for $j \geq 3$. If $c_2 < \bar{\bar{a}}$ then since $\Sigma_1^s c_i = \Sigma_1^s b_i$ and $b_1 \geq c_1 = \bar{a}$ there exists $j \geq 3$ with $b_j < c_j$. Thus $b_2 = \bar{\bar{a}} > c_2$ and $b_j < c_j$ but $p_2^*/p_j^* > p_2''/p_j''$, contradicting population monotonicity. Therefore $c_2 = \bar{\bar{a}}$ and $\mathbf{p}^*$ has the desired property. $\square$

This particular $\mathbf{p}^*$ will be used in the proof of the final lemma.

A partial method M^* may admit several different apportionments for a fixed population. When this occurs the subset of states T that receive different numbers of seats in different apportionments are said to be *tied*. Fix $\mathbf{p} > 0$, let $T(p)$ be the set of tied states, and for each i let $\bar{a}_i(\mathbf{p}) = \min a_i$ over all $\mathbf{a} \in M^*(\mathbf{p})$.

LEMMA 4.3. *If M* is population monotone, then* $M^*(\mathbf{p}) = \{\mathbf{a} \geq \mathbf{0} : \Sigma \, a_i = h \text{ with } a_i = \bar{a}_i(\mathbf{p}) \text{ or } \bar{a}_i(\mathbf{p}) + 1 \text{ for all } i \in T(\mathbf{p})\}$.

PROOF. Fix $\mathbf{p} > 0$ and let $T = T(\mathbf{p})$, $\bar{a}_i = \bar{a}_i(\mathbf{p})$ be as defined above. Choose an arbitrary apportionment $\hat{\mathbf{a}} \in M^*(\mathbf{p})$ and fix it for the remainder of the argument. For distinct $i, j \in T$ write $i \to j$ if there is some $\mathbf{a} \in M^*(p)$ for which $a_i < \hat{a}_i$, $a_j > \hat{a}_j$. By population monotonicity, a_i, a_j can be substituted for $\hat{a}_i$, $\hat{a}_j$ in $\hat{\mathbf{a}}$, hence $a_i + a_j = \hat{a}_i + \hat{a}_j$. Thus $i \to j$ means that an alternative apportionment to $\hat{\mathbf{a}}$ can be found by "switching" some number of seats from i to j.

> If $i \to j$, $k \to l$ and $i \neq l$, then $i \to l$; moreover in   (4.8)
> each case the same number of seats are switched.

If $i = k$ or $j = l$ the result is trivial. Otherwise, suppose that $i < j \leq k < l$. Since $k \to l$ there exists an apportionment of form $\mathbf{b} = (\hat{a}_1,\ldots,\hat{a}_k - \beta,\ldots,\hat{a}_l + \beta,\ldots,\hat{a}_s) \in M^*(\mathbf{p})$. Since $i \to j$ there is some $\mathbf{a} \in M^*(\mathbf{p})$ such that $a_i < \hat{a}_i$ and $a_j > \hat{a}_j$. It follows that a_i, a_j may be substituted into $\mathbf{b}$ to obtain $(\hat{a}_1,\ldots,a_i,\ldots,a_j,\ldots,\hat{a}_l + \beta,\ldots,\hat{a}_s) \in M^*(\mathbf{p})$. Thus $i \to l$ and $a_i + \hat{a}_l + \beta = \hat{a}_i + \hat{a}_l$, so i and l also switch β seats.

Since for every $i \in T$ there must exist some $j \in T$ with $i \to j$ or $j \to i$, T may be partitioned into two classes A and B such that $i \to j$ for every $i \in A$ and $j \in B$. Moreover every switch involves exactly β seats, $\beta \geq 1$.

If $\beta = 1$ the characterization of the lemma follows immediately. The proof is completed by showing that $\beta \geq 2$ leads to a contradiction. We consider two cases:

CASE 1. $\hat{a}_i \geq 1$ for all i.

Let $i \rightarrow j$ and consider the s-tuple $\mathbf{c} = (\hat{a}_1, \ldots, \hat{a}_i - 1, \ldots, \hat{a}_j + 1, \ldots, \hat{a}_s)$ $> \mathbf{0}$, where $\hat{a}_i - 1 > \hat{a}_i - \beta \geq 0$. By hypothesis $\mathbf{c} > \mathbf{0}$, so by weak proportionality $M^*(\mathbf{c}) = \{\mathbf{c}\}$. Now $\hat{\mathbf{a}} \in M^*(\mathbf{p})$ and $(\hat{a}_1, \ldots, \hat{a}_i - \beta, \ldots, \hat{a}_j + \beta, \ldots, \hat{a}_s) \in M^*(\mathbf{p})$, hence by population monotonicity $c_i/c_j = p_i/p_j$. But then $(\hat{a}_1, \ldots, \hat{a}_i - \beta, \ldots, \hat{a}_j + \beta, \ldots, \hat{a}_s)$ is also an M^*-apportionment for $\mathbf{c}$, contradicting weak proportionality.

CASE 2. $\hat{a}_j = 0$ for some j.

Let p_j be smallest for all j such that $\hat{a}_j = 0$. If $j \notin T$, increase p_j (always staying in the set $P(\hat{\mathbf{a}})$) until at some point $\mathbf{p}'$, j enters the tied class. This must eventually happen because $a_j = 0$ cannot hold when j is the largest state. $M^*(\mathbf{p}) \subsetneq M^*(\mathbf{p}')$ because the populations of all tied states stayed the same. Therefore for some i, $(\hat{a}_1, \ldots, \hat{a}_i - \beta, \ldots, \hat{a}_j + \beta, \ldots, \hat{a}_s) \in M^*(\mathbf{p}')$, where $\hat{a}_i - 1 > \hat{a}_i - \beta \geq 0$. If $\hat{a}_k \geq 1$ for all $k \neq i, j$, then by weak proportionality $\mathbf{c} = (\hat{a}_1, \ldots, \hat{a}_i - 1, \ldots, \hat{a}_j + 1, \ldots, \hat{a}_s)$ is the unique M^*-apportionment when $\mathbf{p} = \mathbf{c}$, and a contradiction is obtained by comparing $\mathbf{p}$ and $\mathbf{c}$ as in the preceding case. If $\hat{a}_k = 0$ for some $k \neq j$ then by choice of j, k must also be in T. Hence there exist $\mathbf{a}$, $\mathbf{a}' \in M^*(\mathbf{p}')$ such that $a_j = 0$, $a_k = \beta$, $a'_j = \beta$, $a'_k = 0$. But by weak proportionality there is an M^*-apportionment $\mathbf{a}''$ of form $a''_j = a''_k = 1$ (this uses the assumption that $h \geq s$). A contradiction is obtained as before by comparing $\mathbf{p}$ and $\mathbf{a}''$. $\square$

If S is a subset of tied states at $M^*(\mathbf{p})$ and each state in S gets either a_i or $a_i + 1$ seats at $\mathbf{p}$, we say $(\mathbf{p}_S; \mathbf{a}_S)$ is a *tie* and write $t(\mathbf{p}_S; \mathbf{a}_S)$. In particular if $t(p_1, p_2; a_1, a_2)$ in some problem $\mathbf{p}$ then by the preceding lemma $\mathbf{p}$ has M^*-apportionments of form $(a_1 + 1, a_2, b_3, \ldots, b_s)$ and $(a_1, a_2 + 1, b_3, \ldots, b_s)$. Define Π to be the set of all pairs (a, b) that occur in an M^*-apportionment for some $\mathbf{p}$.

LEMMA 4.4. *If* $(a, b) \in \Pi$ *and* $\bar{\bar{a}} \geq a > 1$, $\bar{a} > b \geq 1$, *then there exist* $p', p'', p''' > 0$ *such that* $t(p', p'', p'''; \bar{a}, a - 1, b)$.

PROOF. The first step is to find some $\mathbf{p}$ with an apportionment of form $\mathbf{a} = (\bar{a}, a, b, c_4, \ldots, c_s)$.

If $\bar{a} = 1$, we may choose $\mathbf{a} > \mathbf{0}$ and let $\mathbf{p} = \mathbf{a}$.

Suppose that $\bar{a} = 0$. Since $(a,b) \in \Pi$ there is some apportionment $\mathbf{b}$ with $b_i = a > 0$, $b_j = b > 0$. If some $b_k = 0$ $(k \neq i,j)$ then a permutation of $\mathbf{b}$ yields the desired $\mathbf{a}$. Otherwise $b_k \geq 1$ for all k and by weak proportionality there exists an M^*-apportionment of form $\mathbf{a}' = (1,a,b,\ldots) \geq (1,1,\ldots,1)$. Now $(1,1,1,\ldots,h-s+1)$ is an apportionment by weak proportionality, hence $\bar{a} \geq h - s + 1$. Since $a > 1$ and $b \geq 1$, there exists $k \geq 4$ such that $a_k' < \bar{a}$.

Beginning with $\mathbf{p}' = \mathbf{a}' \in P(\mathbf{a}')$, decrease p_1' always staying in $P(\mathbf{a}')$ until a point $\mathbf{p}'' \in P(\mathbf{a}')$ is reached for which $1 \to j$ for some j. Such a point exists because if p_1' were decreased until $p_1'/p_k' < p_1^*/p_k^*$, where $\mathbf{p}^*$ is the vector of Lemma 4.2 then state 1 would get $\bar{a} = 0$ seats. If $j \geq 4$, then an apportionment of the desired form $(0,a,b,\ldots)$ exists for $\mathbf{p}''$.

If $j = 2$ or 3, begin at $\mathbf{p}''$ and decrease states 1, 2, 3 proportionally (by a common factor α) until a point $\mathbf{p}''' \in M^*(\mathbf{a}')$ is reached for which $i \to l$, $i \leq 3$, $l \geq 4$. Such a point exists by virtue of Lemma 2 and the fact that $a_k' < \bar{a}$. By Lemma 3, $1 \to l$, establishing that an apportionment of form $(0,a,b,\ldots)$ exists for $\mathbf{p}'''$.

Let then $\mathbf{a} = (\bar{a},a,b,c_4,\ldots,c_s)$ and choose any $\mathbf{p} \in P(\mathbf{a})$. Let T_1 consist of state 2 and all other states (if any) tied with state 2 at $\mathbf{p}$. Beginning at $\mathbf{p}$, decrease all states in T_1 proportionally until at some point $\mathbf{p}^1 \in M^*(\mathbf{a})$, $2 \to j$ for some $j \notin T_1$. At this point $\mathbf{p}^1$ let $T_2 \supsetneq T_1$ be the class of tied states. Decrease all states in T_2 proportionally until the tied class again increases at point $\mathbf{p}^2$, etc. The process terminates at some $\mathbf{p}^n$, where all states satisfying $a_i < \bar{a}$ are tied. In particular, states 1 and 3 are tied at $\mathbf{p}^n$. It follows from Lemma 4.2 that

$$(\bar{a},a,b,c_4,\ldots,c_s), \; (\bar{a}+1,a-1,b,c_4,\ldots,c_s), \tag{4.9}$$
$$(\bar{a},a-1,b+1,c_4,\ldots,c_s) \in M^*(\mathbf{p}^n). \; \square$$

The idea of the proof of Theorem 4.2 is the following. If in some problem a state having $\bar{a}$ seats is tied with a state having a seats, i.e. if $t(\bar{p},p; \bar{a},a)$, define $d(a) = p/\bar{p}$. $d(a)$ is well defined because if also $t(\bar{p}',p'; \bar{a},a)$ then population monotonicity implies that $p/\bar{p} = p'/\bar{p}'$. It is an easy exercise to show that if $d(a)$ and $d(b)$ are defined then $a > b$ implies $d(a) > d(b)$, i.e. d is monotone increasing.

Now let $\mathbf{a} \in M^*(\mathbf{p})$ and choose any $i \neq j$ for which $\bar{a} \geq a_i > 1$ and $\bar{a} > a_j \geq 1$. By Lemma 4.4 $t(p',p'',p'''; \bar{a},a_i - 1,a_j)$ for some p', p'', $p''' > 0$. Comparing this with the apportionment $\mathbf{a} \in M^*(\mathbf{p})$, it follows from population monotonicity that $p''/p''' \leq p_i/p_j$. But $p'''/p' = d(a_j)$ and $p''/p' = d(a_i$

$- 1)$ whence $d(a_i - 1)/d(a_j) \leq p_i/p_j$ and

$$p_i/d(a_i - 1) \geq p_j/d(a_j). \qquad (4.10)$$

It remains to show (4.10) when $a_j = \bar{a}$ and/or $a_i = 1$. Now $d(\bar{a})$ has not yet been defined, hence set $d(\bar{a}) = \infty$ and (4.10) holds. If $a_i = 1$ there are two cases to consider. In case $\bar{a} = 0$ then $d(0)$ is defined and equals 1, so (4.10) says that $p_j/p_i \leq d(a_j)$, which is an immediate consequence of the definition of $d(a_j)$ and population monotonicity. Otherwise $\bar{a} = 1$ and $d(0)$ is not yet defined. In this case set $d(0) = 0$ and again (4.10) holds. Thus (4.10) holds in every case. Therefore, since $d(a_i) > d(a_i - 1)$ for all i we can write

$$\mathbf{a} \in M^*(\mathbf{p}) \quad \text{implies} \quad \min_{a_i > 0} p_i/d(a_i - 1) \geq \max_{a_i \geq 0} p_i/d(a_i). \qquad (4.11)$$

Conversely let $\mathbf{a}$ satisfy (4.11) for some $\mathbf{p}$. Since $d(a)$ is strictly monotone increasing, $\mathbf{p}$ may be wiggled slightly to obtain some $\mathbf{p}'$ such that the min-max inequality holds strictly. For such a $\mathbf{p}'$ the only apportionment satisfying the inequality is $\mathbf{a}$, so by (4.11) $\mathbf{a}$ is the unique apportionment for $\mathbf{p}'$. Now construct a sequence of such $\mathbf{p}'$ converging to $\mathbf{p}$ and conclude by completeness that $\mathbf{a} \in M^*(\mathbf{p})$. $\square$

The theorem fails when there are only three states. The reason is that the proof depends on constructing a sufficiently rich collection of 3-way ties, which cannot be done when there is no fourth state to take up the slack. In general, let $e(a,a') = p/p'$ if $t(p,p'; a,a')$; thus $e(a,a')$ is the ratio at which a state having $a + 1$ seats would first give up a seat to a state having a' seats as the former decreases and the latter increases in population. If M^* is a partial divisor method then $e(a,a') = d(a)/d(a')$ and the following multiplicative rule must hold among all pairs on which e is defined:

$$e(a',a'')e(a'',a''') = e(a',a'''). \qquad (4.12)$$

Conversely, if (4.12) holds we can define $d(a) = e(\bar{a},a)$ and immediately derive the min-max inequality from population monotonicity.

(4.12) can be established by constructing 3-way ties of form $t(p',p'',p''';$ $a',a'',a''')$ as in Lemma 4.4, but for fixed h the construction only works if there is at least one more state to absorb the other seats.

To illustrate what can go wrong when $s = 3$, consider the case $h = 7$. A 3-way tie will involve either one or two seats being shifted around. Hence

$t(\mathbf{p}; \mathbf{a})$ means that $\Sigma a_i = 5$ or $\Sigma a_i = 6$ so there are (up to order) the following ten possibilities for $\mathbf{a}$:

$\Sigma a_i = 6$	$\Sigma a_i = 5$
(0,0,6)	(0,0,5)
(0,1,5)	(0,1,4)
(0,2,4)	(0,2,3)
(0,3,3)	(1,1,3)
(1,2,3)	(1,2,2)

Each of these ten triples produces one dependency in the variables $e(a,b)$ of the form (4.12). Also we must have $e(b,a) = 1/e(a,b)$ and $e(a,a) = 1$. Now choose $e(a,0) = 2a + 1$ as in Webster's method. The ten dependencies are redundant and only determine four additional values:

$$e(1,4) = e(1,0)e(0,4) = 1/3$$
$$e(1,5) = e(1,0)e(0,5) = 3/11$$
$$e(2,3) = e(2,0)e(0,3) = 5/7$$
$$e(2,4) = e(2,0)e(0,4) = 5/9$$

There remain $e(1,2)$ and $e(1,3)$, which are related by the expression $e(1,3) = e(1,2)e(2,3) = 5e(1,2)/7$. To be a divisor method $e(1,2)$ must also satisfy $e(1,2) = e(1,0) e(0,2) = 3/5$. But for $h = 7$, the triple $(0,1,2)$ does not occur as a tie, so no such dependency is imposed. In fact, if $e(1,2)$ is chosen close to but not equal to $3/5$ then M^* will be population monotone but not a divisor method. An example with $e(1,2) = 4/5$ is shown in Figure A4.2.

PROPOSITION 4.4. *For* s $= 3$ *and* $3 \leq$ h ≤ 6, *every population monotone partial method is a partial divisor method.*

PROPOSITION 4.5. *If* $1 <$ h $<$ s, *define* M* *such that the largest state always gets* h *seats and the rest get zero seats.* M* *is population monotone but technically is not a partial divisor method, because it cannot be represented by a monotone increasing* d(a).

PROPOSITION 4.6. *Theorem 4.2 also holds in the case of arbitrary minimum requirements* r *and* h $\geq$ *max* (s,Σr$_i$), s $\neq 3$. *The proof may be modified by first defining* ā$_i$ *and* $\bar{\bar{a}}_i$ *to be the minimum and max-*

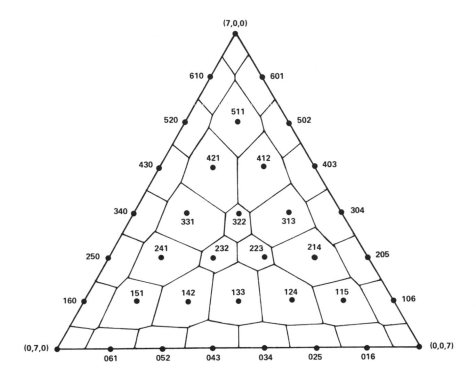

Figure A4.2   A Population Monotone Partial Method on Three States That Is
               Not a Divisor Method

imum apportionments ever received by state i *among all* **a** ∈
M*(**p**), *and then proving the analog of Lemma 4.3. To establish
the analog of Lemma 4.4 suppose without loss of generality that
state* 1 *has the smallest* $\bar{a}_i$, *and state* 2 *the next smallest. Show that
if* **a** ∈ M*(**p**) *and* $\bar{\bar{a}}_i \geq a_i > max \{\bar{a}_i, 1\}$, $\bar{\bar{a}}_j > a_j \geq max \{\bar{a}_j, 1\}$, i, j
≥ 2, *then a 3-way tie of form* t(p′,p″,p‴; $\bar{a}_1, a_i - 1, a_j$) *can be con-
structed. If* t($\bar{p}$,p; $\bar{a}_1$,a) *define* d(a) = p/$\bar{p}$. *This defines* d(a) *for all
relevant* a, $\bar{\bar{a}} > a \geq \bar{a}_2$. *For* $\bar{a}_1 < a < \bar{a}_2$ *construct a tie of form*
t(p,p′; a,$\bar{a}_2$) *and define* d(a) = (p/p′)d($\bar{a}_2$). *Finally, let* d($\bar{\bar{a}}$) = ∞
and d(0) = 0 *if* $\bar{a}_1 > r_1 = 0$. *Now check the well-definition of* d(a)
*and show that the min-max inequality follows from population
monotonicity.*

PROPOSITION 4.7. *For given* minimum *and* maximum *requirements* r
    ≤ r⁺ *Theorem 4.2 may fail even when* s ≥ 4.

Suppose that M is a method such that every restriction to some fixed s and h is population monotone. By Theorem 4.2, every such restriction is a partial divisor method; however, the associated functions $d(a)$ may depend on s and h. For example, M might be Adams's method when $h - s$ is odd and Jefferson's when $h - s$ is even. Of course, such a method is ridiculous, since it does not give consistent results when the house size or number of states changes. Such absurdities are avoided by extending the concept of population monotonicity to allow comparisons between *any* two problems, including ones with different s and h.

A method M is *population monotone* if for any two vectors $\mathbf{p}, \mathbf{p}' > \mathbf{0}$ and $\mathbf{a} \in M(\mathbf{p},h)$, $\mathbf{a}' \subset M(\mathbf{p}',h')$

$$p_i'/p_{j'}' \geqq p_i/p_j \quad \text{implies} \quad \begin{cases} a_{i'}' \geqq a_i \quad \text{or} \quad a_{j'}' \leqq a_j, \\ \text{or} \\ p_{i'}'/p_{j'}' = p_i/p_j \quad \text{and} \quad a_{i'}', a_{j'}' \\ \text{can be substituted for } a_i, a_j \text{ in } \mathbf{a}. \end{cases} \tag{4.13}$$

THEOREM 4.3. *A method is population monotone if and only if it is a divisor method.*

A method M is *house monotone* (i.e., avoids the Alabama paradox) if for every $\mathbf{p}$ and h, $\mathbf{a} \in M(\mathbf{p},h)$ implies $\mathbf{a}' \in M(\mathbf{p},h + 1)$ for some $\mathbf{a}' \geqq \mathbf{a}$.

COROLLARY 4.3.1. *If a method is population monotone then it is house monotone.*

Theorem 4.3 is proved by showing that a single divisor criterion applies to all 2-state problems (use Theorem 4.2) and then showing that the same divisor applies to all problems, including those with $s = 3$. The theorem still holds when (4.13) is modified to allow for minimum and maximum requirements.

Population monotonicity says that as the conditions of a problem change—as populations shift, as the size of house expands or contracts, and states join or secede—apportionments should respond accordingly, i.e., they should not move contrary to the relative changes of states' populations. This is an elementary requirement for any scheme of fair representation – and the only methods that satisfy it are the divisor methods.

It is significant that other fairness ideas follow automatically. Any method that is population monotone avoids the Alabama paradox. Another fairness concept implied by population monotonicity is "uniformity," which says (roughly) that any apportionment should still be valid when restricted to any subgroup of states. This concept is treated in more detail in section 8.

5. BIAS

The decisive conclusion of the preceding section is that the only realistic candidates for methods of apportionment are the divisor methods. The question then becomes, Which of the infinite number of divisor methods should be chosen?

Historical precedent—both the debate of 1832 and the twentieth-century controversy over the methods of Hill and Webster—is that a method is unacceptable if it has a persistent bias in favor either of the large or of the small states. There are several ways to measure "bias," and there are different probabilistic models by which a tendency toward bias can be revealed theoretically. Although no one particular definition or model provides absolute proof that a method is biased or not, the weight of the evidence over a variety of definitions and models is persuasive that Webster's is the only divisor method that is unbiased. Analysis of the historical statistics confirms the theory with experimental fact.

Even a casual inspection of the five "traditional" methods applied to examples shows that in the order Adams (A), Dean (D), Hill (H), Webster (W), and Jefferson (J), they tend increasingly to favor the larger states. This is revealed in Example 1.1 as well as in the more convincing 19 examples of United States history. This observation may be made precise. A method M' *favors small states relative to M* if, for every M-apportionment $\mathbf{a}$ and M'-apportionment $\mathbf{a}'$ for $\mathbf{p}$ and h,

$$p_i < p_j \quad \text{implies either} \quad a_i' \geq a_i \quad \text{or} \quad a_j' \leq a_j.$$

THEOREM 5.1. *If* M *and* M' *are divisor methods with divisor criteria* $d(a)$ *and* $d'(a)$ *satisfying* $d'(a)/d'(b) > d(a)/d(b)$ *for all integers* $a > b \geq 0$, *then* M' *favors small states relative to* M.

PROOF OF THEOREM 5.1. Suppose, by way of contradiction, that for some $\mathbf{a} \in M(\mathbf{p},h)$ and $\mathbf{a}' \in M'(\mathbf{p},h)$, $p_i < p_j$, $a_i' < a_i$, and $a_j' > a_j$. By population monotonicity $a_i' < a_i \leq a_j < a_j'$, so $a_j' - 1 > a_i' \geq 0$ and $d'(a_j' - 1) \geq 1$ because $a \leq d'(a) \leq a + 1$ for all a.

The min-max inequality for $\mathbf{a}'$ implies $p_j/d'(a_j' - 1) \geqq p_i/d'(a_i')$ from which, by the preceding, it follows that $d'(a_i') > 0$. Hence,

$$p_j/p_i \geqq d'(a_j' - 1)/d'(a_i') > d(a_j' - 1)/d(a_i') \geqq d(a_j)/d(a_i - 1),$$

the last by monotonicity of $d(a)$. Thus, $p_j/d(a_j) > p_i/d(a_i - 1)$, contradicting the min-max inequality for $\mathbf{a}$. $\square$

Write $M' > M$ if M' favors small states relative to M.

PROPOSITION 5.1. $A > D > H > W > J$.

Bias has, however, an absolute as well as a relative meaning. Any apportionment that gives a_1 and a_2 seats respectively to states having populations $p_1 > p_2 > 0$ *favors the larger state over the smaller state* if $a_1/p_1 > a_2/p_2$ and *favors the smaller state over the larger state* if $a_1/p_1 < a_2/p_2$. It may be asked whether over many pairs of states a method tends more often to favor the larger over the smaller state or vice versa.

Different meanings may be attached to "many pairs." One simple approach is to consider a pair of populations $p_1 > p_2 > 0$. Two states having these populations could divide any number of seats h between them and, since we are considering only divisor methods, the way in which they would share h seats is determined independently of any other states that may be part of the same problem. Since p_1 and p_2 are rational (or integer) there is a smallest "perfect" house size h^* where both states have integer quotas. A reasonable idea then is to count, for any method M and pair of populations (p_1,p_2), the number $S(p_1,p_2)$ of apportionments favoring the smaller state and the number $L(p_1,p_2)$ of apportionments favoring the larger state, over all M-apportionments (a_1,a_2) such that $a_1 + a_2 \leqq h^*$. The method M is *pairwise unbiased on populations* if for every pair of populations (p_1,p_2), $L(p_1,p_2) = S(p_1,p_2)$.

PROPOSITION 5.2. *Webster's is the only divisor method that is pairwise unbiased on populations.*

This approach to defining and measuring bias has the merit that no assumption need be made about the distribution of populations: *whatever the pair of populations, Webster's is the unique unbiased divisor method.* However, as an empirical test the approach has limitations, for the number of seats shared by a pair of states will typically be much smaller than h^*.

A more realistic approach is to consider a pair of integer apportionments

$a_1 > a_2 > 0$ and ask, If the populations (p_1,p_2) have the M-apportionment (a_1,a_2), how likely is it that the small state (state 2) is favored? Note that the population monotonicity of M guarantees $p_1 \geq p_2$ since $a_1 > a_2$.

Take as a probabilistic model that the populations $(p_1,p_2) = \mathbf{p} > \mathbf{0}$ are uniformly distributed in the positive quadrant. Given integers $\mathbf{a} = (a_1,a_2) > \mathbf{0}$ and a method M, the set of $\mathbf{p}$'s for which $\mathbf{a}$ is an M-apportionment is unbounded. To define a bounded subset of the sample space in a natural way we use the fact that M is a divisor method.

Choose any $x > 0$ representing a hypothetical district size, let $\mathbf{a} > \mathbf{0}$ be an apportionment, and define $R_x(\mathbf{a})$ to be the set of all populations $\mathbf{p} > \mathbf{0}$ which yield the M-apportionment $\mathbf{a}$ using the divisor x:

$$R_x(\mathbf{a}) = \{\mathbf{p} > \mathbf{0} : d(a_i) \geq p_i/x \geq d(a_i - 1)\}$$

where by convention $d(-1) = 0$. Each region $R_x(\mathbf{a})$ is a rectangle containing the point $\mathbf{a}$ and having sides of length $d(a_1) - d(a_1 - 1)$ and $d(a_2) - d(a_2 - 1)$. Figure A5.1 shows these for Dean's method, and Figure A5.2 for Webster's ($x = 1$ in both cases). Figure A5.3 shows them for the somewhat bizarre divisor method that is defined as follows:

$$d(2a) = 2a + 1/5, \qquad d(2a + 1) = 2a + 9/5.$$

A divisor method M is *pairwise unbiased on apportionments* if for *every* $a_1 > a_2 > 0$ and every $x > 0$ the probability that state 1 is favored over state 2 equals the probability that state 2 is favored over state 1, given that $(p_1,p_2) \in R_x(\mathbf{a})$. Note that the probability that one state is favored over the other is independent of the choice of x, so that if a method satisfies the definition for some x then it does for all x.

For each pair $a_1 > a_2 > 0$ the shaded area in the figures shows those populations that favor the smaller state. It is quite evident that Dean's method is systematically biased toward smaller states, whereas both Webster's method and the "1/5–4/5" method are unbiased. However, the latter method is a strange one; indeed it is not proportional. For example, if the populations are in the ratio represented by the ray OAB, they will split 6 seats as 3 and 3, but 4 seats as 3 and 1. Such methods are not reasonable.

PROPOSITION 5.3. *The probability that a state receiving 2 seats is favored over a state receiving 4 seats is: for Adams, 75.0%; Dean, 63.5%; Hill, 57.0%; Webster, 50%; and Jefferson, 25.0%.*

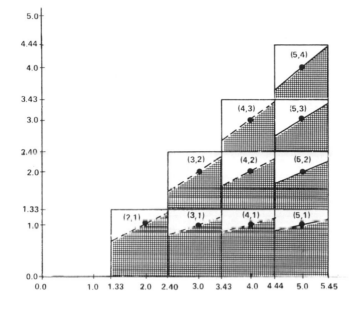

Figure A5.1 Populations Favoring Small and Large States—Dean's Method

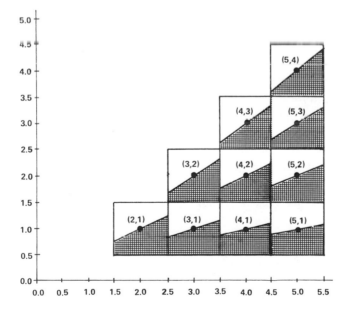

Figure A5.2 Populations Favoring Small and Large States—Webster's Method

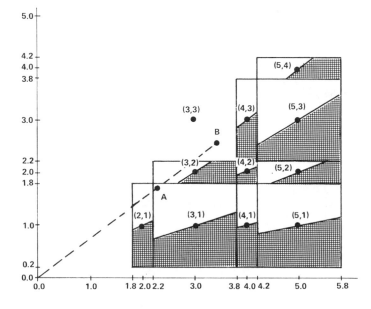

Figure A5.3   Populations Favoring Small and Large States—A Non-Proportional
Method

THEOREM 5.2. *Webster's is the unique proportional divisor method that is pairwise unbiased on apportionments.*

PROOF OF THEOREM 5.2. Given a divisor method M and $a_1 > a_2 > 0$, the ray defined by $a_1/p_1 = a_2/p_2$ divides $R_x(\mathbf{a})$ into the populations favoring state 1 and those favoring state 2. These two sets have equal measure, i.e., the ray *bisects* the rectangle, if and only if it passes through its center, $\mathbf{c} = (c_1, c_2)$. Since

$$c_1 = x(d(a_1 - 1) + d(a_1))/2 \quad \text{and} \quad c_2 = x(d(a_2 - 1) + d(a_2))/2,$$

M is pairwise unbiased if and only if it satisfies the following condition:

$$\frac{d(a_1 - 1) + d(a_1)}{d(a_2 - 1) + d(a_2)} = \frac{a_1}{a_2} \quad \text{for all} \quad a_1 > a_2 > 0. \tag{5.1}$$

In particular, W is pairwise unbiased on apportionments. Conversely, suppose that M satisfies (5.1). Set $a_1 = a \geq 2$, $a_2 = 1$. Then

$$(d(a - 1) + d(a))/a = d(0) + d(1)$$

and, since $a \leqq d(a) \leqq a + 1$ for all a, letting $a \to \infty$ implies

$$d(0) + d(1) = 2.$$

From the two preceding relations it follows that

$$d(2a) = 2a + d(0) \quad \text{and} \quad d(2a + 1) = 2a + 2 - d(0). \qquad (5.2)$$

The assumption of proportionality can be used to show

$$d(b)/d(b - 1) \geq d(b + 1)/d(b) \quad \textit{for all } b > 0. \qquad (5.3)$$

Substituting $b = 2a + 1$ and using (5.2) gives

$$\frac{2a + 2 - d(0)}{2a + d(0)} \geq \frac{2a + 2 + d(0)}{2a + 2 - d(0)}$$

or $4a + 4 \geq (8a + 6)d(0)$. Letting $a \to \infty$ shows that $d(0) \leq 1/2$. Substituting instead $b = 2a$ into (5.3) we find $(8a + 2)d(0) \geq 4a$ and so $d(0) \geq 1/2$. Therefore $d(0) = 1/2$ and we see that M is Webster's method. $\square$

Other probabilistic models of pairwise bias point to the same conclusion. For example, one might assume that all *normalized populations* $p_1 + p_2 = 1$ are equally likely. Given a divisor method M, the populations for which some particular M-apportionment (a_1,a_2), $a_1 > a_2 > 0$, is the solution for h can be represented as a line segment. It is convenient to renormalize so that $p_1 + p_2 = h$; then (a_1,a_2) itself is contained in the segment, and the smaller state is favored in the part of segment lying to the right of (a_1,a_2). Thus in this model M will be pairwise unbiased on apportionments if, for every $a_1 > a_2 > 0$, (a_1,a_2) is the midpoint of its segment. This is manifestly true for Webster, and indeed it may be shown that *Webster's is the unique divisor method that is pairwise unbiased on apportionments in this model.*

The proof follows by observing that $(a_1,a_2) > \mathbf{0}$ is the midpoint of its segment if and only if

$$\frac{a_1}{a_1 + a_2} = \left[\frac{d(a_1 - 1)}{d(a_1 - 1) + d(a_2)} \right] + \left[\frac{d(a_1)}{d(a_2 - 1) + d(a_1)} \right] \bigg/ 2.$$

With $a_1 = a$, $a_2 = a + 1$ we obtain the recursion $d(a + 1) = (2a \cdot 3)d(a - 1)/(2a - 1)$, from which

$$d(2a) = (4a + 1)d(0), \text{ and } d(2a + 1) = (4a/3 + 1)d(1).$$

Now use $2a \leqq d(2a) \leqq 2a + 1$ and let $a \to \infty$ to conclude that $d(0) = 1/2$. Similarly conclude that $d(1) = 3/2$. Hence $d(a)$ is the Webster divisor criterion. Note that only weak proportionality was needed to obtain this result.

The preceding theoretical results suggest the following empirical test for bias. Given a divisor method M, let $\mathscr{P}$ be a collection of 2-state *sample problems* $(p_1,p_2; a_1,a_2)$, where $a_1 > a_2 > 0$ and (a_1,a_2) is an M-apportionment for (p_1,p_2). One way of obtaining such a sample is to select from a larger problem $(p_1,\ldots,p_s; a_1,\ldots,a_s)$ all pairs i, j such that $a_i > a_j > 0$ and consider each such $(p_i,p_j; a_i,a_j)$ as a 2-state problem. This exploits the fact that divisor methods are "uniform," i.e. the way in which a divisor method shares $a_i + a_j$ seats between two states is determined independently of the populations of the other states (see section 8 for a discussion of uniformity). The *bias ratio* is the percentage of pairs $(p; a) \in \mathscr{P}$ for which the small state is favored. One would expect that for sufficiently large samples the bias ratio for Webster is close to 50%, whereas the ratio for other proportional methods is significantly different from 50%.

Analysis of United States historical data fulfills this expectation. However, the congressional apportionment problem requires that a minimum of one seat be given to each state no matter how small its population. This requirement introduces an additional built-in favoritism toward the small states. In order to analyze the actual apportionments that would have resulted by different methods applied to the nineteen historical problems, and yet eliminate this "artificial" bias toward the small, each method was applied with the minimum requirement of 1, but the counts have been made after leaving out all states having a quota less than .5. The *bias ratio over United States history* for any method M was computed by counting, for each census year, the number of pairs of states in which the smaller state would have been favored by this method and dividing by the total number of pairs over all nineteen problems. The results are given in Table A5.1.

TABLE A5.1   Bias Ratio over U.S. History

	Adams	Dean	Hill	Webster	Jefferson
Bias ratio	77.2%	56.6%	54.6%	51.5%	25.0%

The theoretical bias results also hold in the presence of minimum and maximum requirements. It is natural to ask only that a method be unbiased whenever the requirements are not binding. If, for example, $\mathbf{r} = (r_1,\ldots,r_s)$ is a set of minimum requirements for states with populations $\mathbf{p} = (p_1,\ldots,p_s)$, then state i is *free* at h using the method M if $a_i > r_i$ for *some* $\mathbf{a} \in M(\mathbf{p},h)$, and otherwise is *bound*. This definition parallels the previous analysis where $\mathbf{r} = \mathbf{0}$ and the apportionments were confined to $\mathbf{a} > \mathbf{0}$, and Theorems 5.1 and 5.2 (as well as Theorem 5.3 below) still hold.

Problems involving more than two states can also be analyzed for bias by comparing how the larger states and smaller states fare as *groups*. Given a possible apportionment $\mathbf{a} = (a_1,\ldots,a_s) > \mathbf{0}$ for populations $\mathbf{p} - (p_1,\ldots,p_s)$, let L and S be any two disjoint sets of states such that $a_i > a_j$ for every $i \in L$ and $j \in S$. L is a set of *larger states* and S a set of *smaller states*. The apportionment $\mathbf{a} > \mathbf{0}$ *favors the smaller states* if $\Sigma_S a_i / \Sigma_S p_i > \Sigma_L a_j / \Sigma_L p_j$ and *favors the larger states* if $\Sigma_L a_j / \Sigma_L p_j > \Sigma_S a_i / \Sigma_S p_i$.

A divisor method M is *unbiased* if for every $\mathbf{a} > \mathbf{0}$ and divisor $x > 0$, and for any disjoint sets of larger and smaller states L and S, the probability given $\mathbf{p} \subset R_x(\mathbf{a})$ that $(\mathbf{p}, \mathbf{a})$ favors the smaller states equals the probability that it favors the larger states. Note that $R_x(\mathbf{a})$ is an s-dimensional rectangular solid and the condition holds for some x if and only if it holds for all x.

THEOREM 5.3. *Webster's is the unique unbiased proportional divisor method.*

PROOF OF THEOREM 5.3. Let M be a proportional divisor method. Given $\mathbf{a} > \mathbf{0}$ and $x > 0$, let L and S be any disjoint sets of larger and smaller states respectively. The hyperplane $\Sigma_L a_i / \Sigma_L p_i = \Sigma_S a_i / \Sigma_S p_i$ divides $R_x(\mathbf{a})$ into the populations favoring L and those favoring S. These two sets have equal measure, i.e., the hyperplane bisects the rectangular solid $R_x(\mathbf{a})$, if and only if it passes through the center of $R_x(\mathbf{a})$. The center $\mathbf{c}$ has coordinates $c_i = [d(a_i - 1) + d(a_i)]/2$; hence M is unbiased if and only if for all $\mathbf{a} > \mathbf{0}$

$$\sum_L a_i \Big/ \Big(\sum_L d(a_i - 1) + d(a_i)\Big) = \sum_S a_i \Big/ \Big(\sum_S d(a_i - 1) + d(a_i)\Big). \quad (5.4)$$

Conversely, if M satisfies (5.4) for all $\mathbf{a} > \mathbf{0}$, then, in particular, it satisfies it whenever $\mathbf{a} = (a + 1,a)$, $a > 0$. From this it may be concluded as in the proof of Theorem 5.2 that M is Webster's method. $\square$

Note that if it is desired to argue with the number of states s *fixed*, $s \geq 3$, then consider instead an apportionment with s states of form $(a + 1,\ldots,a + 1,a\ldots,a)$, where $a > 0$. Then (5.4) becomes

$$(a + 1)/(d(a) + d(a + 1)) = a/(d(a - 1) + d(a))$$

from which it follows as in the proof of Theorem 5.2 that M must be Webster's method.

This model of bias can be used to provide further convincing empirical evidence that Webster's is the preferred method. A test for a method M is to take the nineteen cases of United States history $(p; a)$, where a is an M-apportionment for p, including minimum requirements of 1, and for each such problem eliminate states with quota less than .5. Divide the remaining states into three approximately equal classes: large (L), middle, and small (S), where the middle class takes up the extras if the number of remaining states is not divisible by three. Counting the number of problems in which the small states are favored one finds: Adams 19 (always), Dean 14, Hill 12, Webster 7, Jefferson 0 (never).

Considerably more insight is obtained by calculating, for each apportionment, the percentage difference β between $k_S = \Sigma_S a_i / \Sigma_S p_i$ and $k_L = \Sigma_L a_j / \Sigma_L p_j$, that is, $\beta = 100 (k_S/k_L - 1)$. β is the *percentage bias* of the apportionment: if positive, the small states are favored; if negative, the large states are favored. Contrasting the apportionments by each of the five traditional methods over the nineteen United States censuses, one finds that in *every* case the percentage bias of Webster's method is no larger in absolute value than that of Hill and, indeed, than that of any of the other methods. The average of the percentage biases of each method over the nineteen problems is given in Table A5.2. A graph of the cumulative average bias of each method may be found in Chapter 3 (Figure 3.5).

TABLE A5.2   Average Percentage Bias over Nineteen U.S. Problems

	Adams	Dean	Hill	Webster	Jefferson
Average bias	18.3%	5.2%	3.4%	0.3%	−15.7%

This model is also convenient for estimating the probability of bias when the number of states s is large (e.g., $s = 50$). Choose $\mathbf{a} > \mathbf{0}$, let L and S be classes of larger and smaller states respectively, and define $a_L = \Sigma_L a_j$ and $a_S = \Sigma_S a_i$. Fix $x > 0$ and let $R = R_x(\mathbf{a})$. The quotients $q_i = p_i/x$ are distributed independently and uniformly in the intervals $d(a_i - 1) \leq q_i \leq d(a_i)$. The mean m_i and variance σ_i of q_i are therefore

$$m_i = (d(a_i) + d(a_i - 1))/2 \text{ and } \sigma_i = (d(a_i) - d(a_i - 1))^2/12.$$

Define the random variable $X = \Sigma_S q_i - (a_S/a_L)\Sigma_L q_j$, where $\mathbf{q} \in R$. X is a sum of independent random variables so its mean and variance are given by

$$m = \sum_S m_i - (a_S/a_L) \sum_L m_j \text{ and } \sigma^2 = \sum_S \sigma_i^2 + (a_S/a_L)^2 \sum_L \sigma_j^2.$$

If the number of states in the set $L \cup S$ is large, the central limit theorem implies that $\bar{X} = (X - m)/\sigma$ is approximately normally distributed with mean 0 and variance 1. So the probability that the small states are favored is $Pr(X \leq 0) = Pr(\bar{X} \leq -m/\sigma)$, which is estimated using standard tables of the normal distribution.

To illustrate, take the *actual* 1970 United States apportionment (see Hill apportionment, 1970). The one-third (i.e., 16) largest states have a total of $a_L = 300$ seats, and the one-third (16) smallest states have $a_S = 27$ seats. $|L \cup S| = 32$, a reasonably large sample for using the normal distribution as an approximation. To conform with our previous historical analysis we assume no quotient can go below .5. For Hill's method we obtain: $\Sigma_S m_i = 26.0861$, $\Sigma_L m_j = 299.8650$, $\Sigma_S \sigma_i^2 = 1.3075$, $\Sigma_L \sigma_j^2 = 1.3342$ so $m = -2.4017$, $\sigma^2 = 1.2565$, and $m/\sigma = -.7886$. Therefore $Pr(X \leq 0) = Pr(\bar{X} \leq .7886) = 78.48\%$. Thus, the odds that Hill favors the small are almost 4 to 1. The results for the five traditional methods are given in Table A5.3.

TABLE A5.3 Estimated Probability of Favoring the Small States for Each of the Five Methods on the Basis of the Actual 1970 Apportionment

Adams	Dean	Hill	Webster	Jefferson
100.0%	93.9%	78.5%	50.0%	0.0%

A similar calculation gives the expected percentage bias for each method. Let $X = \Sigma_S q_i/a_S$ and $Y = \Sigma_L q_i/a_L$. Then $E(X/Y) \approx E(X)/E(Y) + Var(Y)E(X)/E(Y)^3$, the approximation coming from the first terms of a Taylor expansion. $E(X/Y)$ represents the expected ratio by which the large states are overrepresented relative to the small. So, the reciprocal minus 1 gives an estimate of β. For Hill's method, using the previous calculations, we obtain:

$$E(X/Y) = (26.0861/27)/(299.8650/300)$$
$$+ (1.3342/300^2)(26.0861/27)/(299.8650/300)^3$$
$$= .9666,$$

so $\beta = -1 + 1/.9666 = .0346$. Therefore the expected percentage bias in favor of the small by the method of Hill, given the 1970 apportionment, is 3.46%. The results for the five traditional methods are given in Table A5.4. (Compare with the empirical results from United States history given in Table A5.2).

TABLE A5.4   Expected Percentage Bias of Five Methods on the Basis of the Actual 1970 Apportionment

Adams	Dean	Hill	Webster	Jefferson
28.2%	7.0%	3.5%	0.0%	−20.8%

There are many alternative approaches to analyzing the bias of methods over history. For example, instead of defining L and S as the largest and smallest thirds (after dropping states with quotas less than .5) one could use the modified quotas $\bar{q}_i$ as an absolute measure of size. For example if one defines $L = \{i : \bar{q}_i > 8\}$ and $S = \{i : 1 < \bar{q}_i < 4\}$, then the number of problems in which the small states are favored and the average percentage biases are respectively: Adams 19 times and 19.8%; Dean 15 and 5.6%; Hill 14 and 3.7%; Webster 9 and 0.7%; and Jefferson 0 and −21.4%. Webster, when different from Hill, is always less biased. It must not be forgotten however that these 19 problems form a very small series exhibiting significant correlations.

Alternative probabilistic models for the joint distribution of the populations could certainly be chosen; the fact is that no one model is definitive or "most realistic." One obvious choice is to fix the house size h and assume that all quotas $\Sigma q_i = h$ are equally likely. In this model it is not possible to prove that the Webster method is perfectly unbiased. The difficulty results from the fact that a fixed house size forces the sum of the remainders of the quotas to be integer, hence not completely independent. In spite of this, any predicted bias of Webster's method derivable from such a model is so small as to be empirically indistinguishable from the hypothesis of perfect unbias when the number of states is large.

One of the advantages of the probabilistic model we have taken is that it can be applied locally, without assuming gross changes in the relative populations of the states. Thus a method is unbiased only if it is unbiased over *every* set of populations that would yield a prespecified distribution of seats. Other local assumptions may give slightly different numerical results—and may rule out a mathematically perfect method—but the empirical result will not change. The agreement between the theory and the historical statistics seems conclusive that Webster's is the least biased divisor method.

6. STAYING WITHIN THE QUOTA

It seems natural to require that no state's apportionment should deviate from its quota by one or more seats; in other words, no state should get less than its quota rounded down, nor more than its quota rounded up. This property is called *staying within the quota*. The primitive desire to stay within the quota clearly motivated Hamilton's method and it was a key point in Webster's critique of Jefferson's method. Webster's method is closer than any other divisor method to the ideal of staying within the quota. Nevertheless, it does not invariably stay within the quota, as the invented example of Table 10.1 shows. Such examples turn out to be very rare: in practice it is extremely improbable that Webster's method would ever violate quota. Moreover these same examples suggest that staying within the quota may not be such a reasonable idea after all. For example, to give D 26 instead of 25 seats in Table 10.1 would mean taking a seat from one of the smaller states A, B, or C. Such a transfer would penalize the per capita representation of the small state much more—in both absolute and relative terms—than state D is penalized by getting one less than its lower quota. Similar examples can be invented in which some state might reasonably get more than its upper quota. It can be argued that staying within the quota is not really compatible with the idea of proportionality at all, since it allows a much greater variance in the per capita representation of smaller states than it does for larger states. This basic incompatibility between staying within the quota and proportionality is most clearly seen by the following "impossibility theorem," which says that *no* method can be population monotone and stay within the quota.

THEOREM 6.1.   *No partial method exists with* s $\geq$ 4 *and* h $\geq$ s + 3 *that is population monotone and stays within the quota.*

PROOF OF THEOREM 6.1.   Fix $s \geq 4$, $h \geq s + 3$ and suppose M^* is a partial method that is population monotone and stays within the quota. Consider the populations $\mathbf{p} = (5 + \varepsilon, 2/3, 2/3, 2/3 - \varepsilon, b_5, \ldots, b_s)$ where $b_5, \ldots, b_s$ are any *positive* integers whose sum is $h - 7$ and $\varepsilon > 0$ is some small rational number. Since $\Sigma p_i = h$, p_i is i's exact quota for all i. Choose $\mathbf{a} \in M^*(\mathbf{p})$. By the quota assumption, $a_1 \geq 5$ and $a_i = b_i$ for all $i \geq 5$. Therefore $a_2 + a_3 + a_4 = h - 5 - (h - 7) = 2$, so at least one of states 2, 3, 4 gets 0 seats; by population monotonicity it must be state 4.

Now consider the populations $\mathbf{p}' = (4 - \varepsilon, 2 - \varepsilon/2, 1/2 + \varepsilon/2, 1/2 + \varepsilon, b_5, \ldots, b_s)$. Again $\Sigma p_i' = h$ so p_i' is the exact quota of i. Choose $\mathbf{a}' \in$

$M^*(\mathbf{p}')$. By quota, $a_1' \leqq 4$, $a_2' \leqq 2$ and $a_i' = b_i$ for $i \geqq 5$. Hence either state 3 or state 4 gets one seat. By population monotonicity it must be state 4. Therefore $a_4' > a_4$ while $a_1' < a_1$ so by population monotonicity $p_1'/p_4' < p_1/p_4$, that is $(4 - \varepsilon)/(1/2 + \varepsilon) < (5 + \varepsilon)/(2/3 - \varepsilon)$. Simplifying this becomes $\varepsilon > 1/61$, which is false for sufficiently small ε. $\square$

COROLLARY 6.1. *No population monotone method, i.e. no divisor method, stays within the quota for every problem.*

PROPOSITION 6.1. *Every divisor method stays within the quota for all 2-state problems.*

PROPOSITION 6.2. *Webster's method stays within the quota for all 3-state problems.*

PROPOSITION 6.3. *For any divisor method different from Webster's, there is a 3-state problem in which the apportionment does not stay within the quota. (Let* d(a) *be a divisor criterion different from Webster's and choose* a *such that* d(a) $\neq$ a + 1/2. *Let* e = (a + 1/2) $-$ d(a) *and for every integer* b *construct the problem with populations* $\mathbf{p}$ = (a + 1/2,d(a) + e/2,b + 1 + e/2) *and house size* h = 2a + b + 2. *For sufficiently large* b *the answer does not stay within the quota.) It follows from this and the preceding proposition that Webster's method is the* unique *divisor method that stays within the quota for all 3-state problems.*

Population monotonicity is consistent with partial ways of satisfying quota. *M stays above lower quota if* $a_i \geqq \lfloor q_i \rfloor$ for all apportionments $\mathbf{a}$ and *M stays below upper quota if* $a_i \leqq \lceil q_i \rceil$ for all $\mathbf{a}$.

PROPOSITION 6.4. *Jefferson's method is the unique population monotone method that stays above lower quota and Adams's method is the unique population monotone method that stays below upper quota.*

Note that since Jefferson's method is not the same as Adams's this gives another proof that no population monotone method satisfies quota. Another partial quota concept that is satisfied by all divisor methods is the following.

PROPOSITION 6.5. *No divisor method apportionment simultaneously violates upper quota on one state and violates lower quota on another.*

Although no population monotone method stays within the quota *all* of the time, there are population monotone methods that stay within the quota "almost" all of the time; moreover the best from this standpoint is Webster's method. The tendency of different divisor methods to violate quota can be tested using the same basic model used to test for bias. The idea is to fix a hypothetical apportionment **a** and a method *M*, and ask how likely it is that some state violates quota given this particular distribution of seats. Choose an arbitrary but fixed divisor *x* and let $P(\mathbf{a})$ be the set of all populations **p** for which **a** is a resulting *M*-apportionment using the divisor *x*. The simplest and most natural case is to assume that the populations p_i, and hence the quotients p_i/x, are independently and uniformly distributed. The probability that some state *i* violates lower quota can, in principle, be computed from the expression

$$\Pr[a_i + 1 \leq p_i h / \Sigma p_j] = \Pr\left[(h - a_i - 1)\, p_i/x - (a_i + 1) \sum_{j \neq i} p_j/x \geq 0 \right].$$

Similarly, the probability that state *i* violates upper quota can be computed from the expression

$$\Pr[a_i - 1 \geq p_i h / \Sigma p_i] = \Pr\left[(h - a_i + 1)\, p_i/x - (a_i - 1) \sum_{j \neq 1} p_j/x \leq 0 \right].$$

The probability that no state violates quota is at most the sum of all of these probabilities. However, for methods like Webster's these probabilities are extremely small, hence difficult to estimate theoretically. A more practical approach is to estimate the results numerically using a Monte Carlo simulation.

For a problem in which there are many small states, i.e. in which many of the quotients p_i/x are close to zero, methods like Hill's that automatically give every state 1 seat are very likely to violate lower quota on the large states because too many seats will have been used up on the small ones. Thus, the property of automatically giving 1 seat to every state is a serious defect from the point of view of staying within the quota. In 1970 there were 6 states that received only 1 seat using Hill's method; *a priori* these states could be arbitrarily small. However in fact no state had a quota less than .5. To avoid the unrealistic assumption of very small states, it was assumed in estimating the future likelihood of violating quota that no state's quotient would be less than .5. Thus the probability of violating quota was estimated numerically for each of the five traditional methods by choosing

a to be the actual distribution of seats in 1970, and choosing the quotients p_i/x independently from a uniform distribution on the interval max{.5, $d(a_i - 1)$} $\leq p_i/x \leq d(a_i)$. The results are given in Table 10.3. Clearly Webster's is superior to the others in regard to staying within the quota.

In fact Webster did not advocate that a method should always stay within the quota, but asked for something slightly weaker. Namely, he said, it should not be possible to take a seat from one state and give it to another and simultaneously bring *both* of them nearer to their quotas.

That is, there should be no states i and j such that

$$q_i - (a_i - 1) < a_i - q_i \quad \text{and} \quad a_j + 1 - q_j < q_j - a_j. \qquad (6.1)$$

Another way of saying the same thing is that no state can be brought closer to its quota without moving another state further from its quota. Any method with this property is said to be *near quota*. This is similar to the idea of Pareto optimality in economics. It should be further noted that Webster's idea is independent of whether near quota is interpreted in absolute or relative terms. In relative terms it would say that no state can be brought closer to its quota *on a percentage basis* without moving another state further from its quota *on a percentage basis*. In other words for no states i and j do we have

$$1 - \frac{a_i - 1}{q_i} < \frac{a_i}{q_i} - 1 \quad \text{and} \quad \frac{a_j + 1}{q_j} - 1 < 1 - \frac{a_j}{q_j} \qquad (6.2)$$

which is clearly equivalent to (6.1).

The fallacy of Hill's and Huntington's relative difference approach can now be clearly seen: it fails to take into account that there is an *absolute* standard against which the allocation to any state should be compared—namely the quota. Compared to this standard both the relative and the absolute measures of difference lead to the same result—Webster's method.

THEOREM 6.2. *Webster's method is the unique population monotone method that is near quota, interpreted absolutely or relatively.*

PROOF OF THEOREM 6.2. If **a** is not near quota, that is if (6.1) holds for some i and j then rearranging we have

$$1 < 2(a_i - q_i) \quad \text{and} \quad 1 < 2(q_j - a_j)$$

or

$$a_j + 1/2 < q_j \quad \text{and} \quad a_i - 1/2 > q_i$$

or

$$q_j/(a_j + 1/2) > q_i/(a_i - 1/2).$$

Hence the min-max inequality for Webster's method is violated, so a could not be a Webster apportionment. Therefore Webster's method is near quota.

Conversely let M be a population monotone method (i.e. a divisor method) different from Webster's. Then there exists a 2-state problem (p_1, p_2) in which the M-apportionment is uniquely $(a_1 + 1, a_2)$, whereas the W-apportionment is uniquely $(a_1, a_2 + 1)$. By the latter, $p_2/(a_2 + 1/2) > p_1/(a_1 + 1/2)$. At $h = a_1 + a_2 + 1$ the quota of state 1 is

$$q_1 = \frac{p_1 h}{p_1 + p_2} = \frac{p_1(a_1 + 1/2 + a_2 + 1/2)}{p_1 + p_2} < \frac{p_1(a_1 + 1/2) + p_2(a_1 + 1/2)}{p_1 + p_2}$$
$$= a_1 + 1/2.$$

State 2's quota is

$$q_2 \quad (a_1 + a_2 + 1) \quad q_1 > a_2 + 1/2.$$

Therefore the M-apportionment $(a_1 + 1, a_2)$ is not near quota. $\square$

In the case of minimum requirements the notion of quota must be modified because the true quotas of some states may be less than their requirements. Hence it may not be possible to satisfy the requirements *and* have enough left over to give the other states even their lower quotas. Similar problems arise in the case of maximum requirements. The *modified quota* of a state is its proportional share subject to the requirements of *all* states being met. More precisely, let $\mathbf{r} \leq \mathbf{r}^+$ be minimum and maximum requirements with $\Sigma r_i \leq h \leq \Sigma r_i^+$ and let $\mathbf{q}$ be the "ordinary quotas." Choose a multiplier t such that

$$\sum_1^s \text{mid } \{r_i, tq_i, r_i^+\} = h. \tag{6.3}$$

"Mid" again stands for the middle in value of the three arguments. (6.3)

uniquely determines t, and the resulting values $\bar{q}_i = \text{mid}\{r_i, tq_i, r_i^+\}$ are called
the *modified quotas*. The *modified upper quota* of state i is $\lceil \bar{q}_i \rceil$ and the
modified lower quota is $\lfloor \bar{q}_i \rfloor$. The method M *stays within the quota* if for all
requirements $\mathbf{r} \leqq \mathbf{r}^+$ and M-apportionments $\mathbf{a}$, $\lfloor \bar{q}_i \rfloor \leqq a_i \leqq \lceil \bar{q}_i \rceil$ for all i. The
definitions of near quota, staying above lower quota, staying below upper
quota can be similarly extended and Theorems 6.1, 6.2 and Propositions
6.1–6.5 hold as stated.

7. STAYING WITHIN THE QUOTA AND HOUSE MONOTONICITY

The preceding section shows that no population monotone method stays
within the quota or *satisfies quota*. House monotonicity is a weaker property, implied by population monotonicity but not implying it. Up to this
point the only methods discussed that stay within the quota are Hamilton-
like and violate both population monotonicity and house monotonicity. Is
it possible that there are other types of methods that stay within the quota
and are also house monotone? The answer is affirmative.

The simplest of these methods is the Quota method (Balinski and
Young, 1975). The Quota method can also be generalized to obtain *all* house
monotone methods that stay within the quota. In fact, all apportionments
arising from such methods can be described by a system of inequalities,
much as the divisor methods can be described by min-max inequalities. This
approach can be used to adapt traditional methods like those of Adams,
Dean, Hill, Webster, Jefferson, and Hamilton so that they always stay
within the quota. Unfortunately these adaptations suffer from the population
paradox and are rather complicated, so are not to be recommended.

Satisfying quota can be described in a convenient analytical way as
follows: a_i satisfies lower quota for $\mathbf{p}$ and h if and only if $a_i + 1 > q_i = p_i h/p$ and satisfies upper quota if and only if $a_i - 1 < q_i = p_i h/p$, where
$p = \Sigma p_j$. Hence $\mathbf{a}$ satisfies quota if and only if

$$p_i/(a_i + 1) < p/h < p_i/(a_i - 1) \text{ for all } i. \tag{7.1}$$

The most straightforward way of constructing a house monotone apportionment solution f is to define it recursively on h for every given $\mathbf{p}$. For
any apportionment $\mathbf{a}$ of h let $U(\mathbf{p},\mathbf{a})$ be the set of states that are *eligible* to
receive 1 more seat without exceeding their upper quotas at house size
$h + 1$; thus $U(\mathbf{p},\mathbf{a}) = \{i : a_i < p_i(h + 1)/p\}$. Clearly $U(\mathbf{p},\mathbf{a}) \neq \emptyset$ for every

p and **a**. The house monotone solutions generated by the following recursive procedure defines the *Quota method Q*.

> THEOREM 7.1. *Every solution* f *defined as follows is house monotone and stays within the quota:*
>
> (i) $f(\mathbf{p},0) = \mathbf{0}$
> (ii)   *if* $f(\mathbf{p},h) = \mathbf{a}$, *then* $f_k(\mathbf{p},h + 1) = a_k + 1$
>   *for some* k *maximizing* $p_k/(a_k + 1)$ *over all*
> $k \in U(\mathbf{p},\mathbf{a})$, *and* $f_j(\mathbf{p},h + 1) = a_j$ *for all* $j \neq k$.

PROOF OF THEOREM 7.1. It is immediate from the definition that every such *f* is house monotone and that it stays below upper quota.

Suppose, by way of contradiction, that *f* violates lower quota for some problem $(\mathbf{p},h)$. As **p** will be fixed for the remainder of the proof and *f* is single-valued, write $\mathbf{a}^{h'} = f(\mathbf{p},h')$ for every $h' \geq 0$. Also, let $p = \Sigma p_i$. Since some state, say state 1, is below lower quota at h, the set $S = \{i : a_i^h > p_i h/p\}$ is nonempty. For each i let $h_i \leq h$ be the least house size for which $a_i^{h_i} = a_i^h$. Choose $j \in S$ such that $h_j = \max_{i \in S} h_i$; thus j is the last state in S to have reached the apportionment it has at h. Now j did not receive the hth seat, because state 1 was also eligible to get the hth seat and had a higher priority, i.e.,

$$a_1^h + 1 \leq p_1 h/p, \tag{7.2}$$

$$a_j^h > p_j h/p, \tag{7.3}$$

so

$$p_j/a_j^h < p/h < p_1/(a_1 + 1). \tag{7.4}$$

Hence $h_j < h$. Let T be the set of states that receive seats between $h_j + 1$ and h inclusive. By definition of T, $T \cap S = \emptyset$, that is

$$a_i^h \leq p_i h/p \quad \text{for all } i \in T. \tag{7.5}$$

Therefore using (7.3),

$$p_i/(a_i^{h_j} + 1) \geq p_i/a_i^h \geq p/h > p_j/a_j^h = p_j/a_j^{h_j} \quad \text{for all } i \in T.$$

From this and the definition of f it follows that no member of T was eligible to get the h_j^{th} seat:

$$a_i^{h_j-1} = a_i^{h_j} \geq p_i h_j/p \quad \text{for all } i \in T. \tag{7.6}$$

Subtracting (7.6) from (7.5) and summing over T,

$$h - h_j = \sum_T (a_i^h - a_i^{h_j}) \leq (h - h_j) \sum_T p_i/p. \tag{7.7}$$

Dividing by $h - h_j > 0$, conclude that $\Sigma_T\, p_i \geq \Sigma_1^s\, p = p$, a contradiction, since $j \notin T$ and $p_j > 0$. $\square$

Define $\bar{q}_i(h)$ to be the modified quota of state i at house size h.

PROPOSITION 7.1. *Given requirements* $\mathbf{r} \leq \mathbf{r}^+$ *define* $U(\mathbf{p},\mathbf{a}) = \{i : a_i < \bar{q}_i(h + 1)\}$ *whenever* $\mathbf{a}$ *is an apportionment for* h. *Every solution* f *defined recursively as follows is house monotone and stays within the quota:*

(i)
$$f\left(\mathbf{p}, \sum_1^s r_i\right) = \mathbf{r}$$

(ii)   *if* $f(\mathbf{p},h) = \mathbf{a}$ *and* $h < \Sigma r_i^+$, *then* $f_k(\mathbf{p},h + 1) = a_k + 1$
       for some k *maximizing* $p_k/(a_k + 1)$ *over all* $k \in U(\mathbf{p},\mathbf{a})$,
       and $f_j(\mathbf{p},h + 1) = a_j$ *for all* $j \neq k$.

The argument parallels that of Theorem 7.1 and leads to the analog of (7.5) $a_i^h \leq \bar{q}_i(h) = t h p_i/p$ for all $i \in T$. Next deduce that no member of T was eligible to get the h_j^{th} seat. Since every member of T gets at least 1 seat between h_j and h, this means that $r_i^+ > a_i^{h_j-1} = a_i^{h_j} \geq \bar{q}(h_j) = t_j h_j p_i/p$ for all $i \in T$. From these two expressions we obtain

$$(th - t_j h_j) \sum_T p_i/p \geq \sum_T a_i^h - a_i^{h_j} = h - h_j \geq \sum \bar{q}_i(h) - \bar{q}_i(h_j)$$
$$\geq (th - t_j h_j) \sum p_i/p$$

and a contradiction, since $j \notin T$.

Any house monotone method may be described recursively on the house size h by defining which states are eligible to get the "next" seat given the current apportionment. The family $\bar{Q}$ of all apportionment solutions f that are house monotone and stay within the quota may be described in this way using a suitable notion of eligibility.

Fix $\mathbf{p} > 0$, and $\mathbf{a}$ an apportionment of h. For each integer $\alpha \geq 1$ let $S_\alpha = S_\alpha(\mathbf{p},\mathbf{a})$ be the set of states i such that $\lfloor p_i(h + \alpha)/p \rfloor > a_i$, and let $\bar{\alpha} = \bar{\alpha}(\mathbf{p},\mathbf{a})$ be the least $\alpha \geq 1$ such that $\Sigma_{S_\alpha} (\lfloor p_i(h + \alpha)/p \rfloor - a_i) \geq \alpha$. Define $L(\mathbf{p},\mathbf{a}) = S_{\bar{\alpha}}$ or if no such $\bar{\alpha}$ exists, let $L(\mathbf{p},\mathbf{a})$ be the set of all states.

To construct a house monotone sequence of apportionments continuing from $\mathbf{a}$ that stay within the quota, it is clearly necessary that the $(h + 1)^{st}$ seat be given to some state in $L(\mathbf{p},\mathbf{a})$ since otherwise at house size $h + \bar{\alpha}$ some state in $L(\mathbf{p},\mathbf{a})$ would have fallen below its lower quota. It is also clearly necessary that the $(h + 1)^{st}$ seat be given to some state in $U(\mathbf{p},\mathbf{a})$, or else the upper quota would be violated at $h + 1$. It turns out that these two conditions are both necessary *and* sufficient to determine which states are eligible to get the $(h + 1)^{st}$ seat.

THEOREM 7.2. *f is a house monotone solution satisfying quota if and only if for each $\mathbf{p} > 0$ f is constructed recursively as follows:*

(i) $$f(\mathbf{p},0) = 0$$

(ii) *if* $f(\mathbf{p},h) = \mathbf{a}$ *then* $f(\mathbf{p},h + 1)$ *is found by giving* $a_i + 1$ *seats to some one state* $i \in L(\mathbf{p},\mathbf{a}) \cap U(\mathbf{p},\mathbf{a})$ *and* a_j *seats to each* $j \neq i$.

In this recursion the eligibility class $L(\mathbf{p},\mathbf{a}) \cap U(\mathbf{p},\mathbf{a})$ *is never empty.*

PROOF OF THEOREM 7.2. It has already been noted that every $f \in \bar{Q}$ must be defined as in (i) and (ii). Conversely, if f is defined as in (i) and (ii) then it is obviously house monotone and stays below upper quota. Suppose that for some $\mathbf{p}$ and h, $\mathbf{a} = f(\mathbf{p},h)$ violates lower quota. Let $0, \mathbf{a}^1, \ldots, \mathbf{a}^h$ be the apportionments by f up to h, and suppose that $\lfloor p_k h/p \rfloor > a_k^h$. Then $k \in S_1 = S_1(\mathbf{p},\mathbf{a}^{h-1})$ and $\Sigma_{S_1}(\lfloor p_i h/p \rfloor - a_i^{h-1}) \geq \Sigma_{S_1}(\lfloor p_i h/p \rfloor - a_i^h) \geq 1$, so $\bar{\alpha}(\mathbf{p},\mathbf{a}^{h-1}) = 1$ and $S_1 = L(\mathbf{p},\mathbf{a}^{h-1})$. Therefore the hth seat was given to some state in S_1, but not to k, so in fact $\Sigma_{S_1}(\lfloor p_i h/p \rfloor - a_i^{h-1}) > \Sigma_{S_1}(p_i h/p - a_i^h)$ and $\Sigma_{S_1}(\lfloor p_i h/p \rfloor - a_i^{h-1}) \geq 2$.

For each i, $p_i h/p > a_i^{h-1}$ implies $p_i h/p > a_i^{h-2}$, so $S_2 = S_2(\mathbf{p},\mathbf{a}^{h-2}) \supseteq S_1(\mathbf{p},\mathbf{a}^{h-1})$. Therefore $\Sigma_{S_2}(\lfloor p_i h/p \rfloor - a_i) \geq \Sigma_{S_1}(\lfloor p_i h/p \rfloor - a_i) \geq 2$, whence

$\bar{\alpha}(\mathbf{p},\mathbf{a}^{h-2}) \leq 2$. Since $p_i(h - 2 + \bar{\alpha})/p > a_i^{h-2}$ implies $p_i h/p > a_i^{h-2}$ it follows that $L(\mathbf{p},\mathbf{a}^{h-2}) \subseteq S_2$. Therefore the $(h - 1)^{\text{st}}$ seat was given to some state in S_2 but not in S_1, whence $\Sigma_{S_2}(\lfloor p_i h/p \rfloor - a_i^{h-2}) > \Sigma_{S_1}(\lfloor p_i h/p \rfloor - a_i^{h-2}) \geq 2$ and $\Sigma_{S_2}(\lfloor p_i h/p \rfloor - a_i^{h-2}) \geq 3$. Continuing in this manner it follows that for $S_h = S_h(\mathbf{p},\mathbf{0})$, $\Sigma_{S_h}(\lfloor p_i h/p \rfloor - 0) \geq h + 1$, which is impossible.

It remains to show that the eligibility class $L(\mathbf{p},\mathbf{a}) \cap U(\mathbf{p},\mathbf{a})$ must be nonempty at each step of the recursion. If $L = L(\mathbf{p},\mathbf{a})$ is the set of all states, the result holds. Otherwise there is an $\bar{\alpha} = \bar{\alpha}(\mathbf{p},\mathbf{a}) \geq 1$ such that $\Sigma_L(\lfloor p_i(h + \bar{\alpha})/p \rfloor - a_i) \geq \bar{\alpha}$, where $\lfloor p_i(h + \bar{\alpha})/p \rfloor > a_i$ for each $i \in L$. If $\bar{\alpha} = 1$ this says that $p_i(h + 1)/p \geq a_i + 1$, so $i \in L \subseteq U$. If $\bar{\alpha} > 1$ but $L \cap U = \emptyset$, then $p_i(h + 1)/p \leq a_i$ for all $i \in L$ and so

$$p_i(h + \bar{\alpha})/p - a_i \leq p_i(h + \bar{\alpha})/p - p_i(h + 1)/p = (p_i/p)(\bar{\alpha} - 1).$$

By definition of L, $\Sigma_L(p_i(h + \bar{\alpha})/p - a_i) \geq \bar{\alpha}$, hence we obtain $\bar{\alpha} \leq (\Sigma_L p_i/p)(\bar{\alpha} - 1)$ and $\Sigma_L p_i/p \geq \bar{\alpha}/(\bar{\alpha} - 1) > 1$ (since $\bar{\alpha} > 1$), a contradiction. $\square$

To compute the set $L(\mathbf{p},\mathbf{a})$ it is not necessary to consider infinitely many α. In fact, if

$$\alpha > \max_i \left\lceil \frac{a_i - p_i h/p}{p_i/p} \right\rceil,$$

then for every i, $p_i(h + \alpha)/p > a_i$ and

$$\sum_1^s (\lfloor p_i(h + \alpha)/p \rfloor - a_i) < \sum_1^s (p_i(h + \alpha)/p - a_i) = h + \alpha - \sum a_i = \alpha$$

showing that

$$\bar{\alpha}(\mathbf{p},\mathbf{a}) \leq \max_i \left\lceil \frac{a_i - p_i h/p}{p_i/p} \right\rceil$$

if it is defined at all.

Let $\mathbf{a} \in \bar{Q}(\mathbf{p},h)$ if and only if there is a house monotone solution f satisfying quota with $\mathbf{a} = f(\mathbf{p},h)$. The Quota method Q is a submethod of $\bar{Q}$ and is determined by a more stringent criterion of eligibility. But this eligibility criterion is also very simple to compute, as it only "looks ahead" by one seat. Given $\mathbf{a} \in Q(\mathbf{p},h)$, it is only necessary to find those states for which $p_i(h + 1)/p > a_i$; the eligible class at $\mathbf{a}$ is then

$$\{i : p_i/a_i > p/(h + 1) \quad \text{and} \quad p_i/(a_i + 1) \geq p_j/(a_j + 1)$$
$$\text{whenever} \quad p_j/a_j > p/(h + 1)\}.$$

As in the case of rank-index methods, it is also possible to give a "local" characterization of all $\bar{Q}$-apportionments for a given $\mathbf{p}$ and h by a system of inequalities.

THEOREM 7.3. $\mathbf{a} \in \bar{Q}(\mathbf{p},h)$ *if and only if* $\mathbf{a} \geq \mathbf{0}$, $\Sigma a_i = h$ *and*

$$\sum_i max \, (a_i, \lfloor p_i(h + \alpha)/p \rfloor) \leq h + \alpha,$$

$$\sum_i min \, (a_i, \lfloor p_i(h - \beta)/p \rfloor) \geq h - \beta, \quad \text{for all } \alpha, \beta \geq 0.$$

The conditions are feasible for every $\mathbf{p}$ *and* h.

It is easy to verify that if the inequalities hold for

$$0 \leq \alpha \leq \max_i \left\lceil \frac{a_i - p_i h/p}{p_i/p} \right\rceil \quad and \quad 0 \leq \beta \leq \max_j \left\lceil \frac{p_j h/p - a_j}{p_j/p} \right\rceil,$$

then they hold for *all* α, $\beta \geq 0$ (as when computing the set $L(\mathbf{p},\mathbf{a})$).

The conditions are transparently necessary if $\mathbf{a} = f(\mathbf{p},h)$ for some house monotone f that stays within the quota. Sufficiency is established by showing that if $\mathbf{a}$ satisfies the conditions at $h > 0$, then there is an $\mathbf{a}'$, differing from $\mathbf{a}$ by exactly 1 seat, say at state k, such that $\mathbf{a}'$ satisfies the conditions at $h - 1$ and $k \in L(\mathbf{p},\mathbf{a}') \cap U(\mathbf{p},\mathbf{a}')$. The result then follows from an induction argument using Theorem 7.2.

The characterization in Theorem 7.2 suggests an approach first proposed by Still (1979) in which various classical methods, like the divisor methods or Hamilton's method, can be modified so as to be both house monotone and stay within the quota. Let $d(a)$ be a divisor criterion and in the recursion of Theorem 7.2 (ii) give the $(h + 1)^{st}$ seat to some eligible state that maximizes $p_i/d(a_i)$ over all eligible states. In this way we obtain the Quota-Jefferson method (the same as the Quota method), the Quota-Webster method, the Quota-Hill method, etc. Likewise we could define the Quota-Hamilton method by giving the $(h + 1)^{st}$ seat to some eligible state with maximum "remainder" $p_i(h + 1)/p - a_i$.

To illustrate how such methods work, we apply the Quota method to the four-state example shown in Table A7.1.

TABLE A7.1.   Example Illustrating the Quota Method (*starred state gets the next seat*)

State	Population	Quota	Q-Appt.	Quota	Q-Appt.	Quota	Q-Appt.
A	501	4.59	5*	5.01	6	5.43	6
B	394	3.61	4	3.94	4*	4.27	5
C	156	1.43	1	1.56	1	1.69	1
D	149	1.37	1	1.49	1	1.61	1
Total	1200	11.00	11	12.00	12	13.00	13

The rule for computing the Quota method is simpler than the others because (by Theorem 7.1) it is not necessary to calculate the sets $L(\mathbf{p},\mathbf{a})$ at each stage of the recursion. It suffices to maximize $p_i/(a_i + 1)$ over all $i \in U(\mathbf{p},\mathbf{a})$, i.e. the eligible states are those that could get one more seat without violating upper quota at the next larger house size. The recursion begins at $h = 0$ and leads to the solution at $h = 11$ shown in Table A7.1. The quotas at $h = 12$ identify the eligible states at this point to be A, C, and D. Of these $p_A/(a_A + 1)$ is maximum, hence it gets one more seat at house size 12. At this point, B, C, and D are eligible, and state B deserves the next seat according to the Jefferson divisor criterion.

Consider now a variation of the above example in which state B gains in population and all other states stay the same. Table A7.2 illustrates the Quota method calculation for this case, beginning with $h = 11$.

TABLE A7.2.   Example Showing Quota Method Not Population Monotone

State	Population	Quota	Q-Appt.	Quota	Q-Appt.	Quota	Q-Appt.
A	501	4.57	5	4.99	5*	5.40	6
B	400	3.65	4	3.98	4	4.31	4
C	156	1.42	1*	1.55	2	1.68	2
D	149	1.36	1	1.48	1	1.61	1
Total	1206	11.00	11	12.00	12	13.00	13

The solutions at $h = 11$ are the same, but now the only eligible states are C and D, so C gets the next seat. At $h = 12$ states A, B, and D are eligible and A gets the next seat according to the Jefferson divisor criterion. Therefore, while state B gained in population relative to all other states, it actually lost a seat at $h = 13$. Similar examples show that the Quota-Webster method, the Quota-Hill method, and indeed all methods of this type violate population monotonicity and hence are not to be recommended.

PROPOSITION 7.2. *The analog of Theorem 7.2 holds in the presence of minimum and maximum requirements by defining* $U(\mathbf{p},\mathbf{a}) = \{i : a_i < \bar{q}_i (h + 1)\}$ *and* $L(\mathbf{p},\mathbf{a}) = \{i : \bar{q}_i(h + \alpha) > a_i\}$ *for some least* α *such that* $\Sigma_L(\bar{q}_i(h + \alpha) - a_i) \geq \alpha$ *or, if no such* α *exists,* $L(\mathbf{p},\mathbf{a})$ *is the set of all states.*

PROPOSITION 7.3. *Given requirements* $\mathbf{r} \leq \mathbf{r}^+$ *and* $\mathbf{a} \geq \mathbf{0}$, $\Sigma_i a_i = h$, *there is a house monotone solution* f *that stays within the modified quota with* $\mathbf{a} = f(\mathbf{p},h)$ *if and only if*

$$\sum_i max\ (a_i, \lfloor \bar{q}_i(h + \alpha) \rfloor) \leq h + \alpha,$$

and

$$\sum_i min\ (a_i, \lceil \bar{q}_i(h - \beta) \rceil) \geq h - \beta$$

for $0 \leq \alpha \leq \Sigma r_i^+ - h$ *and* $0 \leq \beta \leq h - \Sigma r_i$.

8. UNIFORMITY

The problem of fair representation is but one instance of a problem of *fair division*: How should an inheritance be shared among heirs? How should a public good (e.g., airport capacity) be shared among users (e.g., air carriers)? How should taxes be shared among residents? How should seats in Congress be shared among states? How should seats in a parliament be shared among parties? An inherent principle of any fair division is that *every part of a fair division should be fair*. For example, one property of a fair division of an inheritance should be that no subset of heirs would want to make trades after the division is made. The principle is very general.

In the context of fair representation this principle says that an apportionment that is acceptable to all states must be acceptable if restricted to any subset of states considered alone. The way in which two states share a given number of seats is independent of the populations of *other* states. This is somewhat reminiscent of Arrow's "independence of irrelevant alternatives" axiom in the theory of social choice, but with an important difference: it can be realized. In the context of fair division and even more particularly in apportionment, it is a central consideration, since inevitably each state will compare its representation with each of its sister states.

Specifically, a method M is *uniform* (Balinski and Young, 1978b) if for every t, $2 \leq t \leq s$, $(a_1,\ldots,a_s) \in M((p_1,\ldots,p_s),h)$ implies $(a_1,\ldots,a_t) \in M((p_1,\ldots,p_t),\Sigma_1^t a_i)$, and if also $(b_1,\ldots,b_t) \in M((p_1,\ldots,p_t)\Sigma_1^t a_i)$ then

$(b_1,\dots,b_t,a_{t+1},\dots,a_s) \in M((p_1,\dots,p_s),h)$. In other words, each restriction of a fair apportionment is fair; moreover, if a restriction admits a different apportionment of the same number of seats—that is, if the restricted problem admits a tie—then there is a corresponding tie in the entire apportionment. The min-max description of divisor methods immediately establishes that all divisor methods are uniform.

Uniform methods include more than the divisor methods, however. In fact, the class of uniform methods can be described by generalizing the recursive procedure for computing divisor methods.

Let a *rank-index* $r(p,a)$ be any real-valued function of rational $p > 0$ and integer $a \geq 0$ that is monotone decreasing in $a : r(p,a - 1) > r(p,a)$. Now define a particular house monotone solution f as follows:

(i)   for $h = 0$ let $f(\mathbf{p},0) = \mathbf{0}$.

(ii)   if $f(\mathbf{p},h) = \mathbf{a}$, then $f(\mathbf{p},h + 1)$ is found by giving
            $a_i + 1$ seats to some state i such that $r(p_i,a_i) \geq r(p_j,a_j)$
            and a_j seats to each $j \neq i$.

Let $\mathcal{F}$ be the set of all particular solutions defined recursively by (i) and (ii). The *rank-index method based on* $r(p,a)$ is defined by

$$M(\mathbf{p},h) = \{\mathbf{a} : \mathbf{a} = f(\mathbf{p},h) \text{ for some } f \in \mathcal{F}\}.$$

Divisor methods are just special cases of rank-index methods in which the rank-index has the form $r(p,a) = p/d(a)$. The following theorem shows that the min-max inequality holds also for rank-index methods, hence in particular all rank-index methods are uniform.

THEOREM 8.1. $M(\mathbf{p},h) = \{\mathbf{a} \geq \mathbf{0}: \min_{a_i>0} r(p_i,a_i - 1) \geq \max_{a_i \geq 0} r(p_i,a_i)\}$
            is the rank-index method based on $r(p,a)$.

PROOF OF THEOREM 8.1. First we show that if $\mathbf{a}$ satisfies the inequalities for some given $\mathbf{p}$ and h, then there exists $f \in \mathcal{F}$ with $f(\mathbf{p},h) = \mathbf{a}$. If false, let $\bar{h}$ be the least $h \geq 0$ for which it is false for the given $\mathbf{p}$. Let state i satisfy $r(p_i,a_i - 1) \leq r(p_j,a_j - 1)$ for all $j \neq i$ and define $\mathbf{a}'$ as follows: $a_i' = a_i - 1$ and $a_j' = a_j$ for all $j \neq i$. Then

$$r(p_j,a_j' - 1) \geq r(p_i,a_i') \geq r(p_j,a_j') \text{ for all } j \neq i$$

and

$$r(p_i, a_i' - 1) > r(p_i, a_i').$$

Hence $\mathbf{a}'$ satisfies the inequalities for $\mathbf{p}$ and $h - 1$ and by the induction hypothesis there is some solution $f \in \mathcal{F}$ with $f(\mathbf{p}, h - 1) = \mathbf{a}'$. Let f^{h-1} be the restriction of f up to house size $h - 1$. Since $r(p_i, a_i') \geq r(p_j, a_j')$ for all j, the recursive procedure implies that there is some extension g of f^{h-1} which is in $\mathcal{F}$ and such that $g(\mathbf{p}, h) = \mathbf{a}$.

Conversely, suppose that for some $f \in \mathcal{F}$, $\mathbf{a} = f(\mathbf{p}, h)$ does not satisfy the min-max inequality; say $r(p_i, a_i) > r(p_j, a_j - 1)$ for some $i \neq j$. Let $k \leq h$ be the house size at which (by the recursive procedure constructing f) state j received its a_j^{th} seat. At $k - 1$ state i had $a_i' \leq a_i$ seats and state j had $a_j' = a_j - 1$ seats. But then $r(p_i, a_i') \geq r(p_i, a_i) > r(p_j, a_j')$ so $r(p_j, a_j')$ was not maximum, contradicting the recursive procedure. $\square$

The same rank-index method can be represented by many different rank-indices. In fact any two rank-indices r and r' that are *order equivalent*, in the sense that $r(p, a) \geq r(q, b)$ iff $r'(p, a) \geq r'(q, b)$, yield the same rank-index method, by Theorem 8.1. The converse is true as well.

THEOREM 8.2. *Two rank-indices* r' *and* r" *represent the same rank-index method* M *if and only if* r' *is order equivalent with* r".

PROOF OF THEOREM 8.2. Let M be a rank-index method based on r' and also based on r" We will show that r' is order equivalent to r" Suppose by way of contradiction, that $r'(p, a) > r'(q, b)$ while $r''(p, a) \leq r''(q, b)$ for some pairs (p, a) and (q, b).

Let $(\bar{a}, \bar{b})$ be an M-apportionment of $h = a + b + 1$ seats for the 2-state problem (p, q). If $\bar{a} \leq a$ then $\bar{b} \geq b + 1$ and by the monotonicity of r',

$$r'(p, \bar{a}) \geq r'(p, a) > r'(q, b) \geq r'(q, \bar{b} - 1),$$

but this contradicts the min-max inequality of Theorem 8.1. Hence

$$\bar{a} \geq a + 1 \text{ and } \bar{b} \leq b \text{ for all } M\text{-apportionments } (\bar{a}, \bar{b}). \qquad (8.1)$$

But then

$$r''(p, \bar{a} - 1) \leq r''(p, a) \leq r''(q, b) \leq r''(q, \bar{b})$$

again contradicting the min-max inequality unless these inequalities are all equalities and $\bar{a} = a + 1$, $\bar{b} = b$. Therefore by Theorem 8.1 $(a,b + 1)$ is also an M-apportionment, contradicting (8.1). $\square$

Rank-index methods are not only uniform: they are essentially the *only* methods that are uniform. This is true with conditions that are much weaker than those that have been assumed heretofore. A method M is said to be *balanced* if whenever two states have equal populations then their apportionments do not differ by more than one seat. This is an even less demanding concept than weak proportionality and is satisfied by every non-frivolous method known to the authors. (See Proposition 8.1.) This and symmetry are the only basic assumptions on methods needed for the following theorem.

THEOREM 8.3. *A method is uniform if and only if it is a rank-index method.*

COROLLARY 8.3.1. *Every uniform method is house monotone.*

This surprising corollary is an immediate consequence of the theorem and the definition of a rank-index method. It highlights both the importance and the strength of the uniformity concept.

PROOF OF THEOREM 8.3. We have already noted that a rank-index method is uniform.

To prove the converse we show that a suitably defined priority relation on pairs (p,a) is an order, and that it can be represented by a real-valued, order-preserving function $r(p,a)$.

Suppose that M is uniform, balanced and symmetric. The following must then hold.

> If $(p,q;h)$ has M-apportionment (a,b), and $(p,q;h')$
> has M-apportionment (a',b'), and $a' < a$, $b' > b$,   (8.2)
> then $h = h'$, $a' = a - 1$ and $b' = b + 1$.

Without loss of generality, assume that $a' + b' \geqq a + b$, say $a' + b' = a + b + k$. To prove (8.2) consider first the two cases $k = 0$ and $k = 1$.

$\underline{k = 0}$. Let (x,x',y,y') be an M-apportionment for $(p,p,q,q;2h)$. Since M is balanced, $|x - x'| \leqq 1$ and $|y - y'| \leqq 1$. Either $x + x'$ and $y + y'$ are both even or both are odd. Hence, either $x = x'$ and $y = y'$ or (using symmetry) $x' = x + 1$ and $y' = y - 1$. In either case $x' + y' = x + y = h$ $= h'$. Uniformity implies that (a,b) may be substituted for (x,y) and (a',b')

for (x',y') to obtain the M-apportionment (a,a',b,b'). By balanced, $|a - a'|$ ≤ 1 and $|b - b'| \leq 1$, so, since $a' < a$ and $b' > b$, we have $a' = a - 1$ and $b' = b + 1$.

$\underline{k = 1}$. $a' + b' = a + b + 1$, $b' > b$, $a' < a$ implies $b' \geq b + 2$. Use balanced to deduce that $(p,p,q,q;2h + 1)$ has an M-apportionment either of form $(x,x + 1, y,y)$ or $(x,x,y,y + 1)$ where $x + y = h$. By uniformity it follows that (a,a',b,b') is an M-apportionment. But $b' \geq b + 2$ contradicts balanced.

Therefore, if (a,b) apportions $(p,q;h)$ and (a',b') apportions $(p,q;h + 1)$ then we must have $a' \geq a$ and $b' \geq b$. That is, *every particular M-solution f is house monotone on two states*. It is therefore impossible to have $a' < a$, $b' > b$ and $a' + b' > a + b$. This completes the proof of (8.2).

Consider now the family $\mathcal{P} = \{(p,a) : p > 0,\ a \geq 0,\ p \text{ rational},\ a \text{ integer}\}$. Define a relation $\gtrsim$ on $\mathcal{P}$ as follows:

$$(p,a - 1) \gtrsim (q,b) \text{ if and only if there is some}$$
$$M\text{-apportionment } (\bar{a},\bar{b}) \text{ for } (p,q) \text{ and } h = \bar{a} + \bar{b} \qquad (8.3)$$
$$\text{such that } a \geq \bar{a} > 0,\ \bar{b} \leq b.$$

Intuitively, the method M gives preference for an extra seat to a state having population p and $a - 1$ seats over that of a state having population q and b seats.

Write $(p,a) > (q,b)$ if $(p,a) \gtrsim (q,b)$ and not $(q,b) \gtrsim (p,a)$. Also write $(p,a) \sim (q,b)$ if both $(p,a) \gtrsim (q,b)$ and $(q,b) \gtrsim (p,a)$. Then from (8.2) we have

$$(p,a - 1) > (q,b) \text{ if and only if } a' \geq a \text{ or } b' \leq b \text{ for} \qquad (8.4)$$
$$\text{every } M\text{-apportionment } (a',b') \text{ for } (p,q) \text{ and all } h,$$

and

$$(p,a - 1) \sim (q,b) \text{ if and only if } (a - 1,b + 1) \text{ and } (a,b) \qquad (8.5)$$
$$\text{are both apportionments of } (p,q;\ a + b).$$

Next we show that *the relation $\gtrsim$ is a partial order on $\mathcal{P}$*, that is,

$$(p,a) \gtrsim (q,b) \text{ and } (q,b) \gtrsim (r,c) \text{ implies } (p,a) \gtrsim (r,c). \qquad (8.6)$$

Note, first, that (p,a) and (r,c) are comparable since one can consider the problem $(p,r;\ a + c + 1)$. To prove (8.6) we suppose that $(r,c) > (p,a)$ and derive a contradiction.

Construct the problem $(p,q,r; a + b + c + 1)$. By (8.4) and uniformity *every* apportionment (x,y,z) of this problem satisfies either $z \geqq c + 1$ or $x \leqq a$.

Suppose $z \geqq c + 1$. $(q,b) \gtrsim (r,c)$ implies that *either* $y \geqq b + 1$ (or $z \leqq c$) for every (y,z), *or* that $(b + 1,c)$ and $(b,c + 1)$ are both apportionments for (q,r). If $y \geqq b + 1$ then $x \leqq a - 1$ and so $(q,b) \gtrsim (p,a - 1)$, a contradiction. Otherwise, $(a,b + 1,c)$ must also be an apportionment for (p,q,r), so $(p,a) \gtrsim (q,b)$ implies $(a + 1,b,c)$, again a contradiction.

Suppose, then, that $x \leqq a$ and $z \leqq c$, which means $y \geqq b + 1$. Then $(q,b) \gtrsim (p,a)$, and so $(q,b) \sim (p,a)$ and $(a + 1,b)$ and $(a,b + 1)$ must both be apportionments, a contradiction. This establishes (8.6).

The fact that $\gtrsim$ is a partial order on the countable set $\mathscr{P}$ implies that there exists an order-preserving function r from $\mathscr{P}$ to the real numbers. The function r may be constructed as follows. Let $\pi^0, \pi^1, \pi^2, \ldots$ be an enumeration of all pairs in $\mathscr{P}$, and for each k define an order-preserving function $\phi^k : \{\pi^0, \ldots, \pi^k\} \to R$ such that ϕ^k agrees with ϕ^{k-1} on $\{\pi^0, \ldots, \pi^{k-1}\}$. Define r to be the union of all the ϕ^k's.

Let $\mathbf{a}$ be any M-apportionment for the problem $(\mathbf{p}; h)$. By definition of $\gtrsim$ and uniformity, $(p_i, a_i - 1) \gtrsim (p_j, a_j)$ for all $i \neq j$, $a_i > 0$. Moreover, by balanced $(p_i, p_i; 2a_i)$ has the *unique* apportionment (a_i, a_i), whence $(p_i, a_i - 1) > (p_i, a_i)$. Therefore $\mathbf{a}$ satisfies the min-max inequality

$$\min_{a_i > 0} r(p_i, a_i - 1) \geqq \max_{a_j \geqq 0} r(p_j, a_j) \qquad (8.7)$$

and, moreover,

$$r(p, a - 1) > r(p, a) \text{ for all } p, a > 0. \qquad (8.8)$$

Suppose, conversely, that $\mathbf{a}$ satisfies (8.7), $\Sigma a_i = h$. We must then show that $\mathbf{a}$ is an M-apportionment for $(\mathbf{p}; h)$. Let $\mathbf{b}$ be *some* M-apportionment for $(\mathbf{p}; h)$ and suppose $\mathbf{b} \neq \mathbf{a}$. Choose i and j so that $a_i < b_i$ and $a_j > b_j$. Both $\mathbf{a}$ and $\mathbf{b}$ satisfy (8.7) and $r(p, a)$ is monotone decreasing in $\mathbf{a}$, implying

$$r(p_j, b_j) \geqq r(p_j, a_j - 1) \geqq r(p_i, a_i) \geqq r(p_i, b_i - 1) \geqq r(p_j, b_j),$$

and so all inequalities are equalities. Moreover, by (8.8), $b_j = a_j - 1$ and $b_i = a_i + 1$. But $r(p_i, b_i - 1) = r(p_j, b_j)$ says that $(p_i, b_i - 1) \sim (p_j, b_j)$, so by (8.5) $(b_i - 1, b_j + 1) = (a_i, a_j)$ is an alternative apportionment of $a_i + a_j$ seats between p_i and p_j. By uniformity (a_i, a_j) may be substituted for (b_i, b_j)

in **b** to produce an M-apportionment **b**′ that differs from **a** in fewer components. Continuing in this manner we conclude that **a** itself must be an M-apportionment. This completes the proof of Theorem 8.3.* □

Although uniformity as a property seems innocuous, since so natural, it has surprisingly strong implications even in the absence of completeness. A method M is said to be *weakly population monotone* if for all **p**, $p_i > p_j$ implies $a_i \geq a_j$ for all **a** $\in M(p)$. This very weak notion together with uniformity implies that M must be a divisor method, assuming only that M satisfies the basic conditions of homogeneity, symmetry, and weak proportionality.

THEOREM 8.4. *A method* M *is uniform and weakly population monotone if and only if it is a divisor method.*

PROOF OF THEOREM 8.4. A uniform method that is weakly proportional is balanced (Proposition 8.1). Therefore, M is a rank-index method with some $r(p,a)$ that is monotone decreasing in a. Furthermore, M homogeneous means that $(xp,a) \gtrsim (xq,b)$ for rational $x > 0$ if and only if $(p,a) \gtrsim (q,b)$ and so $r(xp,a) \geq r(xq,b)$ if and only if $r(p,a) \geq r(q,b)$.

Suppose M is weakly population monotone. Then, for any populations $p' > p > 0$ and any integer $a \geq 0$ the 2-state problem $(p',p, 2a + 1)$ has only apportionments of form (a',a), where $a' \geq a + 1$. Therefore, $r(p',a) > r(p,a)$, that is, $r(p,a)$ is monotone increasing in p.

Fix $a \geq 2$. Then $r(1,a) < r(1,1) < r(a + 1,a)$. Let $\mathscr{P}^a = \{p : r(p,a) \geq r(1,1)\}$ and define $p^a = \inf \mathscr{P}^a$. By the preceding inequalities $1 \leq p^a \leq a + 1$, so p^a is finite. It may be irrational; however, in any case, for any increasing sequence of rationals $p^{a(n)} \to p^a$ and any rational $\varepsilon > 0$ there is an $n(\varepsilon)$ so that for $n \geq n(\varepsilon)$

$$r(p^{a(n)},a) \leq r(1,1) < r(p^{a(n)} + \varepsilon,a).$$

Therefore, since M is homogeneous,

$$r(p,a) \leq r(p/p^{a(n)},1) \quad \text{and} \quad r(p/(p^{a(n)} + \varepsilon),1) < r(p,a) \qquad (8.9)$$

for any rational $\varepsilon > 0$ and n sufficiently large.

---

*A variant of this result characterizing rank-index methods by a slightly weaker formulation of uniformity together with house monotonicity is proved in (Balinski and Young, 1977b).

Define $d(a) = p^a$ for $a \geqq 2$ and $d(1) = 1$. If there exists a finite p^0 $= \inf \mathscr{P}^0 > 0$, let $d(0) = p^0$; otherwise, $d(0) = 0$. We claim that by this definition $p/d(a)$ is order equivalent to $r(p,a)$.

Consider, first, the case $d(0) > 0$. Suppose $r(p,a) \leqq r(q,b)$. Then by (8.9), with rational increasing $p^{a(n)} \to p^a$, $q^{b(n)} \to q^b$ and any rational $\varepsilon > 0$,

$$r(p/(p^{a(n)} + \varepsilon),1) < r(p,a) \leqq r(q,b) \leqq r(q/q^{b(n)},1)$$

for n sufficiently large, and so, by weak population monotonicity

$$p/(p^{a(n)} + \varepsilon) < q/q^{b(n)}$$

implying

$$p/p^a \leqq q/q^b \text{ or } p/d(a) \leqq q/d(b).$$

If $r(p,a) = r(q,b)$ then $r(p,a) \leqq r(q,b)$ and $r(q,b) \leqq r(p,a)$ and so $p/d(a)$ $= q/d(b)$.

Consider, then, the case $d(0) = 0$. The same reasoning as above applies for all a, $b > 0$. $d(0) = 0$ means that $r(p,0) > r(1,1)$ for all p, thus $r(p,0)$ $> r(q,b)$ for all $b > 0$ and all p, q. Similarly, $p/d(0) > q/d(b)$ since $d(b)$ > 0. For $a = b = 0$, $r(p,0) \geqq r(q,0)$ if and only if $p \geqq q$, which holds if and only if $p/0 \geqq q/0$ by convention. $\square$

This theorem has strong implications. Notice, first, that without invoking the completeness property one obtains divisor methods, which can trivially be made complete since they are continuous. Most important, the properties that (i) any part of a fair division must be fair (uniformity) and (ii) a greater claim of one player over another guarantees the first at least as great a part of the spoils as the second (weak population monotonicity) are sufficient to characterize divisor methods. This provides yet another way of seeing why divisor methods are really the only ones that are suitable candidates for apportionment.

In the presence of minimum requirements $\mathbf{r}$, *uniformity* means simply that whenever $\mathbf{a}_T$ is the restriction of $\mathbf{a} \in M(\mathbf{r},\mathbf{p},h)$ to some *free* subset of states T and $\mathbf{a}_T \geqq \mathbf{r}'$ for some $\mathbf{r}'$, then $\mathbf{a}_T \in M(\mathbf{r}',\mathbf{p}_T,\sum_T a_i)$; moreover, any alternative solution $\mathbf{b}_T \in M(\mathbf{r}',\mathbf{p}_T,\sum_T a_i)$ can be substituted for $\mathbf{a}_T$ in $\mathbf{a}$.

PROPOSITION 8.1. *If* M *is uniform and weakly proportional, then* M *is balanced.*

In the next four propositions a method M is *only* assumed to be symmetric (see Balinski and Young, 1978a), and quota means modified quota if minimum requirements are present.

PROPOSITION 8.2. M *is the method of Jefferson if and only if it is uniform and satisfies lower quota.*

PROPOSITION 8.3. M *is the method of Adams if and only if it is uniform and satisfies upper quota.*

PROPOSITION 8.4. M *is the method of Webster if and only if it is uniform and is near to quota.*

PROPOSITION 8.5. *There exists no uniform and symmetric method that satisfies quota.*

9. CRITERIA FOR PROPORTIONAL REPRESENTATION

Apportionment in proportional representation (or ''PR'') systems poses the same mathematical problem as for federal systems but raises different issues. In a ''pure'' PR system voters cast a single vote for a party in a multimember district and the problem is to determine the *just* number of representatives due each party. Parties take the place of states and their vote totals the place of populations.

The idea of PR is to achieve party representation more closely proportional to party strength than is realized in federal single-member district systems. Thus at a minimum a PR method must be homogeneous, symmetric, and proportional.

In a PR system the number of parties is constantly changing: some die, new ones are formed, others merge or splinter. In view of this it is necessary to have a method that works for any possible number s of parties. And just as in federal systems it is essential that the method be population monotone. Indeed if anything it is even more essential, for otherwise it would some-

times be possible for one party A to fake some of its votes in favor of a
second party B and thereby increase its own representation at B's expense.
This means that the only acceptable methods for PR are divisor methods
(Theorem 4.3).

An important consideration in PR systems that does not arise in federal
systems is the need to discourage a proliferation of small parties, which
might lead to political instability. This need is customarily met in two ways:
by setting percentage thresholds below which a party does not qualify for
any representation, and choosing a method that implicitly encourages parties
to form coalitions. Specifically, consider an apportionment by a method M
in which some party with $\bar{p}$ votes gets $\bar{a}$ seats and another with p^* votes
gets a^* seats. If these two parties form a coalition party having $\bar{p} + p^*$ votes
how many seats does it obtain? M encourages coalitions if there is an M-
apportionment that gives at least $\bar{a} + a^*$ seats to the coalition. Similarly,
M encourages schisms if there is an M-apportionment that gives at most $\bar{a}$
$+ a^*$ seats to the coalition.

Various people have observed through the years that Jefferson's
method—the divisor method most favorable to the larger parties—encourages coalitions. Erlang proved it in 1907 (Erlang, 1907) and further asserted
a characterization of Jefferson's method that is correct in spirit but wrong
in detail (see Hylland, 1975, Balinski and Young, 1978b, 1979a). A very
simple characterization is the following.

THEOREM 9.1. *Jefferson's is the unique method that is population
monotone and encourages coalitions.*

PROOF OF THEOREM 9.1. The demonstration that Jefferson's method
does encourage coalitions is straightforward (see Chapter 12).

Conversely let M be population monotone—hence a divisor method—
with divisor criterion $d(a)$, and suppose M encourages coalitions. Consider
the problem with $n + 1$ parties, vote-vector $(p,p,\ldots,p)$ and $h = n(a + 1)$
$+ a$ seats to distribute. Since a divisor method is balanced, there exists an
M-solution of form $(a,a + 1,\ldots,a + 1)$. Form a coalition of all parties
except the first. M encourages coalitions so there exists a solution (x,y) with
$y \geq na + n$ and $x \leq a$ for the 2-party vote-vector (p,np). By weak proportionality, (a,na) is the unique solution for the smaller house $h' = na$
$+ n$, so since M is house monotone, $x \geq a$. Therefore, $(a,na + n)$ is an M-
solution, implying $np/d(na + n - 1) \geq p/d(a)$, and so

$$a + 1 \geq d(a) \geq d(na + n - 1)/n \geq (na + n - 1)/n = a + 1 - 1/n$$

for any $a \geq 0$ and all n. Letting n grow shows $d(a) = a + 1$. $\square$
Similar reasoning proves:

THEOREM 9.2. *The method of Adams is the unique divisor method that encourages schisms.*

Recall that Jefferson's method may be characterized as the unique uniform method that stays above lower quota (Proposition 8.2); hence the interesting fact that it both encourages coalitions *and* still gives every party, no matter how small, at least the integer part of its quota.

It is natural to ask whether there exists a divisor method that always gives a coalition exactly what its partners got separately. Theorems 9.1 and 9.2 show that this is impossible, since such a method would satisfy the hypotheses of both theorems and so be identical with the methods of Adams and Jefferson, which are different. However, it is possible to have divisor methods in which the coalition party gets what its partners did, plus or minus one seat. In fact the five traditional methods all have this "stability" property. Specifically, if whenever 2 parties with vote totals $\bar{p}$ and p^* get $\bar{a}$ and a^* seats by some M-solution, there is always an M-solution in which the coalesced party $\bar{p} + p^*$ gets no more than $\bar{a} + a^* + 1$ and no less than $\bar{a} + a^* - 1$ seats, then M is said to be *stable*.

THEOREM 9.3. *A divisor method with divisor criterion d is stable if and only if for all $a_1, a_2 \geq 0$*

$$d(a_1 + a_2) \leq d(a_1) + d(a_2) \leq d(a_1 + a_2 + 1).$$

PROOF OF THEOREM 9.3. Let M be a divisor method with divisor criterion $d(a)$ satisfying the given inequalities. Let $\mathbf{a} = (a_1,\ldots,a_s)$ be an M-allocation for vote totals $\mathbf{p} = (p_1,\ldots,p_s)$ and suppose parties 1 and 2 form a coalition having vote total $p_1 + p_2$. We show there is some solution in which the coalition gets between $a_1 + a_2 - 1$ and $a_1 + a_2 + 1$ seats.
First note that for any real numbers $x_1, x_2 \geq 0$, $y_1, y_2 > 0$,

$$\max\{x_1/y_1, x_2/y_2\} \geq (x_1 + x_2)/(y_1 + y_2) \geq \min\{x_1/y_1, x_2/y_2\}.$$

Therefore

$$(p_1 + p_2)/d(a_1 + a_2 - 2) \geq (p_1 + p_2)/(d(a_1 - 1) + d(a_2 - 1))$$
$$\geq \min\{p_1/d(a_1 - 1), p_2/d(a_2 - 1)\} \qquad (9.1)$$
$$\geq \max_{j \neq 1,2} p_j/d(a_j).$$

By assumption,

$$\min_{i \neq 1,2} p_i/d(a_i - 1) \geqq \max_{j \neq 1,2} p_j/d(a_j). \qquad (9.2)$$

Together (9.1) and (9.2) imply that the coalition receives its $(a_1 + a_2 - 1)^{st}$ seat at least as soon as any state $k \neq 1,2$ receives its a_k^{th} seat, hence there is a solution in which the coalition receives at least $a_1 + a_2 - 1$ seats. A similar argument shows that

$$(p_1 + p_2)/d(a_1 + a_2 + 1) \leqq (p_1 + p_2)/(d(a_1) + d(a_2))$$
$$\leqq \max\{p_1/d(a_1), p_2/d(a_2)\}$$
$$\leqq \min_{i \neq 1,2} p_i/d(a_i - 1),$$

and so there is a solution in which the coalition does not receive its $a_1 + a_2 + 2$ seat. Therefore there is a solution in which it receives between $a_1 + a_2 - 1$ and $a_1 + a_2 + 1$ seats.

Conversely, if stability is violated below, then (9.1) is false, from which it follows that $d(a_1 + a_2 - 2) > d(a_1 - 1) + d(a_2 - 2)$. Similarly, if stability is violated above, then $d(a_1) + d(a_2) > d(a_1 + a_2 + 1)$. □

PROPOSITION 9.1. *The five historical divisor methods are stable.*

PROPOSITION 9.2. *Hamilton's method is stable.*

PROPOSITION 9.3. *The divisor method defined by $d(0) = 1$, $d(1) = 2$, and $d(a) = a + 1/2$ for all $a \geqq 2$ is proportional but not stable.*

Another approach to the problem of coalitions and schisms is to ask whether there is a divisor method which is "coalition-neutral" in the sense that a coalition of two parties is just as likely to gain a seat as to lose one. The natural candidate for such a method is obviously Webster's. To see why Webster's method is approximately coalition-neutral we use the same probabilistic model as before: the possible vote-totals are assumed to be uniformly distributed and for mathematical convenience we assume a fixed divisor x instead of a fixed house size. Let $(p_1, \ldots, p_s)$ be the vote totals of s parties and suppose parties 1 and 2 merge. Let r_1 and r_2 be the remainders of the quotients p_1/x and p_2/x. By Webster's method the merged party will get one *less* seat than its partners received separately providing $r_1 \geq .5$, $r_2 \geq .5$, and $r_1 + r_2 \leq 1.5$. Since the remainders are independently and uniformly distributed between 0 and 1 the probability of the coalition losing a seat is $(1/2)^3 = 1/8$. Similarly the coalition gains a seat providing $r_1 \leq .5$, $r_2 \leq .5$ and $r_1 + r_2 \geq .5$ which also has probability 1/8. Thus Webster's method is coalition-neutral, and there is a high probability (75%) that a coalition gets the same as its two partners.

For an arbitrary divisor method with divisor criterion $d(a)$ the probability in this model that two parties with vote totals p_1 and p_2 and seats a_1 and a_2 gain a seat (p^+), or lose a seat (p^-), are

$$p^+ = 1/2[d(a_1) + d(a_2) - d(a_1 + a_2)]^2/[d(a_1) - d(a_1 - 1)][d(a_2) - d(a_2 - 1)]$$

$$p^- = 1/2[d(a_1 + a_2 - 1) - d(a_1 - 1) - d(a_2 - 1)]^2/[d(a_1) - d(a_1 - 1)][d(a_2) - d(a_2 - 1)].$$

Formally we call a method *coalition-neutral* if $p^+ = p^-$.

PROPOSITION 9.4. *Webster's method is the unique coalition-neutral divisor method.*

If the house size h is fixed in advance then Webster's method is only approximately coalition-neutral. The reason is, if the merged party gains a seat using the divisor x then $h + 1$ seats have been allocated and it is necessary to increase x slightly until some party loses a seat. This may or may not be the merged party. Similarly if the merged party loses a seat using x then only $h - 1$ seats have been allocated and x must be decreased until some party gains a seat. Again this might or might not be the merged party. The two cases approximately cancel out, but not exactly. Of course, the larger the number of states, the less likely it is that the merged party will be the one affected by shifting x. Hence the above estimates for p^+ and p^- are accurate for the case of a fixed house size when the number of states is large.

Percentage thresholds below which a party does not qualify for a seat can be imposed *ex ante* and a method such as Jefferson's or Webster's simply applied to all qualifying parties. Some political scientists (e.g., Rokkan, 1968; Rae, 1971) have also been concerned with the thresholds that are "built in" to specific methods: what percentage of the vote does a party have to get to qualify for a seat, or to surely get a seat? With Adams's, Dean's, and Hill's methods every party, however small, gets at least one seat (assuming there are enough to go around). For other methods, like Webster's and Jefferson's, the answer depends on the house size h and number of parties.

PROPOSITION 9.5. *Jefferson's method denies party* i *a seat if* $p_i/p < 1/(h + s - 1)$ *and guarantees it a seat if* $p_i/p \geq 1/h$.

PROPOSITION 9.6. *Webster's method denies party* i *a seat if* $p_i/p < 1/(2h + s - 1)$ *and guarantees it a seat if* $p_i/p \geq 1/(2h - s + 1)$.

REFERENCES FOR APPENDIX A

M. L. Balinski and H. P. Young. 1974. A New Method for Congressional Apportionment. *Proceedings of the National Academy of Sciences, USA* 71: 4602–06.

———. 1975. The Quota Method of Apportionment. *American Mathematical Monthly* 82: 701–30.

———. 1977a. Apportionment Schemes and the Quota Method. *American Mathematical Monthly* 84: 450–55.

———. 1977b. On Huntington Methods of Apportionment. *SIAM Journal on Applied Mathematics—Part C.* 33, no. 4: 607–18.

———. 1978a. The Jefferson Method of Apportionment. *SIAM Review* 20, no. 2: 278–84.

———. 1978b. Stability, Coalitions and Schisms in Proportional Representation Systems. *American Political Science Review,* 72, no. 3: 848–58.

———. 1979a. Criteria for Proportional Representation. *Operations Research,* 27, no. 1: 80–95.

———. 1979b. Quotatone Apportionment Methods. *Mathematics of Operations Research* 4, no. 1: 31–38.

———. 1980. The Webster Method of Apportionment. *Proceedings of the National Academy of Sciences, USA* 77, no. 1: 1–4.

G. Birkhoff. 1976. House Monotone Apportionment Schemes. *Proceedings of the National Academy of Sciences, U.S.A.* 73, 684–86.

G. A. Bliss, E. W. Brown, L. P. Eisenhart, and Raymond Pearl. 1929. Report to the President of the National Academy of Sciences. February 9, 1929. In *Congressional Record,* 70th Congress, 2nd Session, 70: 4966–67, March 2, 1929. Also in U.S., Congress, House, Committee on the Census. *Apportionment of Representatives: Hearings*. 76th Congress, 3rd Session, 1940.

O. R. Burt and C. C. Harris, Jr. 1963. Apportionment of the U.S. House of Representatives: a minimum range, integer solution, allocation problem. *Operations Research* 11: 648–52.

J. M. Cotteret and C. Emeri. 1970. *Les Systemes electoraux*. Paris: Presses Universitaires de France.

P. Diaconis and D. Freedman. 1978. On Rounding Percentages. Technical Report No. 106, Department of Statistics, Stanford University, Stanford, California.

A. K. Erlang. 1907. Flerfoldsvalg efter rene partilister. *Nyt Tidskrift for Matematik* Afdeling B, 18: 82–83.

J. Hill. 1911. Letter to William C. Huston, Chairman, House Committee on the Census, dated April 25, 1911. In U.S., Congress, House, *Apportionment of Representatives*, House Report 12, 62nd Congress, 1st Session, April 25, 1911.

V. d'Hondt. 1878. *La Representation proportionelle des partis par un électeur*. Ghent.

———. 1882. *Systeme pratique et raisonné de représentation proportionnelle*. Brussels: Muquardt.

E. V. Huntington. 1921. The Mathematical Theory of the Apportionment of Representatives. *Proceedings of the National Academy of Sciences, U.S.A.* 7: 123–27.

———. 1928. The Apportionment of Representatives in Congress. *Transactions of the American Mathematical Society* 30: 85–110.

———. 1940. *A Survey of Methods of Apportionment in Congress*. U.S., Congress, Senate Document no. 304, 76th Congress, 3rd Session.

A. Hylland. 1975. En merknad til en artikkel fra 1907 om forholdsvalg. *Nordisk Matematisk Tidskrift* 23: 15–19.

———. 1978. Allotment methods: procedures for proportional distribution of indivisible entities. Doctoral Dissertation, Harvard University, Cambridge, Mass.

J.-P. Leyvraz. 1977. Le Problème de la répartition proportionnelle. Ecole Polytechnique Fédérale de Lausanne, Thèse de Docteur ès Sciences, Départment de Mathématiques, Lausanne, Switzerland.

J. P. Mayberry. 1978a. Quota Methods for Congressional Apportionment Are Still Non-unique. *Proceedings of the National Academy of Sciences, U.S.A.* 75: 3537–39.

———. 1978b. A Spectrum of Quota Methods for Legislative Apportionment and Manpower Allocation. Brock University, St. Catharines, Ontario (mimeographed).

M. Morse, John von Neumann, and L. P. Eisenhart. 1948. Report to the

President of the National Academy of Sciences. Princeton, N.J., May 28, 1948.

F. W. Owens. 1921. On the Apportionment of Representatives. *Quarterly Publication of the American Statistical Association* December: 958–68.

Douglas W. Rae. 1971. *The Political Consequences of Electoral Laws*. Rev. ed. New Haven and London: Yale University Press.

Stein Rokkan. 1968. Elections: Electoral Systems. In *International Encyclopedia of the Social Sciences,* 5: 6–12. New York: Macmillan and Free Lance Press.

Sainte-Lagüe. 1910. La Représentation et la méthode des moindres carrés. *Comptes Rendus de l'Academie des Sciences* 151: 377–78.

J. W. Still. 1979. A Class of New Methods for Congressional Apportionment. *SIAM Journal on Applied Mathematics* 37, no. 2: 401–18.

W. F. Willcox. 1916. The Apportionment of Representatives. *The American Economic Review* 6, no. 1, Supplement (March): 3–16.

———. 1952. Last Words on the Apportionment Problem. *Law and Contemporary Problems* 17: 290–302.

APPENDIX B

Representative Populations and Apportionments for Nineteen United States Censuses, 1791–1970

Following are the representative populations from each of the nineteen United States censuses from 1791 to 1970, with apportionments by six principal methods: Adams's (also known as smallest divisors), Dean's (harmonic mean), Hill's (equal proportions, geometric mean, Huntington's), Webster's (major fractions, Sainte-Lagüe's, odd numbers), Jefferson's (greatest divisors, d'Hondt's, Hagenbach-Bischoff's, highest averages), and Hamilton's (Vinton's, greatest remainders).

The total number of seats is the number apportioned after each census. Several sources for populations were compared, including official census reports in each period, a Census Bureau compendium of past representative populations issued in 1840, data from Lawrence F. Schmeckebier's book *Congressional Apportionment* (The Brookings Institution, Washington, D.C., 1941), and data very kindly supplied to us by the Census Bureau. There are many small discrepancies in these sources, and several rather large ones. Therefore some choice had to be made. The rule generally followed was to use Schmeckebier's numbers unless there was a discrepancy of more than 10 persons with some other source. In this case we tended to side with the official census reports of the period. For example, Schmeckebier reports Ohio's 1830 representative population as 935,884, whereas the other three sources give 937,897, 937,900, and 937,901. Our choice in this case was 937,901, as found in the official 1830 census. In one case, North Carolina in 1820, Kershaw was not counted in the official report, but two other sources gave a population some 10,000 larger including Kershaw that are in perfect agreement: we chose the latter.

At the time of going to press, the 1980 populations and apportionments were still not certain, owing to court cases alleging substantial undercounts in various states.

1790 Congressional Allocations for House Size, 105

State	Population	Quota	Adam	Dean	Hill	Webs	Jeff	Ham
Virginia	630,560	18.310	18	18	18	18	19	18
Massachusetts	475,327	13.803	14	14	14	14	14	14
Pennsylvania	432,879	12.570	12	12	12	13	13	13
North Carolina	353,523	10.266	10	10	10	10	10	10
New York	331,589	9.629	10	10	10	10	10	10
Maryland	278,514	8.088	8	8	8	8	8	8
Connecticut	236,841	6.877	7	7	7	7	7	7
South Carolina	206,236	5.989	6	6	6	6	6	6
New Jersey	179,570	5.214	5	5	5	5	5	5
New Hampshire	141,822	4.118	4	4	4	4	4	4
Vermont	85,533	2.484	3	3	3	2	2	2
Georgia	70,835	2.057	2	2	2	2	2	2
Kentucky	68,705	1.995	2	2	2	2	2	2
Rhode Island	68,446	1.988	2	2	2	2	2	2
Delaware	55,540	1.613	2	2	2	2	1	2
Totals	3,615,920	105.0	105	105	105	105	105	105

1800 Congressional Allocations for House Size, 141

State	Population	Quota	Adam	Dean	Hill	Webs	Jeff	Ham
Virginia	747,362	21.550	21	22	22	22	22	22
Pennsylvania	601,863	17.355	17	17	17	17	18	17
New York	577,805	16.661	17	17	17	17	17	17
Massachusetts	574,564	16.568	16	17	17	17	17	17
North Carolina	424,785	12.249	12	12	12	12	12	12
Maryland	306,610	8.841	9	9	9	9	9	9
South Carolina	287,131	8.280	8	8	8	8	8	8
Connecticut	250,622	7.227	7	7	7	7	7	7
New Jersey	206,181	5.945	6	6	6	6	6	6
Kentucky	204,822	5.906	6	6	6	6	6	6
New Hampshire	183,855	5.302	6	5	5	5	5	5
Vermont	154,465	4.454	5	4	4	4	4	4
Georgia	138,807	4.003	4	4	4	4	4	4
Tennessee	100,169	2.888	3	3	3	3	3	3
Rhode Island	68,970	1.989	2	2	2	2	2	2
Delaware	61,812	1.782	2	2	2	2	1	2
Totals	4,889,823	141.0	141	141	141	141	141	141

1810 Congressional Allocations for House Size, 181

State	Population	Quota	Adam	Dean	Hill	Webs	Jeff	Ham
New York	953,043	26.199	26	26	26	26	27	26
Virginia	817,615	22.476	22	23	23	23	23	23
Pennsylvania	809,773	22.261	22	22	22	22	23	22
Massachusetts	700,745	19.263	19	19	19	19	20	19
North Carolina	487,971	13.414	13	14	14	14	13	14
Kentucky	374,287	10.289	10	10	10	10	10	10
South Carolina	336,569	9.252	9	9	9	9	9	9
Maryland	335,946	9.235	9	9	9	9	9	9
Connecticut	261,818	7.197	7	7	7	7	7	7
Tennessee	243,913	6.705	7	7	7	7	6	7
New Jersey	241,222	6.631	7	7	7	7	6	7
Ohio	230,760	6.344	7	6	6	6	6	6
Vermont	217,895	5.990	6	6	6	6	6	6
New Hampshire	214,460	5.895	6	6	6	6	6	6
Georgia	210,346	5.782	6	6	6	6	6	6
Rhode Island	76,888	2.114	3	2	2	2	2	2
Delaware	71,004	1.952	2	2	2	2	2	2
Totals	6,584,255	181.0	181	181	181	181	181	181

1820 Congressional Allocations for House Size, 213

State	Population	Quota	Adam	Dean	Hill	Webs	Jeff	Ham
New York	1,368,775	32.503	31	32	32	33	34	33
Pennsylvania	1,049,313	24.917	24	25	25	25	26	25
Virginia	895,303	21.260	21	21	21	21	22	21
Ohio	581,434	13.807	13	14	14	14	14	14
North Carolina	556,821	13.222	13	13	13	13	13	13
Massachusetts	523,287	12.426	12	12	12	12	13	12
Kentucky	513,623	12.197	12	12	12	12	12	12
South Carolina	399,351	9.483	9	9	9	9	10	9
Tennessee	390,769	9.279	9	9	9	9	9	9
Maryland	364,389	8.653	9	9	9	9	9	9
Maine	298,335	7.084	7	7	7	7	7	7
Georgia	281,126	6.676	7	7	7	7	7	7
Connecticut	275,208	6.535	7	6	7	7	6	7
New Jersey	274,551	6.520	7	6	6	7	6	7
New Hampshire	244,161	5.798	6	6	6	6	6	6
Vermont	235,764	5.598	6	6	6	6	5	6
Indiana	147,102	3.493	4	4	3	3	3	3
Louisiana	125,779	2.957	3	3	3	3	3	3

1820 Congressional Allocations for House Size, 213 (*continued*)

State	Population	Quota	Adam	Dean	Hill	Webs	Jeff	Ham
Alabama	111,147	2.639	3	3	3	3	2	3
Rhode Island	83,038	1.972	2	2	2	2	2	2
Delaware	70,943	1.685	2	2	2	2	1	2
Missouri	62,496	1.484	2	2	2	1	1	1
Mississippi	62,320	1.480	2	2	2	1	1	1
Illinois	54,843	1.302	2	1	1	1	1	1
Totals	8,969,878	213.0	213	213	213	213	213	213

1830 Congressional Allocations for House Size, 240

State	Population	Quota	Adam	Dean	Hill	Webs	Jeff	Ham
New York	1,918,578	38.593	37	38	39	39	40	39
Pennsylvania	1,348,072	27.117	26	27	27	27	28	27
Virginia	1,023,503	20.588	20	21	21	21	21	21
Ohio	937,901	18.867	18	19	19	19	19	19
North Carolina	639,747	12.869	13	13	13	13	13	13
Tennessee	625,263	12.578	12	13	13	13	13	13
Kentucky	621,832	12.509	12	12	12	12	13	12
Massachusetts	610,408	12.279	12	12	12	12	12	12
South Carolina	455,025	9.153	9	9	9	9	9	9
Georgia	429,811	8.646	9	9	9	9	9	9
Maryland	405,843	8.164	8	8	8	8	8	8
Maine	399,454	8.035	8	8	8	8	8	8
Indiana	343,031	6.900	7	7	7	7	7	7
New Jersey	319,922	6.435	7	6	6	6	6	6
Connecticut	297,665	5.988	6	6	6	6	6	6
Vermont	280,657	5.646	6	6	6	6	5	6
New Hampshire	269,326	5.418	6	5	5	5	5	5
Alabama	262,508	5.281	6	5	5	5	5	5
Louisiana	171,904	3.458	4	4	3	3	3	3
Illinois	157,147	3.161	4	3	3	3	3	3
Missouri	130,419	2.623	3	3	3	3	2	3
Mississippi	110,358	2.220	3	2	2	2	2	2
Rhode Island	97,194	1.955	2	2	2	2	2	2
Delaware	75,432	1.517	2	2	2	2	1	2
Totals	11,931,000	240.0	240	240	240	240	240	240

1840 Congressional Allocations for House Size, 223

State	Population	Quota	Adam	Dean	Hill	Webs	Jeff	Ham
New York	2,428,919	34.048	33	34	34	34	35	34
Pennsylvania	1,724,007	24.167	23	24	24	24	25	24
Ohio	1,519,466	21.300	21	21	21	21	22	21
Virginia	1,060,202	14.862	15	15	15	15	15	15
Tennessee	755,986	10.597	10	11	11	11	11	11
Massachusetts	737,699	10.341	10	10	10	10	10	10
Kentucky	706,925	9.910	10	10	10	10	10	10
Indiana	685,865	9.614	10	10	10	10	10	10
North Carolina	655,092	9.183	9	9	9	9	9	9
Georgia	579,014	8.116	8	8	8	8	8	8
Maine	501,793	7.034	7	7	7	7	7	7
Alabama	489,343	6.859	7	7	7	7	7	7
Illinois	476,051	6.673	7	7	7	7	6	7
South Carolina	463,583	6.498	7	7	7	7	6	7
Maryland	434,124	6.085	6	6	6	6	6	6
New Jersey	373,036	5.229	5	5	5	5	5	5
Missouri	360,406	5.052	5	5	5	5	5	5
Connecticut	310,008	4.346	5	4	4	4	4	4
Mississippi	297,567	4.171	4	4	4	4	4	4
Vermont	291,948	4.092	4	4	4	4	4	4
Louisiana	285,030	3.995	4	4	4	4	4	4
New Hampshire	284,574	3.989	4	4	4	4	4	4
Michigan	212,267	2.976	3	3	3	3	3	3
Rhode Island	108,828	1.526	2	2	2	2	1	2
Arkansas	89,600	1.256	2	1	1	1	1	1
Delaware	77,043	1.080	2	1	1	1	1	1
Totals	15,908,376	223.0	223	223	223	223	223	223

1850 Congressional Allocations for House Size, 234

State	Population	Quota	Adam	Dean	Hill	Webs	Jeff	Ham
New York	3,097,394	33.186	32	33	33	33	34	33
Pennsylvania	2,311,786	24.769	24	25	25	25	26	25
Ohio	1,980,329	21.218	20	21	21	21	22	21
Virginia	1,232,649	13.207	13	13	13	13	13	13
Massachusetts	994,499	10.655	11	11	11	11	11	11
Indiana	988,416	10.590	10	11	11	11	11	11
Tennessee	906,933	9.717	10	10	10	10	10	10
Kentucky	898,012	9.622	10	10	10	10	10	10

1850 Congressional Allocations for House Size, 234 (*continued*)

State	Population	Quota	Adam	Dean	Hill	Webs	Jeff	Ham
Illinois	851,470	9.123	9	9	9	9	9	9
North Carolina	753,620	8.074	8	8	8	8	8	8
Georgia	753,512	8.073	8	8	8	8	8	8
Missouri	647,074	6.933	7	7	7	7	7	7
Alabama	634,514	6.798	7	7	7	7	7	7
Maine	583,188	6.248	6	6	6	6	6	6
Maryland	546,887	5.859	6	6	6	6	6	6
South Carolina	514,513	5.513	6	5	6	6	5	6
New Jersey	489,466	5.244	5	5	5	5	5	5
Mississippi	482,595	5.171	5	5	5	5	5	5
Louisiana	419,824	4.498	5	5	4	4	4	4
Michigan	397,654	4.251	4	4	4	4	4	4
Connecticut	370,791	3.973	4	4	4	4	4	4
New Hampshire	317,964	3.407	4	3	3	3	3	3
Vermont	314,120	3.366	4	3	3	3	3	3
Wisconsin	305,391	3.272	4	3	3	3	3	3
Iowa	192,214	2.059	2	2	2	2	2	2
Arkansas	191,057	2.047	2	2	2	2	2	2
Texas	189,327	2.028	2	2	2	2	2	2
California	165,000	1.768	2	2	2	2	1	2
Rhode Island	147,544	1.581	2	2	2	2	1	2
Delaware	90,619	0.971	1	1	1	1	1	1
Florida	71,721	0.768	1	1	1	1	1	1
Totals	21,840,083	234.0	234	234	234	234	234	234

1860 Congressional Allocations for House Size, 241

State	Population	Quota	Adam	Dean	Hill	Webs	Jeff	Ham
New York	3,880,735	31.650	30	31	32	32	33	32
Pennsylvania	2,906,215	23.702	23	24	24	24	25	24
Ohio	2,339,511	19.080	18	19	19	19	20	19
Illinois	1,711,951	13.962	13	14	14	14	14	14
Virginia	1,399,972	11.418	11	11	11	11	12	11
Indiana	1,350,428	11.014	11	11	11	11	11	11
Massachusetts	1,231,066	10.040	10	10	10	10	10	10
Missouri	1,136,039	9.265	9	9	9	9	9	9
Kentucky	1,065,490	8.690	9	9	9	9	9	9
Tennessee	999,513	8.152	8	8	8	8	8	8
Georgia	872,406	7.115	7	7	7	7	7	7
North Carolina	860,197	7.015	7	7	7	7	7	7

1860 Congressional Allocations for House Size, 241 (*continued*)

State	Population	Quota	Adam	Dean	Hill	Webs	Jeff	Ham
Alabama	790,169	6.444	7	6	6	6	6	6
Wisconsin	775,881	6.328	6	6	6	6	6	6
Michigan	749,113	6.110	6	6	6	6	6	6
Iowa	674,913	5.504	6	6	6	6	5	6
New Jersey	672,027	5.481	6	5	5	6	5	6
Maryland	652,173	5.319	5	5	5	5	5	5
Maine	628,279	5.124	5	5	5	5	5	5
Mississippi	616,652	5.029	5	5	5	5	5	5
Louisiana	575,311	4.692	5	5	5	5	5	5
South Carolina	542,745	4.426	5	4	4	4	4	4
Texas	531,188	4.332	5	4	4	4	4	4
Connecticut	460,147	3.753	4	4	4	4	4	4
Arkansas	391,004	3.189	3	3	3	3	3	3
California	362,196	2.954	3	3	3	3	3	3
New Hampshire	326,073	2.659	3	3	3	3	2	3
Vermont	315,098	2.570	3	3	3	3	2	3
Rhode Island	174,620	1.424	2	2	2	1	1	1
Minnesota	172,023	1.403	2	2	1	1	1	1
Florida	115,726	0.944	1	1	1	1	1	1
Delaware	111,496	0.909	1	1	1	1	1	1
Kansas	107,206	0.874	1	1	1	1	1	1
Oregon	52,465	0.428	1	1	1	1	1	1
Totals	29,550,028	241.0	241	241	241	241	241	241

1870 Congressional Allocations for House Size, 292

State	Population	Quota	Adam	Dean	Hill	Webs	Jeff	Ham
New York	4,382,759	33.576	32	33	34	34	35	34
Pennsylvania	3,521,951	26.981	26	27	27	27	28	27
Ohio	2,665,260	20.418	20	20	20	20	21	20
Illinois	2,539,891	19.458	19	19	19	20	20	20
Missouri	1,721,295	13.187	13	13	13	13	14	13
Indiana	1,680,637	12.875	12	13	13	13	13	13
Massachusetts	1,457,351	11.165	11	11	11	11	11	11
Kentucky	1,321,011	10.120	10	10	10	10	10	10
Tennessee	1,258,520	9.641	9	10	10	10	10	10
Virginia	1,225,163	9.386	9	9	9	9	10	9
Iowa	1,194,020	9.147	9	9	9	9	9	9
Georgia	1,184,109	9.071	9	9	9	9	9	9
Michigan	1,184,059	9.071	9	9	9	9	9	9

1870 Congressional Allocations for House Size, 292 (*continued*)

State	Population	Quota	Adam	Dean	Hill	Webs	Jeff	Ham
North Carolina	1,071,361	8.208	8	8	8	8	8	8
Wisconsin	1,054,670	8.080	8	8	8	8	8	8
Alabama	996,992	7.638	8	8	8	8	8	8
New Jersey	906,096	6.942	7	7	7	7	7	7
Mississippi	827,922	6.343	6	6	6	6	6	6
Texas	818,579	6.271	6	6	6	6	6	6
Maryland	780,894	5.982	6	6	6	6	6	6
Louisiana	726,915	5.569	6	6	6	6	5	6
South Carolina	705,606	5.406	6	5	5	5	5	5
Maine	626,915	4.803	5	5	5	5	5	5
California	560,247	4.292	5	4	4	4	4	4
Connecticut	537,454	4.117	4	4	4	4	4	4
Arkansas	484,471	3.711	4	4	4	4	3	4
West Virginia	442,014	3.386	4	3	3	3	3	3
Minnesota	439,706	3.369	4	3	3	3	3	3
Kansas	364,399	2.792	3	3	3	3	2	3
Vermont	330,551	2.532	3	3	3	3	2	3
New Hampshire	318,300	2.438	3	3	2	2	2	2
Rhode Island	217,353	1.665	2	2	2	2	1	2
Florida	187,748	1.438	2	2	2	1	1	1
Delaware	125,015	0.958	1	1	1	1	1	1
Nebraska	122,993	0.942	1	1	1	1	1	1
Oregon	90,923	0.697	1	1	1	1	1	1
Nevada	42,491	0.326	1	1	1	1	1	1
Totals	38,115,641	292.0	292	292	292	292	292	292

1880 Congressional Allocations for House Size, 325

State	Population	Quota	Adam	Dean	Hill	Webs	Jeff	Ham
New York	5,082,871	33.459	32	34	34	34	35	34
Pennsylvania	4,282,891	28.193	27	28	28	28	29	28
Ohio	3,198,062	21.052	20	21	21	21	22	21
Illinois	3,077,871	20.261	20	20	20	20	21	20
Missouri	2,168,380	14.274	14	14	14	14	15	14
Indiana	1,978,301	13.023	13	13	13	13	13	13
Massachusetts	1,783,085	11.738	12	12	12	12	12	12
Kentucky	1,648,690	10.853	11	11	11	11	11	11
Michigan	1,636,937	10.776	11	11	11	11	11	11
Iowa	1,624,615	10.694	11	11	11	11	11	11
Texas	1,591,749	10.478	10	11	11	11	11	11

1880 Congressional Allocations for House Size, 325 (*continued*)

State	Population	Quota	Adam	Dean	Hill	Webs	Jeff	Ham
Tennessee	1,542,359	10.153	10	10	10	10	10	10
Georgia	1,542,180	10.152	10	10	10	10	10	10
Virginia	1,512,565	9.957	10	10	10	10	10	10
North Carolina	1,399,750	9.214	9	9	9	9	9	9
Wisconsin	1,315,497	8.660	9	9	9	9	9	9
Alabama	1,262,505	8.311	8	8	8	8	8	8
Mississippi	1,131,597	7.449	7	7	7	7	7	7
New Jersey	1,131,116	7.446	7	7	7	7	7	7
Kansas	996,096	6.557	7	7	7	7	6	7
South Carolina	995,577	6.554	7	7	7	7	6	7
Louisiana	939,946	6.187	6	6	6	6	6	6
Maryland	934,943	6.155	6	6	6	6	6	6
California	864,694	5.692	6	6	6	6	5	6
Arkansas	802,525	5.283	5	5	5	5	5	5
Minnesota	780,773	5.140	5	5	5	5	5	5
Maine	648,936	4.272	5	4	4	4	4	4
Connecticut	622,700	4.099	4	4	4	4	4	4
West Virginia	618,457	4.071	4	4	4	4	4	4
Nebraska	452,402	2.978	3	3	3	3	3	3
New Hampshire	346,991	2.284	3	2	2	2	2	2
Vermont	332,286	2.187	3	2	2	2	2	2
Rhode Island	276,531	1.820	2	2	2	2	1	2
Florida	269,493	1.774	2	2	2	2	1	2
Colorado	194,327	1.279	2	1	1	1	1	1
Oregon	174,768	1.150	2	1	1	1	1	1
Delaware	146,608	0.965	1	1	1	1	1	1
Nevada	62,266	0.410	1	1	1	1	1	1
Totals	49,371,340	325.0	325	325	325	325	325	325

1890 Congressional Allocations for House Size, 356

State	Population	Quota	Adam	Dean	Hill	Webs	Jeff	Ham
New York	5,997,853	34.490	33	34	34	34	36	34
Pennsylvania	5,258,014	30.236	29	30	30	30	31	30
Illinois	3,826,351	22.003	21	22	22	22	23	22
Ohio	3,672,316	21.117	20	21	21	21	22	21
Missouri	2,679,184	15.406	15	15	15	15	16	15
Massachusetts	2,238,943	12.875	13	13	13	13	13	13
Texas	2,235,523	12.855	13	13	13	13	13	13
Indiana	2,192,404	12.607	12	13	13	13	13	13

1890 Congressional Allocations for House Size, 356 (*continued*)

State	Population	Quota	Adam	Dean	Hill	Webs	Jeff	Ham
Michigan	2,093,889	12.041	12	12	12	12	12	12
Iowa	1,911,896	10.994	11	11	11	11	11	11
Kentucky	1,858,635	10.688	10	11	11	11	11	11
Georgia	1,837,353	10.565	10	11	11	11	11	11
Tennessee	1,767,518	10.164	10	10	10	10	10	10
Wisconsin	1,686,880	9.700	10	10	10	10	10	10
Virginia	1,655,980	9.523	9	10	10	10	9	10
North Carolina	1,617,947	9.304	9	9	9	9	9	9
Alabama	1,513,017	8.700	9	9	9	9	9	9
New Jersey	1,444,933	8.309	8	8	8	8	8	8
Kansas	1,427,096	8.206	8	8	8	8	8	8
Minnesota	1,301,826	7.486	8	7	7	7	7	7
Mississippi	1,289,600	7.416	7	7	7	7	7	7
California	1,208,130	6.947	7	7	7	7	7	7
South Carolina	1,151,149	6.620	7	7	7	7	6	7
Arkansas	1,128,179	6.487	7	6	6	6	6	6
Louisiana	1,118,587	6.432	7	6	6	6	6	6
Nebraska	1,058,910	6.089	6	6	6	6	6	6
Maryland	1,042,390	5.994	6	6	6	6	6	6
West Virginia	762,794	4.386	5	4	4	4	4	4
Connecticut	746,258	4.291	5	4	4	4	4	4
Maine	661,086	3.801	4	4	4	4	3	4
Colorado	412,198	2.370	3	2	2	2	2	2
Florida	391,422	2.251	3	2	2	2	2	2
New Hampshire	376,530	2.165	3	2	2	2	2	2
Washington	349,390	2.009	2	2	2	2	2	2
Rhode Island	345,506	1.987	2	2	2	2	2	2
Vermont	332,422	1.912	2	2	2	2	1	2
South Dakota	328,808	1.891	2	2	2	2	1	2
Oregon	313,767	1.804	2	2	2	2	1	2
North Dakota	182,719	1.051	1	1	1	1	1	1
Delaware	168,493	0.969	1	1	1	1	1	1
Montana	132,159	0.760	1	1	1	1	1	1
Idaho	84,385	0.485	1	1	1	1	1	1
Wyoming	60,705	0.349	1	1	1	1	1	1
Nevada	45,761	0.263	1	1	1	1	1	1
Totals	61,908,906	356.0	356	356	356	356	356	356

1900 Congressional Allocations for House Size, 386

State	Population	Quota	Adam	Dean	Hill	Webs	Jeff	Ham
New York	7,264,183	37.606	36	37	37	37	39	38
Pennsylvania	6,302,115	32.625	31	32	32	32	34	33
Illinois	4,821,550	24.960	24	25	25	25	26	25
Ohio	4,157,545	21.523	21	21	21	21	22	21
Missouri	3,106,665	16.083	16	16	16	16	16	16
Texas	3,048,710	15.783	15	16	16	16	16	16
Massachusetts	2,805,346	14.523	14	14	14	14	15	14
Indiana	2,516,462	13.027	13	13	13	13	13	13
Michigan	2,420,982	12.533	12	12	12	12	13	12
Iowa	2,231,853	11.554	11	11	11	12	12	11
Georgia	2,216,331	11.474	11	11	11	11	11	11
Kentucky	2,147,174	11.116	11	11	11	11	11	11
Wisconsin	2,067,385	10.703	11	11	11	11	11	11
Tennessee	2,020,616	10.460	10	10	10	10	10	10
North Carolina	1,893,810	9.804	10	10	10	10	10	10
New Jersey	1,883,669	9.751	10	10	10	10	10	10
Virginia	1,854,184	9.599	10	10	10	10	10	10
Alabama	1,828,697	9.467	9	9	9	9	9	9
Minnesota	1,749,626	9.058	9	9	9	9	9	9
Mississippi	1,551,270	8.031	8	8	8	8	8	8
California	1,483,504	7.680	8	8	8	8	8	8
Kansas	1,470,495	7.613	8	8	8	8	7	8
Louisiana	1,381,625	7.152	7	7	7	7	7	7
South Carolina	1,340,316	6.939	7	7	7	7	7	7
Arkansas	1,311,564	6.790	7	7	7	7	7	7
Maryland	1,188,044	6.150	6	6	6	6	6	6
Nebraska	1,066,300	5.520	6	5	6	5	5	5
West Virginia	958,800	4.964	5	5	5	5	5	5
Connecticut	908,420	4.703	5	5	5	5	4	5
Maine	694,466	3.595	4	4	4	4	3	3
Colorado	539,103	2.791	3	3	3	3	2	3
Florida	528,542	2.736	3	3	3	3	2	3
Washington	515,572	2.669	3	3	3	3	2	3
Rhode Island	428,556	2.219	3	2	2	2	2	2
Oregon	413,536	2.141	3	2	2	2	2	2
New Hampshire	411,588	2.131	2	2	2	2	2	2
South Dakota	390,638	2.022	2	2	2	2	2	2
Vermont	343,641	1.779	2	2	2	2	1	2

1900 Congressional Allocations for House Size, 386 (*continued*)

State	Population	Quota	Adam	Dean	Hill	Webs	Jeff	Ham
North Dakota	314,454	1.628	2	2	2	2	1	2
Utah	275,277	1.425	2	2	1	1	1	1
Montana	232,583	1.204	2	1	1	1	1	1
Delaware	184,735	0.956	1	1	1	1	1	1
Idaho	159,475	0.826	1	1	1	1	1	1
Wyoming	92,531	0.479	1	1	1	1	1	1
Nevada	40,670	0.211	1	1	1	1	1	1
Totals	74,562,608	386.0	386	386	386	386	386	386

1910 Congressional Allocations for House Size, 433

State	Population	Quota	Adam	Dean	Hill	Webs	Jeff	Ham
New York	9,108,934	43.308	41	43	43	43	45	43
Pennsylvania	7,665,111	36.444	35	36	36	36	38	36
Illinois	5,638,591	26.809	26	27	27	27	28	27
Ohio	4,767,121	22.665	22	22	22	22	23	23
Texas	3,896,542	18.526	18	18	18	18	19	18
Massachusetts	3,366,416	16.006	16	16	16	16	16	16
Missouri	3,293,335	15.658	15	16	16	16	16	16
Michigan	2,810,173	13.361	13	13	13	13	14	13
Indiana	2,700,876	12.841	13	13	13	13	13	13
Georgia	2,609,121	12.405	12	12	12	12	13	12
New Jersey	2,537,167	12.063	12	12	12	12	12	12
California	2,376,561	11.299	11	11	11	11	11	11
Wisconsin	2,332,853	11.091	11	11	11	11	11	11
Kentucky	2,289,905	10.887	11	11	11	11	11	11
Iowa	2,224,771	10.578	11	11	11	11	11	11
North Carolina	2,206,287	10.490	10	10	10	10	11	10
Tennessee	2,184,789	10.388	10	10	10	10	10	10
Alabama	2,138,093	10.166	10	10	10	10	10	10
Minnesota	2,074,376	9.863	10	10	10	10	10	10
Virginia	2,061,612	9.802	10	10	10	10	10	10
Mississippi	1,797,114	8.544	9	8	8	8	9	9
Kansas	1,690,949	8.040	8	8	8	8	8	8
Oklahoma	1,657,155	7.879	8	8	8	8	8	8
Louisiana	1,656,388	7.875	8	8	8	8	8	8
Arkansas	1,574,449	7.486	8	7	7	7	7	7
South Carolina	1,515,400	7.205	7	7	7	7	7	7
Maryland	1,295,346	6.159	6	6	6	6	6	6
West Virginia	1,221,119	5.806	6	6	6	6	6	6

1910 Congressional Allocations for House Size, 433 (*continued*)

State	Population	Quota	Adam	Dean	Hill	Webs	Jeff	Ham
Nebraska	1,192,214	5.668	6	6	6	6	5	6
Washington	1,140,134	5.421	6	5	5	5	5	5
Connecticut	1,114,756	5.300	6	5	5	5	5	5
Colorado	798,572	3.797	4	4	4	4	3	4
Florida	752,619	3.578	4	4	4	4	3	4
Maine	742,371	3.530	4	4	4	4	3	3
Oregon	672,765	3.199	4	3	3	3	3	3
South Dakota	575,676	2.737	3	3	3	3	2	3
North Dakota	574,403	2.731	3	3	3	3	2	3
Rhode Island	542,610	2.580	3	3	3	3	2	3
New Hampshire	430,572	2.047	2	2	2	2	2	2
Utah	371,864	1.768	2	2	2	2	1	2
Montana	366,338	1.742	2	2	2	2	1	2
Vermont	355,956	1.692	2	2	2	2	1	2
Idaho	323,440	1.538	2	2	2	2	1	1
Delaware	202,322	0.962	1	1	1	1	1	1
Wyoming	144,658	0.688	1	1	1	1	1	1
Nevada	80,293	0.382	1	1	1	1	1	1
Totals	91,072,117	433.0	433	433	433	433	433	433

1920 Congressional Allocations for House Size, 435

State	Population	Quota	Adam	Dean	Hill	Webs	Jeff	Ham
New York	10,380,589	42.919	41	42	42	43	45	43
Pennsylvania	8,720,017	36.053	34	36	36	36	37	36
Illinois	6,485,280	26.814	26	27	27	27	28	27
Ohio	5,759,394	23.813	23	24	24	24	25	24
Texas	4,663,228	19.280	19	19	19	19	20	19
Massachusetts	3,852,356	15.928	16	16	16	16	16	16
Michigan	3,668,412	15.167	15	15	15	15	15	15
California	3,426,031	14.165	14	14	14	14	14	14
Missouri	3,404,055	14.074	14	14	14	14	14	14
New Jersey	3,155,900	13.048	13	13	13	13	13	13
Indiana	2,930,390	12.116	12	12	12	12	12	12
Georgia	2,895,832	11.973	12	12	12	12	12	12
Wisconsin	2,631,305	10.879	11	11	11	11	11	11
North Carolina	2,559,123	10.581	10	10	10	11	11	11
Kentucky	2,416,630	9.992	10	10	10	10	10	10
Iowa	2,404,021	9.940	10	10	10	10	10	10
Minnesota	2,385,656	9.864	10	10	10	10	10	10

1920 Congressional Allocations for House Size, 435 (*continued*)

State	Population	Quota	Adam	Dean	Hill	Webs	Jeff	Ham
Alabama	2,348,174	9.709	10	10	10	10	10	10
Tennessee	2,337,885	9.666	10	10	10	10	10	10
Virginia	2,309,187	9.547	9	9	9	10	10	10
Oklahoma	2,028,283	8.386	8	8	8	8	8	8
Louisiana	1,798,509	7.436	8	7	7	7	7	7
Mississippi	1,790,618	7.403	7	7	7	7	7	7
Kansas	1,769,257	7.315	7	7	7	7	7	7
Arkansas	1,752,204	7.245	7	7	7	7	7	7
South Carolina	1,683,724	6.961	7	7	7	7	7	7
West Virginia	1,463,701	6.052	6	6	6	6	6	6
Maryland	1,449,661	5.994	6	6	6	6	6	6
Connecticut	1,380,631	5.708	6	6	6	6	6	6
Washington	1,354,596	5.601	6	6	6	6	5	6
Nebraska	1,296,372	5.360	6	5	5	5	5	5
Florida	968,470	4.004	4	4	4	4	4	4
Colorado	939,161	3.883	4	4	4	4	4	4
Oregon	783,389	3.239	4	3	3	3	3	3
Maine	768,014	3.175	3	3	3	3	3	3
North Dakota	643,953	2.662	3	3	3	3	2	3
South Dakota	631,239	2.610	3	3	3	3	2	3
Rhode Island	604,397	2.499	3	3	3	2	2	2
Montana	541,511	2.239	3	2	2	2	2	2
Utah	448,388	1.854	2	2	2	2	1	2
New Hampshire	443,083	1.832	2	2	2	2	1	2
Idaho	430,442	1.780	2	2	2	2	1	2
New Mexico	353,428	1.461	2	2	2	1	1	1
Vermont	352,428	1.457	2	2	2	1	1	1
Arizona	309,495	1.280	2	1	1	1	1	1
Delaware	223,003	0.922	1	1	1	1	1	1
Wyoming	193,487	0.800	1	1	1	1	1	1
Nevada	75,820	0.313	1	1	1	1	1	1
Totals	105,210,729	435.0	435	435	435	435	435	435

1930 Congressional Allocations for House Size, 435

State	Population	Quota	Adam	Dean	Hill	Webs	Jeff	Ham
New York	12,587,967	44.849	43	45	45	45	47	45
Pennsylvania	9,631,299	34.315	33	34	34	34	36	34
Illinois	7,630,388	27.186	26	27	27	27	28	27
Ohio	6,646,633	23.681	23	24	24	24	25	24
Texas	5,824,601	20.752	20	21	21	21	21	21
California	5,668,241	20.195	20	20	20	20	21	20

1930 Congressional Allocations for House Size, 435 (*continued*)

State	Population	Quota	Adam	Dean	Hill	Webs	Jeff	Ham
Michigan	4,842,052	17.251	17	17	17	17	18	17
Massachusetts	4,249,598	15.141	15	15	15	15	15	15
New Jersey	4,041,319	14.399	14	14	14	14	15	14
Missouri	3,629,110	12.930	13	13	13	13	13	13
Indiana	3,238,480	11.538	11	11	12	12	12	12
North Carolina	3,167,274	11.285	11	11	11	11	11	11
Wisconsin	2,931,721	10.445	10	10	10	10	11	10
Georgia	2,908,446	10.362	10	10	10	10	10	10
Alabama	2,646,242	9.428	9	9	9	9	9	9
Tennessee	2,616,497	9.322	9	9	9	9	9	9
Kentucky	2,614,575	9.315	9	9	9	9	9	9
Minnesota	2,551,583	9.091	9	9	9	9	9	9
Iowa	2,470,420	8.802	9	9	9	9	9	9
Virginia	2,421,829	8.629	9	9	9	9	9	9
Oklahoma	2,382,222	8.487	9	8	9	9	8	9
Louisiana	2,101,593	7.488	8	7	8	8	7	8
Mississippi	2,008,154	7.155	7	7	7	7	7	7
Kansas	1,879,498	6.696	7	7	7	7	7	7
Arkansas	1,854,444	6.607	7	7	7	7	6	7
South Carolina	1,738,760	6.195	6	6	6	6	6	6
West Virginia	1,729,199	6.161	6	6	6	6	6	6
Maryland	1,631,522	5.813	6	6	6	6	6	6
Connecticut	1,606,897	5.725	6	6	6	6	6	6
Washington	1,552,423	5.531	6	6	6	6	5	6
Florida	1,468,191	5.231	5	5	5	5	5	5
Nebraska	1,375,123	4.899	5	5	5	5	5	5
Colorado	1,034,849	3.687	4	4	4	4	3	4
Oregon	950,379	3.386	4	3	3	3	3	3
Maine	797,418	2.841	3	3	3	3	2	3
Rhode Island	687,497	2.449	3	3	2	2	2	2
North Dakota	673,340	2.399	3	2	2	2	2	2
South Dakota	673,005	2.398	3	2	2	2	2	2
Montana	524,729	1.870	2	2	2	2	1	2
Utah	505,741	1.802	2	2	2	2	1	2
New Hampshire	465,292	1.658	2	2	2	2	1	2
Idaho	441,536	1.573	2	2	2	2	1	2
New Mexico	395,982	1.411	2	2	1	1	1	1
Arizona	389,375	1.387	2	2	1	1	1	1
Vermont	359,611	1.281	2	1	1	1	1	1
Delaware	238,380	0.849	1	1	1	1	1	1
Wyoming	223,630	0.797	1	1	1	1	1	1
Nevada	86,390	0.308	1	1	1	1	1	1
Totals	122,093,455	435.0	435	435	435	435	435	435

1940 Congressional Allocations for House Size, 435

State	Population	Quota	Adam	Dean	Hill	Webs	Jeff	Ham
New York	13,479,142	44.757	43	45	45	45	47	45
Pennsylvania	9,900,180	32.873	32	33	33	33	34	33
Illinois	7,897,241	26.222	25	26	26	26	27	26
Ohio	6,907,612	22.936	22	23	23	23	24	23
California	6,907,387	22.936	22	23	23	23	24	23
Texas	6,414,824	21.300	21	21	21	21	22	21
Michigan	5,256,106	17.453	17	17	17	18	18	17
Massachusetts	4,316,721	14.333	14	14	14	14	15	14
New Jersey	4,160,165	13.814	14	14	14	14	14	14
Missouri	3,784,664	12.567	12	13	13	13	13	13
North Carolina	3,571,623	11.859	12	12	12	12	12	12
Indiana	3,427,796	11.382	11	11	11	11	12	11
Wisconsin	3,137,587	10.418	10	10	10	10	11	10
Georgia	3,123,723	10.372	10	10	10	10	10	10
Tennessee	2,915,841	9.682	10	10	10	10	10	10
Kentucky	2,845,627	9.449	9	9	9	9	9	9
Alabama	2,832,961	9.407	9	9	9	9	9	9
Minnesota	2,792,300	9.272	9	9	9	9	9	9
Virginia	2,677,773	8.891	9	9	9	9	9	9
Iowa	2,538,268	8.428	9	8	8	8	8	8
Louisiana	2,363,880	7.849	8	8	8	8	8	8
Oklahoma	2,336,434	7.758	8	8	8	8	8	8
Mississippi	2,183,796	7.251	7	7	7	7	7	7
Arkansas	1,949,387	6.473	7	7	7	6	6	7
West Virginia	1,901,974	6.315	7	6	6	6	6	6
South Carolina	1,899,804	6.308	6	6	6	6	6	6
Florida	1,897,414	6.300	6	6	6	6	6	6
Maryland	1,821,244	6.047	6	6	6	6	6	6
Kansas	1,801,028	5.980	6	6	6	6	6	6
Washington	1,736,191	5.765	6	6	6	6	6	6
Connecticut	1,709,242	5.675	6	6	6	6	5	6
Nebraska	1,315,834	4.369	5	4	4	4	4	4
Colorado	1,123,296	3.730	4	4	4	4	3	4
Oregon	1,089,684	3.618	4	4	4	4	3	4
Maine	847,226	2.813	3	3	3	3	2	3
Rhode Island	713,346	2.369	3	2	2	2	2	2
South Dakota	642,961	2.135	3	2	2	2	2	2
North Dakota	641,935	2.132	3	2	2	2	2	2
Montana	559,456	1.858	2	2	2	2	1	2
Utah	550,310	1.827	2	2	2	2	1	2
New Mexico	531,818	1.766	2	2	2	2	1	2
Idaho	524,873	1.743	2	2	2	2	1	2
Arizona	499,261	1.658	2	2	2	2	1	2
New Hampshire	491,524	1.632	2	2	2	2	1	2

1940 Congressional Allocations for House Size, 435 (*continued*)

State	Population	Quota	Adam	Dean	Hill	Webs	Jeff	Ham
Vermont	359,231	1.193	2	1	1	1	1	1
Delaware	266,505	0.885	1	1	1	1	1	1
Wyoming	250,742	0.833	1	1	1	1	1	1
Nevada	110,247	0.366	1	1	1	1	1	1
Totals	131,006,184	435.0	435	435	435	435	435	435

1950 Congressional Allocations for House Size, 435

State	Population	Quota	Adam	Dean	Hill	Webs	Jeff	Ham
New York	14,830,192	43.038	41	43	43	43	45	43
California	10,586,223	30.722	29	30	30	31	32	31
Pennsylvania	10,498,012	30.466	29	30	30	30	31	30
Illinois	8,712,176	25.283	24	25	25	25	26	25
Ohio	7,946,627	23.061	22	23	23	23	24	23
Texas	7,711,194	22.378	22	22	22	22	23	22
Michigan	6,371,766	18.491	18	18	18	18	19	18
New Jersey	4,835,329	14.032	14	14	14	14	14	14
Massachusetts	4,690,514	13.612	13	14	14	14	14	14
North Carolina	4,061,929	11.788	12	12	12	12	12	12
Missouri	3,954,653	11.477	11	11	11	11	11	11
Indiana	3,934,224	11.417	11	11	11	11	11	11
Georgia	3,444,578	9.996	10	10	10	10	10	10
Wisconsin	3,434,575	9.967	10	10	10	10	10	10
Virginia	3,318,680	9.631	10	10	10	10	10	10
Tennessee	3,291,718	9.553	10	9	9	9	9	10
Alabama	3,061,743	8.885	9	9	9	9	9	9
Minnesota	2,982,483	8.655	9	9	9	9	9	9
Kentucky	2,944,806	8.546	9	8	8	8	8	8
Florida	2,771,305	8.042	8	8	8	8	8	8
Louisiana	2,683,516	7.788	8	8	8	8	8	8
Iowa	2,621,073	7.606	8	8	8	8	7	8
Washington	2,378,963	6.904	7	7	7	7	7	7
Maryland	2,343,001	6.799	7	7	7	7	7	7
Oklahoma	2,233,351	6.481	7	6	6	6	6	6
Mississippi	2,178,914	6.323	6	6	6	6	6	6
South Carolina	2,117,027	6.144	6	6	6	6	6	6
Connecticut	2,007,280	5.825	6	6	6	6	6	6
West Virginia	2,005,552	5.820	6	6	6	6	6	6
Arkansas	1,909,511	5.541	6	6	6	6	5	5
Kansas	1,905,299	5.529	6	6	6	5	5	5
Oregon	1,521,341	4.415	5	4	4	4	4	4

1950 Congressional Allocations for House Size, 435 (*continued*)

State	Population	Quota	Adam	Dean	Hill	Webs	Jeff	Ham
Nebraska	1,325,510	3.847	4	4	4	4	4	4
Colorado	1,325,089	3.845	4	4	4	4	4	4
Maine	913,774	2.652	3	3	3	3	2	3
Rhode Island	791,896	2.298	3	2	2	2	2	2
Arizona	749,587	2.175	3	2	2	2	2	2
Utah	688,862	1.999	2	2	2	2	2	2
New Mexico	681,187	1.977	2	2	2	2	2	2
South Dakota	652,740	1.894	2	2	2	2	1	2
North Dakota	619,636	1.798	2	2	2	2	1	2
Montana	591,024	1.715	2	2	2	2	1	2
Idaho	588,637	1.708	2	2	2	2	1	2
New Hampshire	533,242	1.547	2	2	2	2	1	2
Vermont	377,747	1.096	2	1	1	1	1	1
Delaware	318,085	0.923	1	1	1	1	1	1
Wyoming	290,529	0.843	1	1	1	1	1	1
Nevada	160,083	0.465	1	1	1	1	1	1
Totals	149,895,183	435.0	435	435	435	435	435	435

1960 Congressional Allocations for House Size, 435

State	Population	Quota	Adam	Dean	Hill	Webs	Jeff	Ham
New York	16,782,304	40.884	39	41	41	41	42	41
California	15,717,204	38.290	37	38	38	38	40	38
Pennsylvania	11,319,366	27.576	26	27	27	27	28	28
Illinois	10,081,158	24.559	24	24	24	24	25	25
Ohio	9,706,397	23.646	23	24	24	24	24	24
Texas	9,579,677	23.338	22	23	23	23	24	23
Michigan	7,823,194	19.059	18	19	19	19	20	19
New Jersey	6,066,782	14.780	14	15	15	15	15	15
Massachusetts	5,148,578	12.543	12	12	12	13	13	13
Florida	4,951,560	12.063	12	12	12	12	12	12
Indiana	4,662,498	11.359	11	11	11	11	11	11
North Carolina	4,556,155	11.100	11	11	11	11	11	11
Missouri	4,319,813	10.524	10	10	10	10	11	10
Virginia	3,966,949	9.664	10	10	10	10	10	10
Wisconsin	3,951,777	9.627	10	10	10	10	10	10
Georgia	3,943,116	9.606	10	10	10	10	10	10
Tennessee	3,567,089	8.690	9	9	9	9	9	9
Minnesota	3,413,864	8.317	8	8	8	8	8	8
Alabama	3,266,740	7.958	8	8	8	8	8	8
Louisiana	3,257,022	7.935	8	8	8	8	8	8
Maryland	3,100,689	7.554	8	8	8	8	7	8

1960 Congressional Allocations for House Size, 435 (*continued*)

State	Population	Quota	Adam	Dean	Hill	Webs	Jeff	Ham
Kentucky	3,038,156	7.401	7	7	7	7	7	7
Washington	2,853,214	6.951	7	7	7	7	7	7
Iowa	2,757,537	6.718	7	7	7	7	7	7
Connecticut	2,535,234	6.176	6	6	6	6	6	6
South Carolina	2,382,594	5.804	6	6	6	6	6	6
Oklahoma	2,328,284	5.672	6	6	6	6	5	6
Kansas	2,178,611	5.307	5	5	5	5	5	5
Mississippi	2,178,141	5.306	5	5	5	5	5	5
West Virginia	1,860,421	4.532	5	5	5	5	4	4
Arkansas	1,786,272	4.352	5	4	4	4	4	4
Oregon	1,768,687	4.309	5	4	4	4	4	4
Colorado	1,753,947	4.273	5	4	4	4	4	4
Nebraska	1,411,330	3.438	4	3	3	3	3	3
Arizona	1,302,161	3.172	3	3	3	3	3	3
Maine	969,265	2.361	3	2	2	2	2	2
New Mexico	951,023	2.317	3	2	2	2	2	2
Utah	890,627	2.170	3	2	2	2	2	2
Rhode Island	859,488	2.094	2	2	2	2	2	2
South Dakota	680,514	1.658	2	2	2	2	1	2
Montana	674,767	1.644	2	2	2	2	1	2
Idaho	667,191	1.625	2	2	2	2	1	2
Hawaii	632,772	1.542	2	2	2	2	1	2
North Dakota	632,446	1.541	2	2	2	2	1	1
New Hampshire	606,921	1.479	2	2	2	1	1	1
Delaware	446,292	1.087	2	1	1	1	1	1
Vermont	389,881	0.950	1	1	1	1	1	1
Wyoming	330,066	0.804	1	1	1	1	1	1
Nevada	285,278	0.695	1	1	1	1	1	1
Alaska	226,167	0.551	1	1	1	1	1	1
Totals	178,559,219	435.0	435	435	435	435	435	435

1970 Congressional Allocations for House Size, 435

State	Population	Quota	Adam	Dean	Hill	Webs	Jeff	Ham
California	20,098,863	42.847	41	42	43	43	44	43
New York	18,338,055	39.093	37	39	39	39	41	39
Pennsylvania	11,884,314	25.335	24	25	25	25	26	25
Texas	11,298,787	24.087	23	24	24	24	25	24
Illinois	11,184,320	23.843	23	24	24	24	25	24
Ohio	10,730,200	22.875	22	23	23	23	24	23
Michigan	8,937,196	19.052	19	19	19	19	20	19
New Jersey	7,208,035	15.366	15	15	15	15	16	15

1970 Congressional Allocations for House Size, 435 (*continued*)

State	Population	Quota	Adam	Dean	Hill	Webs	Jeff	Ham
Florida	6,855,702	14.615	14	15	15	15	15	15
Massachusetts	5,726,676	12.208	12	12	12	12	12	12
Indiana	5,228,156	11.145	11	11	11	11	11	11
North Carolina	5,125,230	10.926	11	11	11	11	11	11
Missouri	4,718,034	10.058	10	10	10	10	10	10
Virginia	4,690,742	10.000	10	10	10	10	10	10
Georgia	4,627,306	9.864	10	10	10	10	10	10
Wisconsin	4,447,013	9.480	9	9	9	9	9	9
Tennessee	3,961,060	8.444	8	8	8	8	8	8
Maryland	3,953,698	8.428	8	8	8	8	8	8
Minnesota	3,833,173	8.172	8	8	8	8	8	8
Louisiana	3,672,008	7.828	8	8	8	8	8	8
Alabama	3,475,885	7.410	8	7	7	7	7	7
Washington	3,443,487	7.341	7	7	7	7	7	7
Kentucky	3,246,481	6.921	7	7	7	7	7	7
Connecticut	3,050,693	6.503	7	6	6	7	6	7
Iowa	2,846,920	6.069	6	6	6	6	6	6
South Carolina	2,617,320	5.580	6	6	6	6	5	6
Oklahoma	2,585,486	5.512	6	6	6	6	5	6
Kansas	2,265,846	4.830	5	5	5	5	5	5
Mississippi	2,233,848	4.762	5	5	5	5	5	5
Colorado	2,226,771	4.747	5	5	5	5	4	5
Oregon	2,110,810	4.500	5	5	4	5	4	5
Arkansas	1,942,303	4.141	4	4	4	4	4	4
Arizona	1,787,620	3.811	4	4	4	4	4	4
West Virginia	1,763,331	3.759	4	4	4	4	3	4
Nebraska	1,496,820	3.191	4	3	3	3	3	3
Utah	1,067,810	2.276	3	2	2	2	2	2
New Mexico	1,026,664	2.189	3	2	2	2	2	2
Maine	1,006,320	2.145	3	2	2	2	2	2
Rhode Island	957,798	2.042	2	2	2	2	2	2
Hawaii	784,901	1.673	2	2	2	2	1	2
New Hampshire	746,284	1.591	2	2	2	2	1	2
Idaho	719,921	1.535	2	2	2	2	1	2
Montana	701,573	1.496	2	2	2	1	1	1
South Dakota	673,247	1.435	2	2	2	1	1	1
North Dakota	624,181	1.331	2	1	1	1	1	1
Delaware	551,928	1.177	2	1	1	1	1	1
Nevada	492,396	1.050	1	1	1	1	1	1
Vermont	448,327	0.956	1	1	1	1	1	1
Wyoming	335,719	0.716	1	1	1	1	1	1
Alaska	304,067	0.648	1	1	1	1	1	1
Totals	204,053,325	435.0	435	435	435	435	435	435

Notes

CHAPTER 1

1. White v. Weiser, 412 U.S. 783 (1973).

CHAPTER 2

1. J. A. O. Larson, *Representative Government in Greek and Roman History* (Berkeley and Los Angeles: University of California Press, 1955). It is interesting to note that in the case of the Boeatian Confederacy of Greek City States (447–386 B.C.) representation in the federal assembly and courts was allocated proportionally to populations, and taxes were in turn proportional to representation.

2. John Locke, *Two Treatises of Government* (New York: Mentor Book, 1965), first published 1689, Second treatise, chapter 13, para 158, pp. 419–20.

3. Max Farrand ed., *The Records of the Federal Convention of 1787* (New Haven: Yale University Press, 1911), 1: 485.

4. Farrand, ed., *Records,* 1: 580. From statement of Edmund Randolph of Virginia.

5. Joseph Story, *Commentaries on the Constitution of the United States,* 2nd. ed. (Boston: Charles C. Little & James Brown, 1851), 1: 441–42.

6. See *Elections to the European Parliament by Direct Universal Suffrage,* Draft Convention (Doc. 368/74). Resolution adopted January 14, 1975. The minima were: Germany, United Kingdom, Italy and France, each 36, The Netherlands and Belgium, each 14; Denmark and Ireland, each 10; and Luxembourg, 6.

7. Farrand, ed., *Records,* 2: 10. From statement of James Wilson of Pennsylvania.

CHAPTER 3

1. The initial distribution is given in article I, section 2:

and until such enumeration shall be made, the State of New Hampshire shall be entitled to chuse three; Massachusetts, eight; Rhode Island and Providence Plantations, one; Connecticut, five; New York, six; New Jersey, four; Pennsylvania, eight; Delaware, one; Maryland, six; Virginia, ten; North Carolina, five; South Carolina, five; and Georgia, three.

2. The prominent role of the ratio 30,000 is underlined by the language found in the first of the twelve amendments introduced by James Madison in 1789 and accepted by Congress:

> After the first enumeration required by the first article of the Constitution, there shall be one Representative for every thirty thousand, until the number shall amount to one hundred, after which the proportion shall be so regulated by Congress that there shall not be less than one hundred Representatives, nor less than one Representative for every forty thousand persons, until the number of Representatives shall amount to two hundred; after which, the proportion shall be so regulated by Congress that there shall not be less than two hundred Representatives, nor more than one Representative for every fifty thousand persons.

Ten states ratified the proposed amendment; eleven were necessary. The ten amendments that received the requisite eleven assents—and which the Federalists had pledged to introduce to gain further adherents to the Constitution—are collectively known as the Bill of Rights.

3. Douglas Southall Freeman, *George Washington: A Biography* (New York: Charles Scribner's Sons, 1954), 6: 343–49.

4. *Debates and Proceedings in the Congress of the United States,* vol. 3 (Washington, D.C.: Gales and Seaton, 1849). From speech of Representative John Page of Virginia, November 15, 1791, pp. 179–80.

5. Ibid. From speech of Representative Theodore Sedgwick of Massachusetts, December 13, 1791, p. 248.

6. Ibid. From speech of Representative William B. Giles of Virginia, November 11, 1791, p. 179.

7. Ibid. From speech of Representative John Laurance of New York, November 10, 1791, p. 172.

8. Joseph Story, *Commentaries,* 1: 445–46.

9. *Debates,* from speech of Representative Fisher Ames of Massachusetts, December 19, 1791, 3: 254–62.

10. Gaillard Hunt, ed., *The Writings of James Madison* (New York and London: G. P. Putnam's Sons, 1906), 6: 96–97.

11. Freeman, *George Washington,* 6: 345.

12. Harold C. Syrett, ed., *The Papers of Alexander Hamilton* (New York and London: Columbia University Press, 1966), 11: 226–30.

13. Hamilton's calculations are at variance with his words. Instead of calculating the true quotas, as he advocated in point II, he apparently erred in dividing the states' populations by 30,000 instead of 30,133 (i.e., 3,615,920 divided by 120). This gives the fractions shown in Table 3.2 and only eight states are assigned additional seats.

14. Thomas Jefferson, "Opinion on the Bill Apportioning Representation," in *The Works of Thomas Jefferson,* ed. Paul Leicester Ford (New York and London: G. P. Putnam's Sons, 1904), 6: 463–64 and 465–66.

15. Thomas Jefferson, *The Anas* in *The Writings of Thomas Jefferson,* ed. Andrew A. Lipscomb, (Washington, D.C.: Thomas Jefferson Memorial Association, 1904), 1: 333.

16. Ibid., p. 307–308.

17. John C. Fitzpatrick, ed., *The Writings of George Washington* (Washington, D.C.: U.S. Government Printing Office, 1931–44) 32: 16–17.

18. Jefferson, *The Anas*, p. 308.

19. Jefferson, "Opinion on the Bill Apportioning Representation," p. 469.

CHAPTER 4

1. *Debates and Proceedings in the Congress of the United States,* 17th Congress, 1st Session (Washington, D.C.: Gales and Seaton, 1855). From speech of Representative William Lowndes of South Carolina, February 1, 1822, 38:871.

2. The change from 48,000 to 47,000 enhanced the fortunes of three states. The quotient of Georgia went from 8.954 to 9.011, of Kentucky from 12.955 to 13.036, and of New York from 39.970 to 40.222. The respective current delegations of these three were 7, 12, and 34, a total of 53 votes in a House of 213.

3. *Register of Debates in Congress,* 22nd Congress, 1st Session (Washington, D.C.: Gales and Seaton, 1833). From speech of Representative Robert Craig of Virginia, January 13, 1832, 8: 1545.

4. John Quincy Adams, *The Memoirs of John Quincy Adams,* ed. Charles Francis Adams (Philadelphia: J. B. Lippincott & Co., 1876), 8: 474.

5. Ibid., pp. 471–72.

6. Letter dated February 28, 1832, House of Representatives. In Microfilm edition of the Papers of Daniel Webster, Ann Arbor, Mich., University Microfilms in Collaboration with Dartmouth College Library, Hanover, N.H., 1971, reel 8, frames 009886–009894.

7. John Quincy Adams, *Memoirs,* 8: 472.

8. A plaque in the Union Oyster House in Boston states that for lunch Webster habitually downed six dozen oysters, each plate washed down with a tall tumbler of brandy and water.

9. Irving H. Bartlett, *Daniel Webster* (New York: W. W. Norton and Co., 1978).

10. Daniel Webster, *The Writings and Speeches of Daniel Webster,* National Edition (Boston: Little, Brown & Co., 1903), 6: 121. (Extract of letter from James Dean).

11. Ibid., pp. 107–09.

12. Ibid., pp. 111–12.

13. Ibid., p. 120. Webster also proposed the simple rounding rule but recognized it would not work in all cases; indeed it did not for the 1830 case.

14. Ibid., p. 117.

15. *Register of Debates in Congress,* 8: 862. From speech of Senator Mahlon Dickerson of New Jersey, April 25, 1832.

16. Except for the return to 435 seats after the House had temporarily risen to 437 with the addition of Alaska and Hawaii in 1959.

CHAPTER 5

1. U.S. Congress, House, *Congressional Globe,* 42nd Congress, 2nd Session, 1872, p. 110. From speech of Representative Samuel S. Cox of New York, December 13, 1871.

2. The fact was clearly pointed out by the then representative, later president, James A. Garfield: "Suppose we put these nine in and then take the total population . . . and divide it by the new total of the House . . . we are then left with other States having fractions

which, if these nine be admitted, ought equitably to be entitled to additional members.''
Speech, May 8, 1872. Ibid., pp. 3198–99.

3. The decision in the electoral college depended on four states from which rival returns were received. In one of these, Oregon, only one electoral vote was in balance because of a legal technicality. But, in the three Southern states of South Carolina, Florida, and Louisiana the Democrats had won victories, which were later upset by Republican-controlled election boards. Extensive voting irregularities had been practiced by both sides. The event, unanticipated by the Constitution, led to the creation of a special commission consisting of five senators, five representatives and five Supreme Court justices, of which seven were Republicans, seven were Democrats, and one was a justice supposed to be neutral between the parties. The commission voted in all instances in favor of Hayes, eight against seven, the one "neutral" justice joining with the Republicans. Had the Webster or Hamilton method been used and the commission's votes been the same, Tilden would have been the victor instead with 185 electoral votes. There was talk of blocking the inauguration of Hayes, but an agreement was reached at Wormley's Hotel in Washington by which federal troops would be withdrawn from the South and the Reconstruction governments ended. For further discussion see James Evan Shaw, ''The Electoral College and Unstable Congressional Apportionment,'' in *Direct Popular Election of the President and Vice President of the United States:* Hearings on S. J. Res. 28, 96th Congress, 1st session, March 27, 30, April 3, and 9, 1979, pp. 463–476.

4. House, *Congressional Globe,* 42nd Congress, 2nd Session, p. 60. From speech of Representative Ulysses Mercur of Pennsylvania, December 11, 1871.

5. Letter in U.S., Congress, House, *Apportionment Among the Several States, House of Representatives,* 56th Congress, 2nd Session, 1900, H. Rept. 2130. Also in *Congressional Record,* 47th Congress, 1st Session, 1881, 12:704–05. Tables prepared by Seaton in *Congressional Record,* ibid., pp. 776–79.

6. House, *Congressional Record,* ibid., p. 970. From speech of Representative Roger Q. Mills of Texas, February 7, 1882.

7. Ibid., p. 1032. From speech of Representative Samuel Cox of New York, February 9, 1882.

8. Reprinted in House, *Apportionment Among the Several States,* 56th Congress, 2nd Session, 1900. H. Rept. 2130.

9. House, *Congressional Record,* 56th Congress, 2nd Session, 1901, 34: 591–93. From speech of Representative John E. Littlefield of Maine, January 5, 1901.

10. Ibid., pp. 729–30. From speech of Representative Albert J. Hopkins of Illinois, January 8, 1901.

11. See *Congressional Record,* ibid., appendix, pp. 67–68, speech of Representative Edgar D. Crumpacker of Indiana, January 7, 1901. The population data used by the House was different in four figures from the representative populations later published in the census of 1900. Connecticut's representative population was underestimated by 65, New York's by 882; whereas Maryland's was overestimated by 2,006 and Nebraska's by 2,239. Had the final published census figures been used as the basis of apportionment, Iowa would have gained one seat and Nebraska lost one seat by Webster's method. For both sets of data the Webster and Hamilton solutions are different. This difference between the data used by Congress and the data ultimately published by the Census Bureau has confused students of apportionment. Lawrence F. Schmeckebier's book *Congressional Apportionment* (Washington, D.C.: The Brookings Institution, 1941), contains a history in which it is affirmed that the reapportionment of 1900 is a Hamilton solution. But he gives the census

data, not that used by Congress. Moreover, even by the census data the actual apportionment is not a Hamilton solution, so he errs in two ways. The book contains other errors of
similar type.

12. The possibility that a method could harbor such behavior was recognized, however, in just this decade in the context of proportional representation systems. (See A. K.
Erlang, "Flerfoldsvlag efter rene partilister," *Nyt Tidskrift for Matematik,* Afdeling B,
vol. 18 (1907): 82–83.

CHAPTER 6

1. Biographical information concerning Willcox was kindly given to us orally by
Frank W, Notestein, and also comes from his short article, "Walter F. Willcox—An
Appreciation," *Cornell Alumni News* 67 (January 1965): 19.

2. The letter of Walter F. Willcox addressed to E. D. Crumpacker, chairman of the
Committee on the Census, is dated December 21, 1910. It appears, together with the tables
prepared by Willcox, in U.S., Congress, House, *Apportionment of Representatives,* H.
Rept. 1911, 61st Congress, 3rd Session, January 13, 1911.

3. House, *Apportionment of Representatives,* H. Rept. 12, 62nd Congress, 1st
Session, April 25, 1911.

4. Ibid. The letter of Joseph A. Hill addressed to William C. Huston, chairman of
the House Committee on Census, is dated April 25, 1911. It appears, together with the
tables he prepared, in this Report,

5. Hill, in his 1911 letter, had placed the emphasis on the basic criterion, and only
added a computational rule for convenience. His rule proposed to begin, as Hamilton did,
by giving to each state the whole number in its quota, and then allocating the remaining seats
so as to minimize the relative inequality between states. It is, however, possible to find
examples in which an apportionment satisfying the relative difference test gives to some
state less than the whole number in its quota. See, for example, Table 10.1. Such examples
are extremely rare and can be expected almost never to occur in practice. Technically, Hill
did make an error that Huntington corrected.

6. Letter of Edward V. Huntington to Representative Isaac Seigel of New York
dated January 17, 1921, House, *Congressional Record,* 66th Congress, 3rd Session, 1921,
60: 1678–79.

7. House, *Congressional Record,* 70th Congress, 1st Session, 1928, 69: 9087.
From speech of Representative Emmanuel Celler of New York, May 17, 1928.

8. W. F. Willcox, "The Apportionment of Representatives," *American Economic
Review,* vol. 6, Supplement (1916): 1–16. See pp. 7 and 15.

9. E. V. Huntington, "Discussion: The Report of the National Academy of Sciences on Reapportionment," *Science,* May 3, 1929, pp. 471–73.

10. Wesberry v. Sanders, 376 U.S. 1 (1964).

11. If x is a common divisor or ideal constituency size, then $1/x$ is an ideal representation per capita. By Webster's method a state with population p gets b seats if $b - \frac{1}{2} <
p/x < b + \frac{1}{2}$. This is equivalent to $1/x - b/p < (b-)/p - 1/x$ and $b/p - 1/x < 1/x -
(b - 1)/p$, which says simply that the state is closest in absolute terms to the ideal per
capita representation $1/x$ if it gets b seats.

12. If state A has population p and gets a seats, and state B has population q and gets b

seats, and A is the favored state, then Jefferson's method minimizes $a(q/p) - b$, whereas Adams's method minimizes $a - (p/q)b$.

13. E. V. Huntington, "The Apportionment of Representatives in Congress," *Transactions of the American Mathematical Society* 30 (1928): 85–110. See p. 90.

14. E. V. Huntington, "The Apportionment Situation in Congress," *Science,* December 14, 1928, pp. 579–82. See p. 581.

15. U.S., Congress, House, Committee on the Census, *Apportionment of Representatives in Congress Amongst the Several States: Hearing on H. R. 13471,* 69th Congress, 2nd Session, January 10, 1927; ibid., *Apportionment of Representatives: Hearing on H. R. 130,* 70th Congress, 1st Session, February 14, 15, 20, and 21, 1928.

16. The complete exchanges between Walter F. Willcox and Edward V. Huntington published in *Science* are: May 18, 1928, pp. 509–10; June 8, 1928, pp. 581–82; December 14, 1928, pp. 579–82; February 8, 1929, pp. 163–65; March 8, 1929, p. 272; March 29, 1929, pp. 357–58; May 3, 1929, p. 471–73; May 8, 1942, pp. 477–78; May 15, 1942, pp. 501–03.

17. Willcox, *Science,* May 15, 1942, p. 502.

18. House, *Apportionment of Representatives,* 1928, p. 61. From memorandum submitted by Walter F. Willcox, dated February 21, 1928.

19. Hungtington, *Science,* May 18, 1928, pp. 509–10.

20. G. A. Bliss, E. W. Brown, L. P. Eisenhart, and Raymond Pearl, "Report to the President of the National Academy of Sciences," February 9, 1929. In House, *Congressional Record,* 70th Congress, 2nd Session, 1929, 70: 4966–67. Also in House, Committee on the Census, *Apportionment of Representatives: Hearings,* 76th Congress, 3rd Session, February 27, 28, 29, and March 1 and 5, 1940.

21. Huntington, *Science,* May 3, 1929, p. 471.

22. U.S., Congress, Senate, *Congressional Record,* 71st Congress, 1st Session, 1929, 71: p. 2078. From speech of Senator Hugo Black of Alabama, May 28, 1929.

23. Ibid., p. 1336. From speech of Senator Hugo Black of Alabama, May 15, 1929.

24. House, *Congressional Record,* 70th Congress, 2nd Session, 1928, 69: 9009. From speech of Representative Ralph Lozier of Missouri, May 17, 1928.

25. The twentieth amendment to the Constitution made it impossible to comply with the Vandenberg Act because of a change in the date of the opening of regular sessions of Congress. Vandenberg took the steps necessary to amend the Act in order to preserve its substance, and this easily passed both houses, even though the occasion was used to hold new hearings. (House, Committee on the Census, *Apportionment of Representatives in Congress: Hearings,* 76th Congress, 3rd Session, February 27, 28, 29 and March 1, 5, 1940). As explained later by Representative Ed. Gossett of Texas, "rather than go into technical, almost metaphysical calculations of these methods, we concluded to change merely the dates in order to cure the hiatus left by the 'lame duck' amendment." See Senate, Committee on Commerce, *Apportionment of Representatives in Congress: Hearings on H.R. 2665,* 77th Congress, 1st Session, February 27, 28, and March 1, 1941, p. 5.

26. House, *Congressional Record,* 77th Congress, 1st Session, 1941, 87: 1126. From speech of Representative Clare E. Hoffman of Michigan, February 18, 1941.

27. Ibid, p. 1081. From speech of Representative Leland M. Ford of California, February 17, 1941.

28. 46 Stat. 26. See U.S. *Statutes at Large,* 1941–42, vol. 55, part 1, pp. 761–62.

29. Senate, *Congressional Record,* 71st Congress, 1st Session, 1929, 71: 108. From speech of Senator Arthur H. Vandenberg of Michigan, April 18, 1929.

CHAPTER 7

1. To meet minimum requirements, a Hamilton-type method in its traditional interpretation also gives one seat to each state with quota less than 1 (no matter how small) and then uses the priority list of remainders to distribute the seats left over.

2. Thomas Jefferson, "Opinion of the Bill Apportioning Representation," *Works*, p. 409.

3. A state whose quotient is less than its minimum requirement is given its required number of seats and the divisor is chosen so that, with this proviso, the rounding rule apportions the required number of seats.

4. By Dean's method a state with population p gets at least $a+1$ seats if $x - p/(a+1) < p/a - x$. This is equivalent to $p/x > a(a+1)/(a+\frac{1}{2})$, the harmonic mean of a and $a+1$.

5. The name "harmonic mean" originates from Pythagoras' discovery that musical notes are determined by the frequency of vibration of a string. Imagine a violin string anchored at "0." Pythagoras' law says that the tones produced when the string is held at distances "2" and "3," respectively, sound a major fifth—and when the string is pressed at their harmonic mean (2.40) a major third results.

6. By Hill's method a state with population p gets at least $a+1$ seats if $x/(p/(a+1)) < (p/a)/x$. This is equivalent to $p/x > \sqrt{a(a+1)}$, the geometric mean of a and $a+1$.

7. The name "geometric mean" derives from the Pythagoreans' fascination with the problem of taking a plane figure and constructing a square having the same area. This is a natural problem of geometry, the Greek origin of which means "land measurement." The geometric mean of two successive integers, say 2 and 3, is found by constructing a square having the same area as a rectangle with short side 2 and long side 3. The answer is a square with side approximately 2.45—the square root of 2 times 3. The geometric mean can also be understood in another way. Suppose something is growing "geometrically," in other words, is increasing by a certain fixed percentage each year, like money earning compound interest. If an initial deposit of $2.00 grows to $3.00 after some period, then halfway through the period the amount is the geometric mean of 2 and 3, or about $2.45.

8. Whatever divisor method is used, a minimum requirement of 1 seat simply means that the signpost for the first seat is placed at the beginning of the road; a minimum of 2 means the first *and* second signposts are placed at the beginning, and so forth.

9. Jean-Antoine-Nicolas Caritat, Marquis de Condorcet, "Plan de Constitution, presenté à la Convention Nationale les 15 et 16 Fevrier 1793." in *Oeuvres de Condorcet*, vol. 12, ed. A. Condorcet O'Connor and M. F. Arago (Paris: Firmin Didot Frères, 1847).

CHAPTER 8

1. The populations of the states were estimated for each year between censuses by interpolation, using the annual growth rates implied by successive censuses.

CHAPTER 9

1. G. A. Bliss, E. W. Brown, L. P. Eisenhart, and Raymond Pearl, "Report to the President of the National Academy of Sciences," February 9, 1929. Printed in House,

Committee on the Census, *Apportionment of Representatives in Congress: Hearings,* 76th Congress, 3rd Session, February 27, 28, and 29, and March 1 and 5, 1940.

2. Marston Morse, John von Neumann, and Luther P. Eisenhart, "Report to the President of the National Academy of Sciences." May 28, 1948 (mimeograph).

3. Frank W. Notestein, "Walter F. Willcox—An Appreciation," *Cornell Alumni News* 67 (January 1965): 19.

CHAPTER 10

1. E. V. Huntington, "The Apportionment of Representatives in Congress," *Transactions of the Mathematical Society,* 30 (1928): 85–110 (see p. 94).

2. For the censuses of 1790–1840 the quotas and modified quotas are identical because in these cases *no* state had a quota less than 1.

3. Over the nineteen United States censuses the percentage bias of Hamilton's method would have been 0.6% in favor of the large, whereas for the modified method it would have been 0.4% in favor of the small. In each of the six censuses in which the modified Hamilton method differs from its parent it switches seats from larger to smaller states.

CHAPTER 11

1. Wesberry v. Sanders, 376 U.S. 1 (1964).

2. Kirkpatrick v. Preisler, 394 U.S. 526 (1969).

3. White v. Weiser, 412 U.S. 783 (1973).

4. Webster solutions were used seven times, in 1840, 1850, 1880, 1890, 1900, 1910, and 1930; Jefferson solutions five times, 1790 through 1830; Hill's four times, 1940 through 1970. Twice, in 1860 and 1870, no consistent method was used; and once, in 1920, there was no reapportionment.

5. House, *Congressional Record,* 47th Congress, 1st Session, 1882, 12:1179. From speech of Representative John A. Anderson of Kansas, February 16, 1882.

CHAPTER 12

1. Inter-Parliamentary Union, *Parliaments of the World: A Reference Compendium,* prepared by Valentine Herman and Françoise Mendel (London: Macmillan Press, Ltd., 1976).

2. W. Arthur Lewis, *Politics in West Africa* (London: Allen & Unwin, 1965), pp. 71–72.

3. See Stein Rokkan, "Elections: Electoral Systems," in *International Encyclopedia of the Social Sciences* (New York: Macmillan and Free Lance Press, 1968), 5: 6–12.

4. Facts concerning the electoral systems are drawn mainly from *Parliaments of the World,* Table 9, pp. 113–33.

5. Douglas W. Rae, *The Political Consequences of Electoral Laws,* rev. ed. (New Haven and London: Yale University Press, 1971), p. 134.

6. See Rokkan, "Elections: Electoral Systems."

7. There is a good deal of confusion on this point. *Parliaments of the World* refers to the methods of Hagenbach-Bischoff, of d'Hondt, of their use in combination, and of "highest average" as though they were all different. The same occurs in Jean-Marie Cotteret and Claude Emeri, *Les Systemes electoraux* (Paris: Presses Universitaires de France, 1970).

8. V. d'Hondt, *La Représentation proportionnelle des partis par un électeur* (Ghent, 1878); and *Systeme pratique et raisonné de représentation proportionnelle* (Brussels: Murquardt, 1882).

Index

Page numbers in italics refer to definitions of technical terms.